THE GOVERNMENT-CITIZEN DISCONNECT

THE GOVERNMENT- CITIZEN DISCONNECT

Suzanne Mettler

Russell Sage Foundation   NEW YORK

LIBRARY OF CONGRESS CATALOGING-IN-PUBLICATION DATA

Names: Mettler, Suzanne, author.
Title: The government-citizen disconnect / Suzanne Mettler.
Description: New York : Russell Sage Foundation, 2018. | Includes bibliographical references and index.
Identifiers: LCCN 2017061400 (print) | LCCN 2018011822 (ebook) | ISBN 9781610448727 (ebook) | ISBN 9780871546685 (paperback)
Subjects: LCSH: United States—Social policy. | Welfare state—United States. | Political sociology—United States. | United States—Politics and government—Public opinion. | United States—Politics and government—1989- | BISAC: POLITICAL SCIENCE / Public Policy / Social Policy. | POLITICAL SCIENCE / Government / General. | POLITICAL SCIENCE / General. | POLITICAL SCIENCE / Public Policy / Social Services & Welfare. | SOCIAL SCIENCE / Research.
Classification: LCC HN65 (ebook) | LCC HN65 .M47 2018 (print) | DDC 306.0973—dc23
LC record available at https://lccn.loc.gov/2017061400

Text design by Linda Secondari.

RUSSELL SAGE FOUNDATION
112 East 64th Street, New York, New York 10065
10 9 8 7 6 5 4 3 2 1

For Julia

CONTENTS

ILLUSTRATIONS

FIGURES

TABLES

ABOUT THE AUTHOR

SUZANNE METTLER is Clinton Rossiter Professor of American Institutions in the Government Department at Cornell University.

ACKNOWLEDGMENTS

I BEGAN WORK on this book project a very long time ago, and a vast number of people have helped me along the way. It is my great pleasure to mention here at least those who had a formal or enduring role in shaping how the project evolved. I am thankful to each of them, as well as to numerous others—too many to name—with whom conversations, email exchanges, or replies to my published work along the way have influenced my thinking.

I first started thinking about the project nearly two decades ago, when I was well immersed in researching another book. At that time, when I was on the faculty in the Maxwell School at Syracuse University, Andrew Milstein valiantly initiated the immense task of building the dataset that tracks the use and value of federal social policies over time, the basis of chapter 2. Andrew and I published an article on our findings, "American Political Development from Citizens' Perspective: Tracking Federal Government's Presence in Individual Lives over Time," in *Studies in American Political Development,* vol. 21, no. 1 (2007): 110–30. Christina Leigh Deitz ably assisted me in preparing a grant application for the Russell Sage Foundation (RSF), which proved to be successful. The project would have been impossible without the very generous aid provided by RSF, which provided my primary source of support for the project, including the survey I conducted in 2008, the main source of data for chapters 3, 4, and 5. A grant from the Spencer Foundation also covered some of the survey costs.

In the meanwhile, I moved to Cornell University, joining the faculty of the Government Department. Cornell has made my work on this project possible in numerous ways, not least through the study leave and sabbatical time financed by the institution. Judy Virgilio and Dinnie Sloman offered vital guidance to me in administering the RSF and Spencer grants. Laurie Dorsey managed the expenses of the project, and Stacy Kesselring and Jerrica Brown assisted with myriad administrative matters—each of the three of them with a wonderful combination of skill, careful attention, and good cheer.

The Cornell Survey Research Institute (SRI) administered the Social and Governmental Issues and Participation Study in 2008 as well as the recontacting of volunteers for interviews in 2015. I am particularly grateful to SRI's Darren Hearn, Yasamin Miller, and Stephanie Slate for their expertise and attentiveness, which made each of these components successful, and to statistician Kathryn Barger for weighting the survey data. Joanne Miller of the University of Minnesota, the bearer of considerable wisdom about survey design, provided invaluable advice to me as I planned the survey questionnaire. Chase Harrison helped me to think through the appropriate approach to the sampling strategy, oversamples, and incentives. Of course, I am especially thankful to the individuals who served as research subjects— the people in Syracuse who took part in in-person preliminary interviews I conducted to test the survey instrument; the 1,400 individuals who answered the phone and took time to answer the long survey questionnaire; and the 21 people who went above and beyond by participating in follow-up phone interviews many years later. I was honored to interview Lou Clark, whose vantage point in working for change in Syracuse over many decades proved to be tremendously insightful.

Numerous students at Cornell contributed to the project as research assistants. PhD students Richard Barton, Julianna Koch, Claire Leavitt, Michael Miller, and Mallory SoRelle each conducted various aspects of the research, as did undergraduates Beatriz Barros, Rose Beattie, Christopher Cho, Jason Claman, Perry Davidoff, Estevan Ginsburg, Michael Hill, and Jake May. Cara Sierks and AshLee Smith assisted me in conducting many of the open-ended interviews in 2015.

Two PhD students in particular played roles that proved to be indispensable. It has been one of the blessings of my life to have been able to work with Delphia Shanks-Booth, who contributed her methodological savvy to the statistical analysis underlying chapters 4 and 5 and her talents in graph preparation for those chapters as well as chapter 3. I am appreciative beyond measure for everything she contributed to this project: her extraordinary expertise and conscientiousness as a researcher, her boundless generosity with her time and incredible patience with my myriad requests, and of course her delightful humor and good cheer. David De Micheli managed to fit in work on this book in between—and even during—his research trips to Brazil, and his stellar mapping abilities and general talents in making "a picture worth a thousand words" is responsible for several figures in chapters 1, 3, and 5. I am deeply thankful.

I am fortunate to find myself in a community of scholars—or really, a few such communities—and those relationships have contributed greatly to my evolving ideas. I've presented several conference and workshop papers over the years, and the feedback I've received from other scholars at those events has pushed and prodded my analysis forward. Some of these, particularly those late in the game, proved particularly helpful, including a 2015 presentation of a related paper with Delphia Shanks-Booth in the seminar series of the Cornell Center for the Study of Inequality, a presentation of a paper at a 2016 Cornell conference on inequality and politics, and a 2017 workshop at Johns Hopkins University at which I presented two book chapters. Several colleagues offered useful advice and feedback, including: Jane Collins, John Mark Hansen, Devin Judge-Lord, Robert Lieberman, Paul Pierson, Danny Schlozman, Theda Skocpol, Laura Tach, Vesla Weaver, and Kim Weeden. I am very grateful to Steven Maynard-Moody, who directed me to the Bureau of Economic Analysis data, and spurred my thinking about ways to use it. My ongoing collaboration with Larry Jacobs, in our project on the Affordable Care Act, has developed my thinking about policy effects and policy development generally. John Sides and I wrote an op-ed together in 2012, drawing on some of the data utilized here, and that process prompted me to consider it in new ways.

Five people read the entire manuscript and offered tremendously helpful feedback. My incredibly faithful friends and colleagues Jeff Stonecash and Rick Valelly went the extra mile—scratch that, many miles!—by reading the entire manuscript and offering superbly insightful comments, prompting considerable revising. The other three readers were anonymous reviewers for RSF, so I cannot thank them by name, but suffice to say that their detailed and thoughtful questions and suggestions pushed me to improve the book a great deal, on matters ranging from careful checks on the empirical analysis to clarifications of broader aspects of the argument.

Working with RSF director of publications Suzanne Nichols has been a delight. I appreciated her patience with me as the project hovered on the back burner for several years. Once it was ready, she moved it along with remarkable efficiency while sparing no efforts to ensure that it would be as well produced as possible. I truly admire the high standards she sets and her charm and congeniality in enforcing them. Marcelo Agudo, production editor at RSF, has kindly indulged my many questions about the appropriate use of the English language and offered sound advice. I am thankful to the entire team at RSF for their professionalism and care in the production of this book.

My family makes everything possible, not least the joy of each day. Wayne Grove, as always, has discussed every aspect of this book with me, over countless meals (delicious ones that he prepared) over many years. Sophie Mettler-Grove has always stayed abreast of what I've been up to, offering keen interest and ebullient support, and it has been a delight to see her life develop in so many ways over the years I've worked on this book. My siblings have been steadfast supporters as well, and I am so grateful.

Our younger daughter, Julia Mettler-Grove, was just a toddler when I began the project that led to this book, and her life has unfolded as it took shape. Julia has become an amazing young adult, one with a profound interest in public affairs and a commitment to making the world a better place. This book is dedicated to her with endless love, and hope that her generation can find ways to navigate more successfully the challenges described here.

CHAPTER 1

A TIME OF CONTRADICTION

IT WAS A TIME when government was despised; it was a time when more people relied on government than ever before. It was an age of division over the legitimacy of the welfare state; it was an age of unity, with the use of redistributive policies so widespread that social, economic, and political differences were transcended. It was an epoch when citizens voiced strong support for specific social policies; it was an epoch when they elected a great many public officials who sought to eviscerate those same policies.[1]

Over the past four decades, Americans' relationship to the federal government has evolved in a deeply paradoxical manner. As a society, we appear to regard government with ever greater disdain, as evidenced by popular discourse, numerous polls, and election results. Yet people depend on the federal government more than ever to help them attain economic security, health care, and educational opportunity.

Anger at the federal government and alienation from it have fueled mobilization on both the right and the left in recent years, from the Tea Party movement to Occupy Wall Street and among the supporters of both Bernie Sanders and Donald Trump in the 2016 election. It is not only partisan activists who are fed up; frustration is also widespread among ordinary Americans. More than a half-century of tracking polls reveal that evaluations of government have plummeted to all-time lows. Back in the early 1970s, the majority of Americans—upwards of 60 percent—said that they could "trust the government in Washington to do what is right" just about always or most of the time; by 2015, only one in five concurred with that statement. Similarly, four decades ago the public was equally split between those who believed that government is "run for the benefit of all the people" versus "a few big interests looking out for themselves"; by 2015, the percentage voicing the benevolent view of government had fallen to 19 percent.[2] The charge that "the system is rigged" energizes liberals and conservatives alike, as evidenced by the crowds at 2016 election rallies. Only one in four Americans agreed in 1960 that "public officials don't care much what people like me think," but by 2016 three in four agreed; meanwhile, the percentage doubled for those who felt that "I have no say in what government does."[3] The fervor and frustration propelled Trump, the consummate political outsider, to victory, making him the first president in American history who lacked any prior experience in public service, either in elected office, the military, or a cabinet position.

Americans have grown disillusioned not only with governing institutions but with numerous other institutions as well, ranging from the news media (both television and newspapers) to banks and organized religion.[4] Yet the public now regards government with particular scorn, its confidence in it having plummeted most severely. Since the early 1960s, Gallup has asked Americans which is the biggest threat to the country: "big government," "big business," or "big labor." Early on, only 35 percent named "big government," but since then that response has surged to a dubious commanding lead, named by 60 percent.[5] That people would assess so poorly the very set of institutions that are subject to popular control speaks volumes about the relationship between citizens and government.

Yet over these very same decades, Americans have increasingly counted on the federal government's assistance in their personal lives. Nationwide, the share of the average citizen's income that flows from federal social "transfers"—including Social Security, food stamps, the Earned Income Tax Credit (EITC), and more than forty other programs—increased from 7 percent in 1969 to 17 percent in 2014, as seen in figure 1.1. On a per capita basis, the rate grew fairly steadily over time, escalated more quickly with the onset of the 2008 financial downturn, and then declined somewhat more recently. The amount received by the average person increased from $1,852 in 1969 to $7,729 in 2014, in 2014 dollars. As a percentage of all benefits, Social Security (retirement, survivors', and disability) and Medicare payments remain virtually the same in 2014 as in 1969.[6] Even if we exclude these two policies, the increased value of other policies is still impressive, growing from 3 percent of income in 1969 ($790) to 7 percent in 2014 ($3,237), as seen in figure 1.2.

These figures do not include the most generous social benefits, which are

Figure 1.1 Growth of Federal Government Social Transfers, 1969–2014

Source: Author's calculations from U.S. Bureau of Economic Analysis (2016).
Note: BEA data include all transfers to individuals from governments: retirement and disability insurance benefits, medical benefits, income maintenance benefits, unemployment insurance compensation, veterans' benefits, education and training assistance, and other transfer receipts. These data are available in table CA35 of the (regional) local area and personal income and employment data. Averages are computed using population and income figures from table CA1.

Figure 1.2 Growth of Federal Government Social Transfers with Social Security and Medicare Excluded, 1969–2014

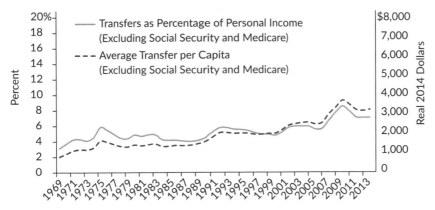

Source: Author's calculations from U.S. Bureau of Economic Analysis (2016).
Note: BEA data include all transfers to individuals from governments: retirement and disability insurance benefits, medical benefits, income maintenance benefits, unemployment insurance compensation, veterans' benefits, education and training assistance, and other transfer receipts. These data are available in table CA35 of the (regional) local area and personal income and employment data. Averages are computed using population and income figures from table CA1.

either channeled through the tax code, such as the home mortgage interest deduction, or provided in tandem with private organizations, such as tax-subsidized, employer-provided health and retirement benefits. These policies serve the same function as social benefits delivered as direct payments or services—such as helping families to afford health care, housing, or education—but in permitting beneficiaries simply to pay less in taxes, they differ in design. If we consider only public social spending or government transfers, the U.S. welfare state is smaller as a percentage of GDP than that of other affluent nations, ranking twenty-fourth worldwide, but if we account also for the social expenditures channeled through the tax code and tax-subsidized payments from employers, the United States has the second-largest welfare state in the world after France.[7]

Although many think of the welfare state as benefiting only a small minority of Americans, mostly the poor, if we account for the full array of twenty-one major federal social policies that assist individuals and families with economic security and educational opportunity, including those located in the tax code—it turns out that usage is widespread.[8] Ninety-six percent of American adults have used at least one such policy, and the remaining 4 percent are mostly young people who have not yet had the occasion to do so. The average adult has utilized 4.47 of these policies, and the pervasiveness of usage spans differences of income, age, race and ethnicity, and partisanship.[9] The share of personal income that flows from the federal government has increased all over the nation, in "red states" on the electoral map even more than in "blue states," and with peak levels in counties with overwhelmingly white populations (surpassing 95 percent). From multiple angles, the pairing of disdain for government with growing reliance on public benefits amounts to a conundrum.

To be sure, skepticism about the federal government is nothing new in the United States. The American experiment itself grew out of the colonists' dissatisfaction with the centralized governing authority of the British crown. They spurned the excesses of King George III and initially created, as the nation's first government, the Articles of Confederation, a loose union of states with a weak central government. When state delegates met in Philadelphia in 1787 and opted to replace that arrangement and fashion a national government with greater authority and capacity, they were viewed with no small measure of suspicion and contempt. The framers of the new U.S. Constitution spearheaded a public relations campaign in the form of *The Federalist Papers,* authored by Alexander Hamilton, John Jay, and James Madison, in order to promote its ratification. Similar cycles have repeated themselves time and again throughout U.S. history when the national government's efforts to respond to widely perceived needs have run up against resistance by citizens wary of federal overreach.[10]

Yet, viewed in historical perspective, contemporary Americans' antipathy to government seems all the more counterintuitive, not less. After all, the Revolution was fought by colonists who objected to a despotic ruler who denied them political authority and civil liberties, never mind social provision. Today, by contrast, Americans boast the world's most long-standing constitution guaranteeing representative government and a wide array of civil liberties and political rights, and nearly all benefit at some point from the nation's large array of social benefits. Not only have most people used such policies, but as we will see in chapter 4, they report having had positive experiences of them. This is not to say that all is well: the United States faces daunting political and economic challenges. Ironically, however, when majorities of Americans in the 1960s and early 1970s reported high levels of confidence in government, it was at a time when the nation actually required *more* of citizens than it does today, through higher federal tax rates and universal conscription of young men, and when it granted citizens considerably *fewer* social benefits.[11]

To put it plainly, contemporary American politics is plagued by what I call a "government-citizen disconnect," a vast and growing gulf between the role the government actually plays in Americans' lives and their overall assessment of and response to it. Even as policies aimed to help individuals and families have increased in number and expanded in coverage, government itself has become more unpopular. Collectively, Americans rely increasingly on a wide array of policies to aid them in times of need or to help with the costs of health care, housing, and college education, and yet elections produce growing numbers of public officials whose principal aim is to terminate, restructure, or sharply reduce the size of several of those very programs.

This book aims to describe the government-citizen disconnect and its emergence, to probe how it is manifested in individual lives, and to assess how it relates to political participation. We will begin by tracking the reach of federal social policies and how it has changed over time. Over the past forty years, job security and wages declined for much of the U.S. workforce, owing to economic and technological transformation and government's abandonment of strong postwar protections for workers, and economic inequality soared. Yet, despite the antigovernment ethos of the period, law-makers managed to preserve social policies and expand the coverage of the vast majority of them.

Next, we will examine how individuals' experiences of these policies accumulate over the course of their lives. This analysis reveals that usage patterns transcend numerous social, economic, and political divisions. Despite the many ways in which U.S. society today appears to be deeply divided, in fact it is united by widespread usage of social policies.

Yet regardless of these ubiquitous experiences of social provision, Americans have become increasingly disenchanted with government. That raises a puzzle: How can government do so much, yet be so despised? To explore this question, I evaluate whether citizens draw broader conclusions about government from their policy experiences, and how other factors influence their views as well. In a previous book, I showed that many contemporary social policies channel public benefits indirectly, through the tax code or private organizations, arrangements I term "the submerged state." These "submerged" policies obscure government's role in social provision from the point of view of citizens, but interest groups that benefit from such policies are keenly aware of them, and when reforms are proposed, such as during the Obama Administration, they influence the policy process and shape the results.[12] In this book, by contrast, I focus entirely on citizens' experiences of policies and broaden the inquiry to examine the full array of federal social policies, submerged and visible, and means-tested and non-means-tested. I explore how accumulated policy usage of these different types affects citizens' views of government, along several dimensions.

I confirm, on the one hand, that policy visibility does matter: policies delivered from government directly to citizens, alone or collectively, can give recipients a sense that government has helped them in times of need or provided opportunities to them. Policies with submerged, indirect designs that camouflage government's role as a provider of benefits routinely fail to convey such information and therefore do not make an impact. Yet, even the impact of multiple visible policies is quite limited. Overall, when Americans evaluate government, few take into consideration the social policies they have benefitted from across their lifetimes.

Instead, contemporary orientations to government are shaped more routinely by people's social identities and political affiliations and the ideas or perspectives they encompass. These shared perspectives compete with or overwhelm the impact of firsthand experiences of social policies. For example, those in the broad middle class, who have seen fading opportunities and stagnating incomes over four decades, deeply dislike welfare, and racial resentment also appears to drive antipathy toward it. I find that those who feel unfavorably toward welfare view it as a microcosm of how government works, and they extrapolate from it to form negative assessments of government generally. Such factors fill the void left by the disconnect between government and citizens.

Some Americans do gain more positive views of government through policy usage, however, and they tend to be supportive of expanded social provision. This finding raises another question: Why are the voices of these Americans not heard more audibly in the political process? Ironically, as we will see, it is typically those who are less cognizant or appreciative of government's role in their lives who speak most frequently in politics, whereas those who are most aware of the difference that government makes in their lives are more likely to refrain. The playing field of politics is tilted such that it overrepresents those who place little value on social benefits, as they happen to be more likely to be mobilized and to participate in numerous political activities, and underrepresents those who could be its best defenders.

The government-citizen disconnect generates contradictory, self-defeating effects. Although it is rooted in dissatisfaction with government, this disconnect inadvertently undermines the very capacities that are necessary for reform. Many contemporary problems, such as rising economic inequality, job insecurity, climate change, and immigration, transcend what families, civic organizations, or businesses can address and solve on their own. These problems cannot be handled effectively except through widespread collective action, coordinated and legitimated by government. Yet the government-citizen disconnect is making the American political system less able to respond to such conundrums. As long as Americans keep waging a war on their own government, the United States will become increasingly less able to muster the political will necessary for self-government to survive.

From Sea to Shining Sea

Americans quite literally "across the map" utilize considerably more social benefits than they did thirty-five years ago. "Federal transfers" include primarily forms of social provision that are distributed fairly directly, such as direct deposits by government into the bank accounts of beneficiaries, as in the case of Social Security, or as services provided at government expense,

Figure 1.3 Federal Government Social Transfers as a Percentage of Personal Income, by State, 1979

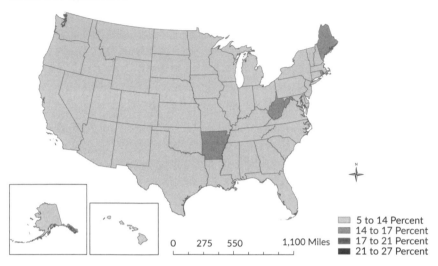

Source: Author's calculations from U.S. Bureau of Economic Analysis (2016).
Note: BEA data include all transfers to individuals from governments: retirement and disability insurance benefits, medical benefits, income maintenance benefits, unemployment insurance compensation, veterans' benefits, education and training assistance, and other transfer receipts. These data are available in table CA35 of the (regional) local area and personal income and employment data. Averages are computed using population and income figures from table CA1.

such as Medicare. Figures 1.3 and 1.4 show the percentage of the average person's income that came from federal transfers, by state, in 1979 and 2014, respectively.[13] In 1979, that percentage surpassed 14 percent in only four states: Arkansas, Maine, Rhode Island, and West Virginia. By 2014, by contrast, in only nine states did individuals receive *less* than 14 percent of their income from federal coffers, and in eight states the federal government contributed more than 22 percent of the average person's income. The states in which income from the federal government exceeded 17 percent represented each region of the country, from Florida to Oregon, from New Mexico to Rhode Island and Michigan. The most striking aspect of federal spending across the states—as well as across counties, as we will see in chapter 3—is that its scope and distribution transcend partisan and demographic divides.

These maps, furthermore, like figures 1.1 and 1.2, do not include the full array of social policies to be analyzed in this book: they omit most of those

Figure 1.4 Federal Government Social Transfers as a Percentage of Personal Income, by State, 2014

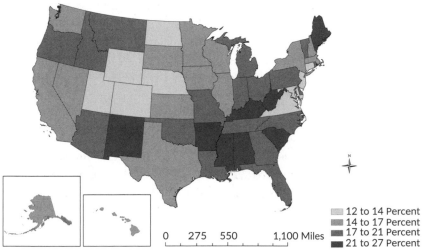

12 to 14 Percent
14 to 17 Percent
17 to 21 Percent
21 to 27 Percent

Source: Author's calculations from U.S. Bureau of Economic Analysis (2016).
Note: BEA data include all transfers to individuals from governments: retirement and disability insurance benefits, medical benefits, income maintenance benefits, unemployment insurance compensation, veterans' benefits, education and training assistance, and other transfer receipts. These data are available in table CA35 of the (regional) local area and personal income and employment data. Averages are computed using population and income figures from table CA1.

channeled through the tax code.[14] "Tax expenditures," as they are called, usually function by allowing beneficiaries to pay less in taxes rather than by sending them a check or delivering a service to them. They include several of the most generous U.S. social policies. From an accounting perspective, there is no meaningful difference between "federal transfers" and "tax expenditures": both bestow benefits on particular individuals and households that are not granted to everyone, and both diminish government's resources, whether by distributing its funds or by not collecting revenues that would otherwise be due. The design features of tax expenditures make government's role as the provider of social benefits less obvious than do other arrangements. As such, these policies have collectively been termed the "hidden welfare state" by Christopher Howard, and when combined with subsidies channeled to or through private organizations, they make up the "submerged state."[15] Policies of these types tend to bestow benefits particularly on the affluent, and several of them also benefit particular industries, such as real estate, home builders, and health insurance companies, which are organized politically to defend them.

If the larger policies in the tax code were also included in the maps in figures 1.3 and 1.4, we would observe still greater uniformity in benefit levels across the states. When it comes to the home mortgage interest deduction, for example, individuals claim it at higher rates in states with higher incomes and property values, which also tend to have the nation's lowest levels of social transfers.[16] The 26 percent of tax filers who claimed this deduction in 2010 were concentrated most heavily in the following states, where over 32 percent claimed it: Colorado, Connecticut, Maryland, Minnesota, New Jersey, Utah, and Virginia. Nationwide, the average claimant benefited to the tune of $2,400, but in coastal states such as California, Maryland, and Virginia, that figure reached $4,000 and above.[17] Many other tax expenditures that, as we will see in chapter 2, benefit primarily households with high incomes are likely to be similarly distributed geographically.

Widespread usage of federal social benefits transcends not only different regions of the country but also—as chapter 3 makes evident—other cleavages, such as income, partisan identity, age, and race or ethnicity. Receiving such benefits at some point in one's life has become a commonplace component of American citizenship.

The Red State–Blue State Puzzle

If there is one divide in American society that we would not expect social policy usage to span, it would be political partisanship. After all, partisan differences with respect to social provision date back to the New Deal—when Democrats became associated with a larger role for government in mitigating inequality and providing opportunity and the Republican Party with greater emphasis on promoting personal responsibility and market-oriented solutions—and they have grown much greater in recent decades with the increase in partisan polarization. In the postwar era, Republican presidents Dwight Eisenhower and Richard Nixon each signed into law expansions of Social Security coverage and landmark legislation granting federal aid to college students, and moderate Republicans in Congress supported maintenance of these and other laws that extended economic security and educational opportunity. Yet, in 1981, newly elected president Ronald Reagan signaled that the party would pursue a different course when he declared, "Government is not the solution to our problem; government is the problem."[18] From that time onward, the GOP sought to distinguish itself by embracing this approach, and efforts to scale back social policies figured front and center in the Republican agenda, from the "Contract with America" approach of the 1990s to the Tea Party demands in 2010 and beyond.

Rank-and-file partisans adopted contrasting views about the norm of personal responsibility as an organizing principle for society, with major implications for government's role.[19] Democrats, influenced by social science research, came to see individuals as being profoundly affected by social forces beyond their control; no amount of hard work can enable individuals to get ahead if they encounter either persistent disadvantages—owing to social conditions based, for example, on class, race, or gender—or structural changes in the economy and technology.[20] In this view, government must mitigate inequalities and dislocations through the use of public policies.[21] Republicans, by contrast, more typically perceive individuals to be in control of their own destinies and capable of succeeding if they exhibit sufficient industriousness and other moral virtues, such as honesty, and embrace marriage and religion. From this perspective, government—in the form of the "nanny state"—is the problem to the extent that it undermines those virtues, robbing people of the incentive to exert their own will and live independently and thus encouraging laziness.[22] Government, in this view, cultivates an "entitlement society," a nation of "victims" and "moochers."[23]

Partisans' views about the welfare state have grown increasingly disparate, more so than on other issues.[24] Between 1956 and 2012, for example, the gap in partisans' views about whether "the government in Washington should see to it that every person has a job and a good standard of living" or "government should just let each person get ahead on his own" widened sharply. While Democrats' views changed little, Republicans became more likely to agree with the latter statement. Similarly, on the question of whether government should help people afford health coverage—asked over the same time period—Republicans increasingly opted for leaving it to the individual.[25]

Yet, despite the emergence of such stark polarization in views about social policy, here is the crux of the matter: rank-and-file supporters of the parties do not differ from each other nearly as much in their actual social program usage as they do in their attitudes about policies. In fact, their policy usage remains sharply at odds with the rhetoric and positions taken by their party leaders and candidates. This disjuncture produces some surprising indicators of the government-citizen disconnect.

For example, much of the strongest electoral support for the contemporary GOP, particularly for many of its most conservative representatives, emanates from states and congressional districts in which people rely most heavily on the federal government's social provisions, particularly through direct transfers.[26] This paradox was manifest in the 2012 presidential campaign, when partisan divisions over the usage of social benefits were highlighted in bold relief. Republicans ran against the Affordable Care Act (ACA), the health care reform policy that represented one of President Barack Obama's major achievements of his first term. Already the U.S. House of Representatives had voted on thirty-three occasions to repeal all or part of the law.[27] In a much-publicized recording of GOP presidential candidate Mitt Romney speaking to donors, he directly criticized those who use government benefits and portrayed them all as political supporters of Obama:

> There are 47 percent of the people who will vote for the president no matter what. All right, there are 47 percent who are with him, who are dependent upon government, who believe that they are victims, who believe the government has a responsibility to care for them, who believe that they are entitled to health care, to food, to housing, to you-name-it. That that's an entitlement. And the government should give it to them. And they will vote for this president no matter what.[28]

With this "47 percent" comment, Romney implied that he stood no chance of gaining votes from beneficiaries of social programs.

Yet on election night, as seen in figure 1.5, the map of the electoral college results found a disproportionate number of the states most dependent on federal social transfers lined up squarely in support of Romney, while those that relied the least on such policies gave a slight edge to Obama. Of the eight states in which federal transfers comprised more than 22 percent of all income, six cast their forty-three electoral votes for Romney.[29] Only the other two, Maine and New Mexico, with just nine electoral votes, went for Obama. The states in which federal transfers made up the smallest percentage of personal income—14 percent or less—split their electoral votes between Obama, who gained fifty-seven from them, and Romney, who netted fifty-five.[30] These results fail to show the supposed political divide between a "blue" America of "takers" and a "red" America of "makers."

Figure 1.5 Federal Government Social Transfers as a Percentage of Personal Income, by State, and State Electoral College Victories by Republican Presidential Candidate Mitt Romney, 2012

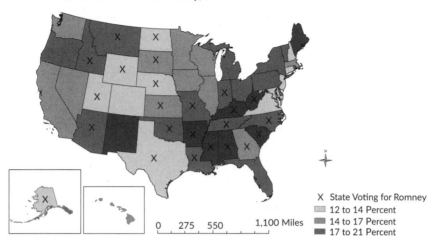

Source: Author's calculations from U.S. Bureau of Economic Analysis (2016). Results of the 2012 election from Federal Election Commission (2012).
Note: BEA data include all transfers to individuals from governments: retirement and disability insurance benefits, medical benefits, income maintenance benefits, unemployment insurance compensation, veterans' benefits, education and training assistance, and other transfer receipts. These data are available in table CA35 of the (regional) local area and personal income and employment data. Averages are computed using population and income figures from table CA1.

The 2016 election of Donald Trump, startling as it was to many, accentuated this pattern even further as a still higher percentage of states that depend more heavily on government aid lined up for the GOP. Six states flipped from "blue" in the 2012 election to "red" in 2016. In four of them, Florida, Michigan, Ohio, and Pennsylvania, with eighty-eight electoral votes, government transfers made up between 18 and 21 percent of average income, as seen in figure 1.4.[31] Highlighting the inherent paradox of the election results, four of the six states that flipped for Trump—Iowa, Michigan, Ohio, and Pennsylvania—had adopted the Affordable Care Act's expanded version of Medicaid and stood to lose the expansion of benefits if the new president held to his promise to repeal the law.[32]

The plot thickens when we drill down and focus on specific states in which the actual use of federal social benefits has soared in recent decades. In Kentucky, for example, as recently as 1989, in only one county did the average amount of personal income from federal transfers top 40 percent;

by 2014, twenty-eight counties held that distinction. Meanwhile, political transformation roiled the state. In the mid-twentieth century, most of Kentucky's congressional districts, in most elections, sent a Democrat to Congress. Its representatives included long-serving progressive leaders who used policies to serve broad public purposes, such as Carl Perkins, a champion for access to college, and Romano Mazzoli, who brokered a bipartisan immigration agreement. By the early 1990s, Republicans had become more likely to triumph, winning most seats in most elections. Today the Kentucky delegation includes some of the most conservative members in a House GOP that is increasingly rightward-leaning and staunchly opposed to government spending.

This pairing of higher program usage with conservative political representation is shown in figure 1.6. The black line indicates that the percentage of the average Kentuckian's income that flowed from federal social transfers grew from 10 percent in the period 1969 to 1971 to 23 percent in the period 2013 to 2015. Meanwhile, the average ideological position of members of the state's congressional delegation, as indicated by DW-NOMINATE scores, shifted from just to the left of the political center in the 1970s and 1980s to just to the right of center in the early and mid-1990s. Then suddenly in the late 1990s, and continuing into the present, the congressional delegation's ideological positions veered sharply in a more conservative direction, in tandem with soaring usage of social provision.

These trends have been accompanied by surprising results at the county level as well. Republican congressman Andy Barr, for example, represents the Sixth District, which includes McCreary and Wolfe Counties. In both counties, 52 percent of income—approximately $12,000 per resident—flows from federal social policies. Barr is a proponent of changing food stamps to make receipt contingent on employment, with lifetime limits on benefits.[33] Tea Party affiliate and congressman Thomas Massie, who represents Kentucky's Fourth District, resides in Lewis County, in which 43 percent of income comes from federal government transfers. He is known as one of the most conservative members of the U.S. House of Representatives and has been dubbed "Mr. No" by *Politico* because he votes against the vast majority of bills that reach the House floor, including those strongly supported by the GOP leadership.[34] Massie stridently opposes social welfare spending, having been among the group of Republicans who forced the end of the long tradition of bipartisan cooperation on the farm bill in 2013 because they opposed its inclusion of the food stamp program.[35] Such puz-

Figure 1.6 Simultaneous Growth of Federal Social Transfers in Kentucky and Ideological Conservatism Among the State's Congressional Delegation, 1969–2015

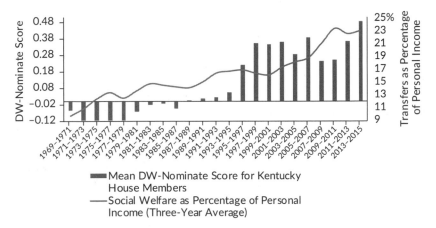

Mean DW-Nominate Score for Kentucky House Members

Social Welfare as Percentage of Personal Income (Three-Year Average)

Source: DW-Nominate scores from Lewis et al. (2017). Author's calculations from U.S. Bureau of Economic Analysis (2016).

Note: BEA data include all transfers to individuals from governments: retirement and disability insurance benefits, medical benefits, income maintenance benefits, unemployment insurance compensation, veterans' benefits, education and training assistance, and other transfer receipts. These data are available in table CA35 of the (regional) local area and personal income and employment data. Averages are computed using population and income figures from table CA1. DW-Nominate scores are provided for a single Congress, spanning three years. BEA data are provided for each calendar year. Three-year means are calculated for the years spanned by each Congress to make social welfare and DW-Nominate data comparable. BEA data are available only through 2014; thus, the 2013–2015 Congress corresponds to a two-year average of social welfare transfers.

zling combinations of high rates of social policy usage and the election of leaders who are staunchly opposed to it have been replicated in many congressional districts and states throughout the country. This trend raises perplexing questions about how Americans' usage of social provision relates to their attitudes about government and participation in politics.

A Policy Feedback Conundrum

Direct, personal experiences of social policies loom large in citizens' everyday lives, giving them firsthand and commonplace demonstrations of how well—and whether—government functions, what difference it makes, how responsive it is to people like them, and how capable they are of influencing it. Personal experience of such policies happens more frequently and routinely for most people than other sorts of interactions with the federal government, such as voting or military service. Moreover, these policies affect individuals' social and economic well-being in transformative ways, influencing such basic matters as whether or not they can afford to pursue a college education, seek health care when they are sick and avoid premature death, retire and stop working, pay the rent rather than get evicted, or even feed their children three meals a day.

Given the frequency, immediacy, and significance of people's experiences of government social policies, we might assume that these policies would influence their attitudes about government generally. It would make sense to expect that as such policies become more widespread, Americans would become *more* affirming of government, not less, and that candidates who aim to protect these policies would enjoy an easier path to office, not a more difficult one. The political scientist Samuel Lubell made this argument in 1952, predicting that the New Deal would have long-term consequences for American politics because large swathes of the public, including the rising middle class, urbanites, and farmers, had come to believe that they had benefited from rising governmental authority and therefore were "not as hostile to 'Big Government'" as older generations had been. Lubell pointed to how the political dynamics were changing from "those of getting" to "those of keeping—to preserve the gains of the past 20 years."[36]

A long tradition in political thought has argued that the expansion of social rights, such as access to health care and education, would foster a deepening of democracy. In 1944, President Franklin D. Roosevelt delivered a State of the Union Address in which he proposed that safeguarding more basic freedoms required the adoption of a "Second Bill of Rights" that would ensure rights such as access to jobs, housing, and health care. He argued, "We have come to a clear realization of the fact that true individual freedom cannot exist without economic security and independence. . . . People who are hungry and out of a job are the stuff of which dictatorships are made."[37] Scholars have elaborated on the likelihood that social rights would foster and preserve democracy. The British sociologist T. H. Marshall anticipated that gaining social rights would facilitate the full incorporation of individuals as citizens and enhance social solidarity because "the claim of all to enjoy these conditions is a claim to be admitted to a share in the social heritage . . . to be accepted as full members of society, as citizens."[38] Others have argued that social rights enable more citizens to gain the capacity to participate meaningfully as citizens. The American political scientist Robert Dahl explained, "In order to exercise the fundamental rights to which citizens in a democratic order are entitled—to vote, speak, publish, protest, assemble, organize, among others—citizens must also possess the minimal resources that are necessary in order to take advantage of the opportunities and to exercise those rights."[39]

The theory of "policy feedback," which has evolved over the past quarter-century, is based in part on such assumptions. Generally, it posits that policies established at earlier points in time can have long-run political consequences, for example by reshaping the political behavior of ordinary citizens.[40] One strand of policy feedback scholarship demonstrates that beneficiaries will act to protect policies they themselves utilize. Paul Pierson, for example, has shown that social policies largely withstood the Reagan Revolution because they had generated constituencies of supporters, such that path-dependent dynamics had taken hold.[41] Focusing particularly on Social Security and Medicare, Andrea Campbell explains that by bestowing valuable resources on senior citizens, these policies elevate seniors' motivation to participate in politics so that such policies will be protected.[42] Other scholars have found that the parents of school-age children are more likely to take part in politics, specifically on issue-based activity related to K-12 education, and that farmers, apparently motivated by government agricultural programs, are more likely to vote.[43]

Another strand of policy feedback scholarship turns attention to our subject here: the effects of public policies on citizens' broader views of government and their relationship to it, and thereby on the health of democracy. Anne Schneider and Helen Ingram argue that policies, through their design, impart messages to beneficiaries "that inform them of their status as citizens and how they and people like themselves are likely to be treated by government." This in turn fosters "a conception of the meaning of citizenship that influences their orientations toward government and their participation."[44] Joe Soss has expanded these ideas into a theory of political learning, arguing that as people take part in government social policies, interacting with agencies in the process, they derive broader lessons about how government generally responds to people like them and about their own capacity as citizens.[45] In my own study of the education and training provisions of the World War II GI Bill, I found that beneficiaries, experiencing the generous terms of program eligibility, its fair and efficient implementation, and its powerful socioeconomic effects, became more fully incorporated as citizens and as a result participated more frequently than veteran nonbeneficiaries in civic organizations and political activities.[46] These studies imply that as more people encounter government through direct and personal experiences of it that make a positive difference in their lives, they develop more salutary views about it.[47]

In sum, political feedback effects are assumed to occur as long as policies convey information to recipients, whether through the resources they offer or messages they transmit through design and implementation. If this occurs, policies may play a democratizing role by making apparent the difference government makes in citizens' lives and fostering civic engagement and participation, which can in turn mitigate political and economic inequality. Yet, today's government-citizen disconnect flies in the face of such expectations by suggesting that some feedback dynamics fail to transpire.[48] The question then becomes: How can we explain why Americans and U.S. politics have been veering in an antigovernment direction at a time when more people than ever are personally benefiting from government? We are faced with a paradox.

Making Sense of a Paradox

In fact, political science is no stranger to the mutual existence of seemingly contradictory phenomena, even within individuals' own attitudes. Scholars long ago discovered an inherent paradox in many Americans' opinions about social policies relative to their broader views of government.[49] In a classic study published in 1968, the political scientists Lloyd A. Free and Hadley Cantril discovered that most Americans espoused conservative values, favoring a "curbing of Federal power," and yet on practical questions of government operations the authors detected "an apparently inexorable trend in liberal directions" ever since the New Deal.[50] In essence, Americans typically articulated *ideologically conservative* views on abstract questions, preferring less government interference and lower taxes and believing that poverty stems largely from lack of effort rather than personal circumstances.[51] Yet they simultaneously sounded like *operational liberals* in their support for specific social programs of the federal government.[52] When it comes to Americans' attitudes about government generally versus social policy in particular, seeming contradictions are nothing new.[53]

Even as antigovernment politics has gained steam over the past several decades, Americans have continued to approve of most social policies, as several studies of public opinion have found. Majorities tell pollsters that they want funding for nearly all such policies at least to be maintained at current levels and in many instances to be increased. These conclusions are based on surveys that have asked the same questions and used identical wording repeatedly, across years and decades.[54] Support for existing policies, however, does not appear to do much to diffuse antigovernment attitudes. As John Hibbing and Elizabeth Theiss-Morse observe, "Pleasure with public policies is hardly a guarantor that people will be pleased with government."[55] Still, the large body of political behavior research has not explained how individuals' actual usage and firsthand experience of social provision might influence their views about government generally.

A voluminous literature on the welfare state details transformations in social policy over the past several decades but refrains, with rare exceptions, from probing the impact of citizens' policy experiences on their perceptions of government. Some studies have specified the changing size and scope of social policy over time.[56] Others have probed the politics underlying these changes.[57] A few analyses examine the impact of policies on poverty or on inequality.[58] Some excellent recent case studies focus on the form that policies take, including their rules, procedures, and manner of administration, which are crucial to understanding how they are experienced and how beneficiaries respond to them.[59] This book, by contrast, takes a "bird's-eye view" of the welfare state, looking across multiple programs to probe Americans' accumulated usage of them and how it relates to their attitudes about government and political participation.

To begin investigating the government-citizen disconnect, we start in chapter 2 by surveying changes in the scope and coverage of the welfare state since 1980. During this long conservative era, when the dominant political discourse favored unleashing markets and scaling back the public sector, two major transformations occurred in tandem.[60] First, businesses largely abandoned their mid-twentieth-century role as partners with government in the social contract. American workers, particularly those with less education, found fewer jobs with good pay, benefits, and job security, and employees of all educational levels experienced greater job insecurity. Economic inequality soared, and mobility deteriorated. Second, government stepped up. Against the tide of efforts to shrink public programs, lawmakers effectively protected most of them, and in a few key instances they found opportunities to create new programs or to expand existing ones, whether by altering eligibility rules to broaden coverage or, less often, by making benefits more generous. Meanwhile, with the aging of the baby boomers and the declining incomes of many people of working age, more Americans than ever began to qualify for several existing benefits. Policies therefore gradually provided coverage to more Americans.

We assess how these policy developments accumulated in the lives of individual Americans in chapter 3. The use of social benefits has become a common experience for Americans, one that unites them across social, political, and geographic divisions. But if Americans of all stripes rely on social provision, then why do antigovernment attitudes and political behavior persist? This brings us to the puzzle that is at the heart of our inquiry.

Delving Deeper into Policy Feedback Effects . . . and Their Limits

Probing the government-citizen disconnect as manifested in individuals' lives requires that we take our understanding of policy feedback to the next level by examining when it does and does not occur and the varied paths it takes. Most of what scholars have learned about policy effects so far concerns how policy design and delivery convey information to recipients, whether through the resources they bestow or the cognitive lessons they impart, and how that may in turn influence attitudes about government generally, support for specific policies, and participation in politics.[61] Programs with broad, inclusive eligibility terms are thought to convey more positive messages and generate greater civic engagement than means-tested programs—those that limit benefits to individuals with incomes below a particular level—as the latter can be stigmatizing and marginalizing.[62] Policies embedded in the tax code or channeled through private organizations (those with "submerged" designs) leave recipients less aware of government's role as a provider of social benefits than do government policies that deliver benefits in more direct and visible ways.[63] To date, however, we have been unable to disentangle the impact of these different design features or to assess how accumulated usage of particular policy types might influence individuals' views of government, broadly understood.[64]

This book explores how individuals' accumulated experiences of these different types of public policies relate to their present attitudes about government. It also probes the association between policy experiences and rates of political participation. A novel data set permits an accounting of individuals' lifetime usage of twenty-one different federal social policies, distinguishing between all four possible combinations of means-tested versus non-means-tested and visible versus submerged designs. I also examine past usage of a few specific policies—for instance, by comparing the Earned Income Tax Credit, which channels means-tested benefits to less-advantaged Americans through the tax code, with public assistance, which makes government's role more obvious. I probe how these and other policy experiences relate to a wide array of citizens' attitudes about government.

To preview briefly, the extent to which policy designs make government's role visible in some instances influences recipients' inclination to credit government with helping them or providing opportunities. Use of the GI Bill and Pell Grants, for example, or multiple uses of visible means-tested policies are associated with positive effects. By contrast, in the case of the EITC, despite the generous resources committed to this policy and its success in lifting people out of poverty, its design—submerged in the tax code—leaves recipients unaware that government has come to their aid. Still, what is most striking is how rarely multiple firsthand experiences of government largesse, not only of policies with hidden designs but even of those with seemingly visible designs, yield an impact on beneficiaries' attitudes about government.

If such direct, personal experiences of policies bear so little relationship to attitudes about government, what does make a difference? Overall, I found that Americans view government as if they are all wearing different eyeglasses that influence what they see. Individuals' lenses are refined only in part through their personal accumulated policy experiences and the information about government they have gleaned through them. Instead, shared identities and the perspectives they convey often prove more influential in determining how individuals perceive government. These different lenses reveal "government-in-action" to differing extents and depict it in very different ways. Some individuals perceive government as visible and valuable in their lives while for a great many others it is barely visible at all.

Among those who overlook government's role in their own lives, their focus is drawn elsewhere. Some adopt their social group's view of government, often reflecting historic legacies of how that group has fared vis-à-vis government, even if the group's earlier experiences are different from an individual's own experience. Others focus not on the policies that have benefitted them, but instead on what they perceive as government's inappropriate role in aiding "undeserving" others, through programs they associate with "welfare." These views emanate particularly from middle-income Americans who have incomes above the cutoff for such benefits, and whose lives have been buffeted by rising economic inequality. Racism also appears to drive antipathy to welfare, continuing its long entanglement in the United States with perceptions of social provision for citizens deemed the "undeserving poor."[65] What is striking is that those who hold such perceptions of welfare extrapolate from them to adopt a negative orientation to government generally: their disdain for welfare feeds into a broader dislike of government and sense of alienation from it.

During recent decades, the growing usage of government social provision has done little to spark more widespread political activity aimed at protecting, preserving, and expanding those programs. To be sure, those who are most aware and appreciative of government's role in their lives through social benefits are most likely to favor broad expansions of social provision. Yet, ironically, these same individuals participate significantly less in politics than others, both in elections and in other political activities. By contrast, those who use social benefits but exhibit little cognizance of government's role in providing them are very likely to participate routinely in politics, as are those who are most hostile to government. The loudest political voices belong to those who have benefited from policies but who give government little credit for their economic well-being, which they tend to see as a matter of their own deservingness. This leads to electoral outcomes that undermine the political capacity to strengthen social policies while fueling the efforts of those who seek to weaken them. As a result, it has become more difficult for the U.S. political system to respond effectively to rising economic inequality. The government-citizen disconnect undermines the political support necessary to update and improve existing policies so that they can better meet Americans' needs. More fundamentally, this disconnect frays the bonds that make representative government and democracy possible.

Yet, it doesn't have to be this way. Not only visible policy designs but also membership groups and organizations can do much to make government's role more evident to individuals by illuminating what difference it makes. For citizens who already recognize how government matters, groups and organizations can point the way toward means of participating in politics, so that they can make their voices heard. By finding ways to reconnect citizens and government, we can improve the health of democracy.

Charting the Journey

The mystery of the unabated growth of antigovernment attitudes in an age when more and more citizens rely on government presents a ripe topic for investigation. The scholar who has addressed this conundrum most directly is the sociologist Arlie Russell Hochschild, in her fascinating book *Strangers in Their Own Land: Anger and Mourning on the American Right*. Like me, Hochschild perceived a paradox at work in the increasingly antigovernment attitudes of many Americans—a paradox that she defines as "the need for help and a principled refusal of it."[66] To make sense of it, she traveled to Louisiana and conducted in-depth interviews over a five-year period, probing what she terms the "deep story" of the feelings that underlie politics. This book, by contrast, offers a systematic inventory of individuals' specific interactions with social policies. I have collected data that permit statistical aggregation and analysis, so that it is possible to evaluate how such policy experiences relate to broader attitudes about government, controlling for other aspects of personal experiences.[67] Hochschild's approach complements my own, and her deeply insightful analysis illuminates some of my key findings, which I discuss later in the book.

This book draws on three major sources of evidence. First, I collected data from myriad government agencies and constructed a large data set that specifies, over time, the percentage of Americans covered by each of twenty-one federal social policies and the real value of those benefits at the individual or household level.[68] These data, presented in chapter 2, permit us to assess the changing size and scope of the American welfare state over time.

Second, to describe how social benefits are utilized across time and place, I used data available through the U.S. Bureau of Economic Analysis (BEA) in the Department of Commerce. These data illustrate the change in the percentage of personal income that flows from the federal government, across time, by state and county. They are the basis of the figures and maps shown earlier in this chapter and of county-level maps and some other evidence presented in chapters 3 and 5.

Third, I analyzed the results of a national survey I conducted in 2008, through the Cornell Survey Research Institute, that explores Americans' attitudes about government and policies, their participation in politics, and how these relate to their lifetime usage and policy experiences of the twenty-one federal social policies. The Social and Governmental Issues and Participation Study (SGIP), a telephone survey of 1,400 Americans, remains unique in that it includes questions about both political attitudes and participation as well as program experiences, whereas most surveys ask either one type of question or the other, but not both. The combination of these questions in a single survey is what makes it possible to evaluate how accumulated experiences of usage as well as use of particular policies relate to attitudes about government and rates of political involvement. A description of the design and procedures for the survey appears in appendix A, the questionnaire itself appears in appendix B, and a discussion of the response rates and a comparison to other surveys appear in appendix C.

It is important to note the limitations and appropriate uses of the SGIP data. Asking individuals questions at one point in time about the policies they have ever used previously raises questions about how reliably people can remember these past experiences. To minimize these concerns, I took several measures in designing the survey to facilitate respondents' recall, as explained in appendix A. Furthermore, I utilized the policy usage data gleaned from the survey to explore patterns among different groups of individuals, not to provide definitive usage rates among the U.S. population; I rely on the administrative data noted earlier to provide the latter.

Research about how policy experiences affect political behavior also faces challenges of sorting out cause and effect, given that some prior characteristic of beneficiaries may influence both their policy usage and their subsequent attitudes or participation, or because they may exhibit behavior after usage that they already exhibited previously. To detect these dynamics, ideally we would have access to panel data, collected from the same individuals over time, or data from field experiments; such data sources would permit us to isolate the impact of policy usage while holding other factors constant.[69] Yet such data remain extremely rare. None of the existing sources, moreover, permit us to consider use of the large number of policies explored in the SGIP study.

Because the SGIP data were collected at one moment in time, they must be analyzed cautiously. I do so in three ways. In chapter 3, I use them descriptively to show cumulative patterns of usage among individuals with different characteristics. In chapter 4 and the beginning of chapter 5, I explore how policy usage shapes political attitudes. This analysis is facilitated by the survey questions that investigate whether individuals have *ever* used specific policies, probing the past, and attitudinal questions that investigate their current views of government and public policies, that is, at the time of the data collection. We can infer that past experiences may influence subsequent attitudes, while exercising caution given the concerns noted earlier. When it comes to political participation, however, the survey does not permit us to disentangle the timing of it and policy usage, so we consider only associations, in the latter parts of chapter 5, not causal relationships.

In addition to the data sets used for the actual analysis in the book, I also sought a means of illustrating how ordinary citizens think about social benefits and discuss them in their own words. Toward that end, and with the help of two research assistants, I conducted follow-up open-ended, qualitative interviews with a small number of survey respondents.[70] In 2015, we wrote to respondents to the original survey who had indicated a willingness to be recontacted, requesting the opportunity to conduct a follow-up interview. We limited our contacts to respondents of working age, defined as those who had been born since 1950 (age sixty-five or younger), and those who had answered the survey question about income. We interviewed twenty-one of those who responded.[71] Their responses provide elaboration on some of the attitudes and experiences explored here. Where they are quoted or discussed, pseudonyms are used. The questionnaire used for these interviews appears in appendix D.

It should be noted that this book conceptualizes the welfare state broadly, encompassing both direct, visible programs and those channeled through the tax code. The BEA data, used for the mapping and other spatial analysis, excludes most of the tax expenditures, with the exception of the EITC, the child tax credits, and a few other smaller ones. The SGIP data, by contrast, include both types, as does the data set drawn from the wide array of government agencies; both investigate the same twenty-one policies. In combination, these sources permit us to chart the size and scope of the American welfare state, how its coverage has changed over time, how usage of its programs accumulates in individuals' lives, and how it relates to Americans' views about government and participation in politics.

The United States today faces a paradoxical crisis. In some respects, the nation has responded inadequately to—and even exacerbated—rising economic inequality. In other ways, policymakers have stepped up and existing policies have been broadened to provide greater social provision for families struggling from declining and stagnant incomes and the loss of incomes. Yet, in the meantime, Americans have lost faith in their own government, and confidence in it has declined to all-time lows. The use of social benefits has done little to stem the tide of growing antipathy toward public institutions as many Americans increasingly turn away from government.

At the least, these developments make American politics more and more divisive and impotent, turning some people off from participating at all. At the worst, rising frustration with government appears to be making some Americans less protective of basic principles of the Constitution and more willing to support a leader who rules through personal power, with little respect for the rule of law.[72] What is at stake here is not only the future of American social provision but, more importantly, the well-being of democratic governance.

CHAPTER 2

THE MARKET RECEDES, GOVERNMENT RESPONDS

WHEN LOU CLARK started working for the Urban League in Syracuse in 1969 to help find jobs for young African American residents, opportunities were on the rise. Numerous manufacturers offered positions with good pay, benefits, and chances for promotion—jobs that, as Lou puts it, "could support a family." Companies were willing to offer necessary training even to prospective employees who lacked high school diplomas. Lou founded the Black Employment Council, a network of African American professionals working in the personnel departments of locally based corporations who shared information about job openings with each other and sought to help young people find and attain those positions.[1]

But as the 1970s advanced, employers began to leave the region and jobs disappeared with them. Over the next three decades, employer after employer announced layoffs and, worse yet, plant closures: Allied Chemical, General Electric, General Motors, Carrier, and numerous others. Lou now belongs to 100 Black Men, a group that pursues similar goals to the now defunct Black Employment Council's, but encounters far greater challenges. In the atrophied labor market, the group lacks the personal connections of the past, and the high school graduates it assists are fortunate if they can find work at a fast-food restaurant, typically for the minimum wage of $9 per hour. There are some better-paying jobs in the suburbs, but city residents often lack the transportation to get to them. Most new jobs in the region are positions such as home health aides and restaurant cooks that offer annual pay hovering around $22,000; the few growth areas offering salaries of more than $40,000 per year require substantial advanced education.[2]

As decent jobs vanished in Syracuse, the poverty rate soared from 18 percent in 1979 to 35 percent in 2014.[3] All racial and ethnic groups experienced worsening conditions. As the percentage of African Americans living below the poverty line grew from 33 to 44 percent, upward mobility that had only barely begun ground to a halt. Among Hispanics, poverty rates skyrocketed from 35 to 56 percent. White poverty rose from 15 to 26 percent, but meanwhile the actual size of the white population diminished by more than half, as many who could afford to relocate did so.[4] Overall, economic conditions in Syracuse declined, particularly among working-age adults and most of all for children, exactly half of whom were living in poverty by 2014.[5]

With the market increasingly failing to provide sufficient employment, more people experienced greater need, and safety net programs responded. The percentage of the population using some form of cash public assistance nearly doubled, from 11 percent in 1979 to 20 percent in 2014.[6] The percentage of the population receiving food stamps grew from 20 percent in 2005 to 32 percent in 2014, and 48 percent of the households receiving food stamps included children under age eighteen. By 2014, 45 percent of city residents had gained government-sponsored health coverage, predominantly through Medicaid or Medicare.[7]

While conditions worsened in deindustrialized Rust Belt cities such as Syracuse, they also deteriorated in many of the rural counties surrounding them. Long-term changes in the economy and population trends led to rising poverty rates in these nonmetropolitan areas as well, and as a result, the percentage of the rural population relying on social transfers also increased.[8]

In many different types of communities throughout the nation, the strong patterns of economic growth of the postwar era came to an end and life became more difficult for low- and middle-income Americans. Each locality and people at different points on the economic spectrum faced distinct challenges, yet none were exempt from broad national trends. Average family income growth had increased across the income spectrum throughout the postwar era from 1947 to 1979, a period when, as President John F. Kennedy said of the soaring economy, "the rising tide lifts all the boats."[9] From 1979 onward, by contrast, overall growth slowed considerably for all but those in the top 5 percent, with the worst losses in absolute and relative terms being felt lower down the economic distribution.

The market, though much lauded by conservative politicians and intellectuals, failed to deliver expanded economic security and well-being for most Americans, and inequality soared. Although the strong economy of the late 1990s briefly mitigated the long-term trends, by the early 2000s growth slowed once again. The recession that began in 2007 brought greater income losses, particularly for the bottom 80 percent.[10] Since 2009, the nation's economy has gradually improved, but inequality has increased all the more, with the richest 1 percent seeing their fortunes rise by 7.7 percent by 2015 while the incomes of the bottom 99 percent increased by only 3.9 percent.[11] CEO compensation has skyrocketed since the 1970s, when it averaged thirty times the pay of the average worker, to two hundred times the pay of the average worker today.[12]

Despite the antigovernment discourse of this era, several social policies were expanded to meet the growing needs of low- and middle-income Americans. The task here is to step back and survey the broader policy landscape and how it changed over time by amassing data to identify aggregate trends in the coverage and value of social benefits. As the market receded, public policies that in the mid-twentieth century had strengthened American workers' earning capacity began to deteriorate. Against the odds, government stepped up with new and expanded social provision, offering some minimal level of economic security and well-being to a greater proportion of the population than ever before. Still, gaping holes remain today as existing policies have failed to provide sufficiently for many in need.

This chapter uses the social policy benefit data I collected from government agencies to chart usage and benefit generosity in twenty-one federal social policies. The aim is to measure the changing impact of government in citizens' lives. To gauge program coverage relative to the size of the population over time, I used current population data and calculated the percentage of all Americans who utilize benefits in each program each year. To assess the value of benefits over time, I applied the Consumer Price Index (CPI) and transformed average benefit amounts per individual or household into constant or real terms.

Market Failure . . . and Glorification

After the United States emerged from World War II, economic growth soared and jobs with good pay and benefits proliferated. Americans across the income spectrum experienced upward social mobility, and inequality reached its lowest point in the twentieth century.[13] Opportunities abounded for white men, including those who lacked college degrees, who found jobs a few rungs higher up the socioeconomic ladder than those their fathers had held.[14] Following the civil rights achievements of the 1950s and 1960s, black men began to find more openings in the job market as well.[15]

Public policies bolstered the strong postwar economy. Prior to the New Deal, Americans lacked meaningful rights in the workplace, as labor unions remained unsanctioned by government and the Supreme Court had invalidated state-level protective labor laws except those for women only. That changed in 1935 when Congress enacted the National Labor Relations Act (NLRA), which granted unions the right to organize and engage in collective bargaining; the NLRA was followed in 1938 by the Fair Labor Standards Act (FLSA), which guaranteed minimum wage and maximum hours laws. In a reversal from the past, the Supreme Court upheld both laws as well as new state-level laws protecting workers.[16] As a result of the NLRA, in the 1950s and 1960s, labor unions reached their strongest point in American history, with one in four workers among their members. Their activity boosted the wages even of workers who did not belong to them.[17] In addition, labor strength helped make employer-provided health and retirement benefits the norm in most jobs. In 1950, General Motors signed the "Treaty of Detroit," a contract with the United Auto Workers (UAW) that ensured employees' receipt of these benefits and became emblematic of the era's prevailing approach to social provision for workers: the private sector providing benefits subsidized by government. Accordingly, President Dwight Eisenhower advanced the tax-free status of all employer-provided health benefits as an important component of social provision, and this approach became law when he signed the Revenue Act of 1954.[18]

In the early 1970s, however, tectonic shifts began to alter the American job market. The first tremors were felt in 1973, when the economy was rocked by oil shocks that led to soaring energy prices. The nation also faced mounting international competition from Asia, particularly Japan. The economy slowed and inflation grew, particularly as the Federal Reserve increased the cost of borrowing, which in turn spurred unemployment.[19]

The market receded from the impressive role it had played for decades in providing for Americans' well-being. The ranks of the jobless, which throughout the entire postwar era had only on three brief occasions crested 6 percent, spiked to 9 percent in 1975 as the economy launched into recession, and to 11 percent as it did so again in 1982.[20] Manufacturing companies in northeastern cities such as Syracuse pulled up stakes, either closing plants and relocating in southern states with lower labor costs and lower rates of labor organization or leaving the country to operate else-where.[21] Jobs in the sector plummeted from one in four in 1973 to one in ten in 2010.

The nation's overall employment rates had rebounded by the late 1980s, but the new jobs offered much less to workers than had the manufacturing jobs of the past, particularly to those with less education. Job growth in more recent decades has been concentrated in low-wage service sectors, with pay over the last decade hovering between $9 and $13 per hour.[22] Men's wages, compared to their high-water mark in 1973, deteriorated for those in the middle of the earnings distribution and below. Family incomes held steady largely because of the growing participation of women in the work-force.[23] While women experienced some real wage growth over the period, particularly in the bottom quintile of the earnings distribution, their wages nevertheless continued to lag behind men's. Overall, the gender wage gap—women's hourly earnings relative to men's—diminished from 69 percent in 1979 to 83 percent in 2015.[24]

Paradoxically, just when the actual market was leaving so many Ameri-cans behind, a new public philosophy emerged that featured as its center-piece a venerated ideal of the market. This approach, which aimed to re-place Keynesianism, eschewed government intervention and advanced a faith that the market, left to its own devices, would naturally and sponta-neously maximize the preferences of individuals and generate positive out-comes.[25] As the historian Daniel T. Rodgers points out, "The puzzle of the era's enchantment of the market idea is that it was born not out of success but out of such striking market failure."[26]

For conservatives, who had long been seeking to overcome their margin-alized status, the economic crisis provided a political opportunity and the embrace of the market offered a useful heuristic for a more limited ap-proach to governance. New conservatism had been percolating at the state and local levels and in think tanks for decades, but when Ronald Reagan was elected to the presidency, it gained a charismatic national leader in the quest to dismantle the New Deal regime.[27] Advocates of this approach began to pursue policy changes, particularly aiming to relax the obligations of business toward workers.

From the late 1970s to the present, public officials condoned the deterio-ration of policies that previously had bolstered workers' leverage in the po-litical economy, and in several respects they pursued the demise of these policies. During the Carter administration, Congress considered a bill to improve and update the moribund National Labor Relations Act. That bill would have repealed provisions of the Labor Management Relations Act of 1947 (the Taft-Hartley Act), which permitted states to adopt "right to work" rules that discouraged unionizing, and it would have allowed "card-check" procedures for enlisting new union members, an easier method than those inscribed in the NLRA. Although the bill sailed through the House, it became the victim of a Senate filibuster, falling one vote shy of the supermajority required to bring it to a vote.[28] Next, in a highly symbolic act, Reagan became the first president to take an openly combative stance toward organized labor. When eleven thousand air traffic control workers went on strike, he responded forcefully by firing them outright and banning them from future jobs in the federal government.[29] With public officials no longer offering firm support of labor rights, management proceeded to push the limits, putting workers increasingly on the offensive.[30] Public unions remained strong long after private-sector unions were decimated, but since 2011, GOP governors and legislatures in several states have put them on the defensive as well by aggressively seeking to scale back their collective bargaining rights.[31]

As a result, the ranks of organized labor have declined precipitously, falling from 24 percent of the workforce in 1979 to 11 percent in 2015, as shown by figure 2.1. This transformation has yielded profound consequences: the economist Richard Freeman claims that it accounts for 20 percent of the rise in inequality—a much more significant role than that played by globalization, the more frequently cited explanation.[32] Unions, when they are strong, play a powerful role in reducing inequality by granting a union wage premium to those employed in highly organized sectors, which in turn increases wage scales for non-union workers as well, elevating wages particularly among less-educated and blue-collar workers.[33] They also mobilize people to take part in elections, boosting turnout in particular among their low-income members, and thus promote greater responsiveness on the part of elected officials.[34] Labor's demise has left it far less capable of achieving such goals.

Meanwhile, the federal minimum wage plummeted in real value as lawmakers failed to update it sufficiently. Because it lacks the protection of automatic cost-of-living adjustments, the minimum wage necessarily deteriorates owing to inflation unless lawmakers agree to boost the rate. Each president who served from 1938 to 1978, both Democrats and Republicans, approved an increase. That pattern ended with Reagan, who called the

Figure 2.1 The Rise and Fall of Union Membership and the Minimum Wage, 1930–2015

Source: Data are reported by the U.S. Department of Labor and the U.S. Bureau of Labor Statistics (BLS). For the minimum wage, 1938–2015, see "History of Federal Minimum Wage Rates under the Fair Labor Standards Act, 1938–2009," Wage and Hour Division, U.S. Department of Labor, Washington, D.C., http://www.dol.gov/whd/minwage/chart.htm (accessed February 15, 2018). For union membership, 1938–1983, see U.S. Department of Labor (1975), 389; Bureau of National Affairs (1997), 10; and Jacobs and Ryan (2003), 378–79. For the period 1983–2015, see BLS, "Databases, Tables, and Calculators, by Subject," http://www.bls.gov/data/#historical-tables (accessed February 15, 2018).

minimum wage an injustice that was responsible for "more misery and unemployment than anything since the Great Depression."[35] The modest increases approved during subsequent administrations failed to make up for lost ground. As seen in figure 2.1, the minimum wage fell from its peak value in 1968, when it was worth $10.89 in 2015 dollars, to $7.25 in 2015. Its demise represents another major source of rising inequality, an outcome mitigated in other English-speaking nations, such as Great Britain and Australia, which offer significantly higher rates.[36] Economists predict that a boost in the minimum wage from its current rate of $7.25 to $9.80 would directly benefit 15.3 percent of the workforce and indirectly benefit another 7.0 percent of the workforce, those who earn just above $7.25, who would be likely to see a boost in their paychecks as well. Among those who would benefit, 55 percent are women, and contrary to the assumption that teenage workers would be most affected, 88 percent of those earning the minimum wage are over age twenty.[37]

Making matters worse for workers at the low end of the income scale,

Figure 2.2 Rising Inequality in Employer-Provided Health Insurance Coverage, by Wage Group, 1979–2010

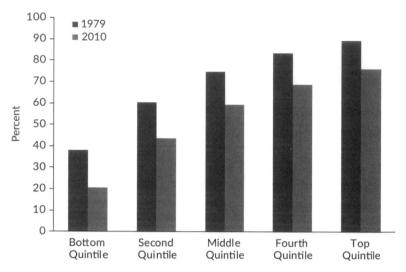

Source: Mishel et al. (2012), 200.
Note: Includes only private-sector wage and salary workers ages eighteen to sixty-four who worked twenty hours a week or more, twenty-six weeks a year or more.

fewer and fewer jobs offered health and retirement benefits over this period. The share of workers whose employers provided health coverage dropped from over 70 percent in the early 1980s to 56 percent in 2010.[38] Low-wage workers, already the least likely to possess such benefits, experienced the most precipitous declines in coverage, in both real and absolute terms. As seen in figure 2.2, coverage rates for the lowest quintile dropped by 46 percent, from 37.9 percent to 20.5 percent. Fewer jobs offered secure retirement benefits of any kind, and the share of private-sector employees with "defined benefit" plans financed solely by their employers fell from 28 percent in 1980 to 3 percent in 2011.[39] Overall, the inequality in employee benefits grew faster than the inequality in wages.[40]

In sum, contrary to the tenets of the new conservatism, the market has actually receded from its role of providing jobs with good pay and benefits, particularly for those who are less well-off. Employers have scaled back their role in the social contract, and government itself has sanctioned their retreat as lawmakers have loosened the regulations that bound them to that contract. Today it is only those in the upper quintile of the labor market who still enjoy working conditions that resemble those that were widely accessible at midcentury, and even they encounter more frequent spells of joblessness. In his 2016 State of the Union Address, President Barack Obama told Congress, "It's not too much of a stretch to say that some of the only people in America who are going to work the same job, in the same place, with a health and retirement package for 30 years are sitting in this chamber."[41] Although the president exaggerated to make a point, it was undeniable that the market, left to its own devices, had yielded an unimpressive record as the single-handed "solution to our problem."

Expanding Social Provision

Over the past thirty-five years, lawmakers have faced a conundrum. On the one hand, the public philosophy of the age has called for scaling back government and terminating citizens' dependence on it. On the other hand, the changing job market and weakened social contract between government and workers have put Americans in greater need of public social provision.

During the Great Depression, in 1934, President Franklin D. Roosevelt told the nation, "If, as our Constitution tells us, our Federal Government was established among other things, 'to promote the general welfare,' it is our plain duty to provide for that security upon which welfare depends." The New Deal directed public policies toward—in Roosevelt's words—"the forgotten man at the bottom of the economic pyramid," not only through its policies for workers but also by creating several social policies, including Old-Age and Survivors Insurance (OASI, or Social Security), Unemployment Insurance (UI), and Aid to Dependent Children (ADC), which became known as "welfare." In subsequent decades, public officials further expanded the federal government's capacity to respond to ordinary citizens—for example, through student loans and grants for college students, signed into law by Eisenhower, Johnson, and Nixon, and through Medicare and Medicaid, championed by Johnson.

From the Reagan administration through the emergence of the Tea Party after the election of Barack Obama, conservatives have gone on the offensive to diminish the welfare state. Yet most social policies, though they have endured long periods of neglect and some outright cuts, have proven fairly resilient over these decades. Certainly many of these policies contain features that make them inaccessible to many Americans who need them. Overall, moreover, they do much less than they could to reduce inequality;

in fact, many feature an upward redistributive tilt. And several policies have been subject to restructuring or drift that undermines their capacity to accomplish their original goals, whether to alleviate deep poverty or to promote upward mobility. Given the politics of the past few decades, however, what is remarkable is that most such programs have survived and been expanded to meet some measure of growing needs.

All of the social policies examined here are listed in table 2.1, by type. The first column lists the percentage of the entire population utilizing the policy during 2015 or the most recent year with available data. The second column lists the value of the average benefits to individuals. These details are drawn primarily from the historical data set compiled for this book, which examines changes in both the scope and the value of benefits over time; figures from this data set are mentioned throughout the following discussion. The third column lists the basic eligibility criteria.

Policies for Seniors Grow Stronger

As the nation's most expensive domestic program, Social Security appeared at first to make an alluring target for conservative budget-cutters. During Reagan's first six months in office, the Office of Management and Budget (OMB) put forward a White House budget that proposed trimming Social Security by $45 billion, in the form of 25 percent reductions in benefits for early retirees, tighter disability requirements, delayed cost-of-living adjustments, and a slowdown in the growth of future benefits. Although Reagan himself did not champion the cuts, he had in the past suggested that contributing to Social Security should be voluntary, and he favored private alternatives.[42] The initiative to slash benefits provoked a firestorm, a pronounced example of what Andrea Campbell calls the "participation-policy cycle."[43] Within three days after the cutbacks were announced, Campbell reports, "mail poured into Congress and the White House. Besieged by calls from angry constituents, members of both parties attacked the proposals."[44] Once the GOP-controlled Senate passed a resolution rejecting the proposal by a vote of 96–0 and the House followed suit, Reagan withdrew his proposals.

Public officials floated additional proposals for scaling back both Social Security and Medicare on a few other occasions later in the 1980s, and since then, but senior citizens protested them vigorously each time. As a result, the two policies have remained largely intact to the present, notwithstand-

Table 2.1 Current Federal Social Policy Benefits by Coverage, Value, anc Eligibility Criteria

	PERCENTAGE OF THE POPULATION COVERED IN 2015 (OR IN MOST RECENT YEAR AVAILABLE)	AVERAGE VALUE OF INDIVIDUAL BENEFITS OVER TWELVE MONTHS (ONE YEAR), 2015 (OR MOST RECENT YEAR AVAILABLE)	BASIC ELIGIBILITY REQUIREMENTS
Visible policies			
Medicaid	23.3%	$5,149[a]	Low income limit
Medicare	17.0[b]	10,300[c]	Workforce history
Social Security retirement benefits	15.3	16,128[d]	Workforce history
Food stamps (SNAP)	14.2	1,522	Low income limit
Social Security Disability Insurance (SSDI)	3.4	16,188[d]	Disability, workforce history
Pell Grants	2.8[a]	3,692	Low income limit, college attendance
Supplemental Security Income (SSI)	2.6	8,796	Disability, low income limit
Subsidized housing	1.46	7,068[e]	Low income limit
Veterans' benefits	1.3[d]	13,895	Military service
Unemployment Insurance (UI)	1.1[f]	14,964	Workforce history
Temporary Assistance to Needy Families (TANF)	0.9	5,184[g]	Low income limit, workforce participation
GI Bill	0.3[d]	30,230[h]	Military service
Head Start	0.3	8,771	Low income limit
Submerged policies			
Tax-subsidized, employer-provided health benefits	47.8[i]	2,030[i]	Workforce participation
Tax-subsidized, employer-provided retirement benefits	38.6[i]	2,710[i]	Workforce participation
Home mortgage interest deduction	23.5[h]	2,156	Homeownership, mortgage debt
Earned Income Tax Credit (EITC)	18.5[h]	2,469	Workforce participation, low income limit
American Opportunity Tax Credit, Lifetime Learning Credit, and student loan interest deduction	9.9[i]	900[i]	Income limits, college attendance

(continued)

Table 2.1 (*continued*)

	PERCENTAGE OF THE POPULATION COVERED IN 2015 (OR IN MOST RECENT YEAR AVAILABLE)	AVERAGE VALUE OF INDIVIDUAL BENEFITS OVER TWELVE MONTHS (ONE YEAR), 2015 (OR MOST RECENT YEAR AVAILABLE)	BASIC ELIGIBILITY REQUIREMENTS
Child and Dependent Care Tax Credit	4.2[h]	711	Incurred care expenses
Student loans[k]	2.8[l]	10,807[j]	College attendance
529 plans and Coverdells	n/a	Various, typically worth a few hundred dollars[c]	Saving for education

Source: All data in table for which sources are not cited in the following notes are from the author's historical data set collected from U.S. government sources.

[a] 2013.

[b] Medicare coverage data come from Kaiser Family Foundation, "Medicare Beneficiaries as a Percent of Total Population" (2011–2015), http://kff.org/medicare/state-indicator/medicare-beneficiaries-as-of-total-pop/?activeTab=graph&currentTimeframe=0&startTimeframe=4&selectedDistributions=medicare-beneficiaries-as-a-share-of-total-population (accessed February 15, 2018).

[c] Medicare average benefit for the aged (not the disabled). For 529s and Coverdells, it is difficult to list a meaningful number, since individuals may have them for multiple dependents.

[d] 2014.

[e] 2010 data from Johnson, Renwick, and Short (2010), 19.

[f] 2012.

[g] Median monthly benefit in states in 2016, multiplied by 12; data from Floyd 2016, 12.

[h] The GI Bill estimate calculated using average tuition and fees at public colleges ($9,420), as reported in College Board (2016, 3), plus the average housing allowance multiplied by 12 ($20,172) and half of the maximum book allowance of $1,000; see Military.com, "Post-9/11 GI Bill Overview," http://www.military.com/education/gi-bill/new-post-911-gi-bill-overview.html (accessed February 15, 2018).

[i] "Percentage of the population covered" is actually the percentage of tax returns filed claiming the benefit, which is approximately the percentage of "households."

[j] 2016. Data on employer-provided benefits and education tax expenditures come from the Urban-Brookings Tax Policy Center. The amounts shown are the tax savings only, not the additional value of the benefit itself.

[k] Student loans are categorized as "submerged" because their design made them so from 1965 to 2010, and thus they are treated as such in the analysis of the SGIP data, which was collected in 2008.

[l] Student loan data come from the College Board (2016) and show Stafford loans, subsidized and unsubsidized, for graduate and undergraduate students. While these are listed as a benefit, they must be repaid.

ing some important changes that trimmed access to Social Security for the least well-off and siphoned off some Medicare beneficiaries into private-sector plans.[45]

Coverage and benefit rates (see table 2.1 for current figures) reveal that both programs have not only endured but even grown in some key respects. Demographic shifts—namely, the aging of the baby boom generation—have increased the percentage of Americans benefiting from Social Security. As of 2015, 15.3 percent of the population received Social Security in the form of retirement checks or benefits for spouses and survivors, up from 13.5 percent in 1980. The cost-of living adjustment feature, which Nixon signed into law in 1971, ensured that benefits would retain their value; in fact, the average retired worker in 2014 collected $16,128 annually in program benefits, up from $11,772 in 1980 (2015 dollars). The percentage of the public enrolled in Medicare had grown to 17 percent by 2015.[46] Due to the mounting costs of medical care, average annual benefits increased, in real terms, from $5,148 in 1980 to $10,300 in 2013.[47]

In sum, even during a long era when the welfare state has been under attack, Social Security and Medicare have endured reasonably well. Certainly conservatives continue to seek cuts in both programs; the George W. Bush administration (unsuccessfully) promoted the partial privatization of Social Security in 2005, and Representative Paul Ryan (R-WI) regularly advances budget plans that would curtail both. Yet these two popular programs benefit from the strong political support they have developed over many decades, along with a financing structure—through payroll taxes—that makes the deservingness of recipients explicit. The widespread perception that eligibility for these programs is an earned right of those who have spent many years in the paid workforce bolsters their strength, and to date that perception has helped them remain fairly resilient.

Visible Policies for Nonseniors Survive Against the Odds

Visible policies for working-age Americans and their children have faced far greater political challenges over recent decades than those targeted to seniors. They are less likely to enjoy the support of mobilized constituencies that advocate on their behalf to protect and maintain benefits.[48] Nonetheless, not only have most of these policies survived, but their coverage rates have grown. Their growth owes in part to the impact on jobs and wages of the sluggish economy, which has left more people in circumstances that qualify them for benefits. Economists have praised the policies for performing their intended function as a safety net, particularly during the 2008 downturn and its aftermath: these policies covered the larger portion of the population that qualified for benefits, lifted people out of poverty, and provided a countercyclical force.[49] Coverage rates have also increased because lawmakers have managed, in a few instances, to muster enough political support to expand the terms of eligibility for existing policies. Yet the limits of these policies' capacity to provide sufficiently for those in need have also become increasingly evident, for reasons to be discussed later in this chapter.

The New Deal–era policy that did not survive the conservative onslaught—the exception to the rule—was the policy most identified with the welfare state itself: Aid to Families with Dependent Children (AFDC), otherwise known as "welfare," which policymakers terminated in 1996. Originally called Aid to Dependent Children when it was created in 1935 as an income support policy for families that lacked a male "breadwinner", AFDC had increasingly come under fire from critics who, without evidence, blamed it for the rise in births to single mothers.[50] As more married women with young children entered the workforce, moreover, the public grew increasingly dissatisfied with the policy's bestowal of benefits on mothers who were not employed. Already in 1976, when Reagan campaigned in the presidential primary, his stump speech included a reference to the "welfare queen"—a profligate individual who freely took advantage of government benefits and even engaged in fraud.[51] Images of welfare recipients, advanced by journalists and others, racialized the policy and conveyed the impression that most beneficiaries were African American.[52] Social scientists showed these stereotypes to be misleading, given that the typical welfare recipient was white, most beneficiaries used the program for a short period when they were in between jobs, and fraud was extremely rare. Nonetheless, the public increasingly expressed disfavor with welfare, even as it continued to support government help for the poor generally.[53]

By the time Bill Clinton ran for president in 1992, he had broken with the Democratic Party's tradition of defending the policy and promised to "end welfare as we know it." After vetoing the first two welfare reform bills sent to his desk by the GOP-controlled Congress, he signed the third, during the 1996 presidential election. The Personal Responsibility and Work Opportunity Reconciliation Act became law, replacing AFDC with Temporary Assistance for Needy Families (TANF). The policy imposed bold new federal requirements: time limits that restrict lifetime usage to sixty months and work limits that mandate employment by recipients after twenty-four months of benefit receipt.[54] These features epitomized the ascent of a liberal, individualist view of self-reliance applied in a genderless manner, replacing the more traditional New Deal approach, which had aimed to permit single mothers to serve primarily as caretakers rather than as breadwinners.[55]

Given the strong economy of the late 1990s, the welfare rolls had already begun to diminish even before Clinton signed the law, and they continued to fall afterward. Supporters of welfare reform claimed credit for their demise. As time wore on, however, the recession of 2001, the sluggish recovery, and from 2007 to 2009 the worst downturn since the Great Depression led to growing concern about those who no longer had access to welfare benefits. Low-income people reported that they sought to avoid using the stigmatized program for fear of using up their eligibility when the future might find them even worse off, and those who did use the benefits incurred a sense of shame for having done so.[56] Some believed erroneously that the program no longer existed.[57] Also, Congress and state legislatures did little to make more TANF funds available even during the worst years of the recession.[58] As a result of such forces, as seen in figure 2.3, the percentage of TANF beneficiaries has plummeted, from a high of 5.5 percent of the population in 1993 to less than 1 percent (0.94) in 2015. The value of benefits varies from state to state, but it has eroded nationwide; by 2015, benefits were worth less than half the value of income at the poverty line in all states, and less than 20 percent of that rate in sixteen states.[59]

Meanwhile, coverage rates in several programs aside from TANF grew, with the uptick beginning well before the 2008 recession, and no policy has increased its reach as dramatically as Medicaid. Originally, this policy targeted individuals who already qualified for other social benefits, including the aged, the blind, disabled individuals, and those in single-parent families using AFDC.[60] During the 1980s, Congress expanded the law several times so that it would reach more children in low-income families who did not qualify for AFDC, and by 1990 it covered anyone under age eighteen who lived below the poverty line.[61] Already Medicaid coverage had increased from 9.5 percent of the population in 1980 to 21.2 percent in 2010, as seen in figure 2.3. The Affordable Care Act, signed into law by President Obama in 2010, further enlarged Medicaid to cover families with incomes up to 133 percent of the poverty level ($26,720 for a family of three in 2015), though

Figure 2.3 Beneficiaries of Selected Social Policies as a Percentage of the U.S. Population, 1973–2015

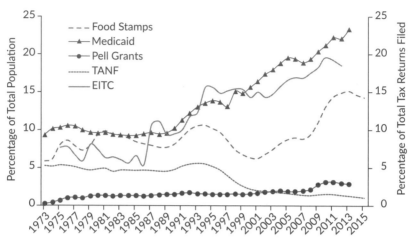

Source: Food stamps: U.S. Department of Agriculture, Food and Nutrition Service, "Supplemental Nutrition Assistance Program (SNAP): National Level Annual Summary," http://www.fns.usda.gov/pd/snapsummary.htm (accessed February 15, 2018). *EITC:* Congress of the United States, Joint Committee on Taxation, "Publications on Tax Expenditures" (individual year reports), https://www.jct.gov/publications.html?func =select&id=5 (accessed February 15, 2018). *Medicaid:* Social Security Administration (2015). *TANF:* payment data from 1936 to 2004 gathered from Social Security Administration (2006), table 9.G; data for 2005 to 2015 come from individual-year caseload reports of the U.S. Department of Health and Human Services, Office of Family Assistance, "Data and Reports: Caseload Data," http://www.acf.hhs.gov/programs/ofa /programs/tanf/data-reports (accessed February 15, 2018). *Pell Grants:* data come from the *Federal Pell Grant Program End-of-Year Reports* provided by the U.S. Department of Education, https://www2.ed.gov/finaid/prof/resources/data/pell-data.html (accessed February 15, 2018).
Note: Data reported here are those most recently reported at the time of data collection: for EITC, until 2012; for Pell Grants and Medicaid, until 2013; for TANF and food stamps until 2015.

in a 2012 decision, the U.S. Supreme Court made the expansion of Medicaid by states optional. To date, thirty-three states have adopted the expanded program and accepted the federal funding to facilitate it.[62] Overall, Medicaid coverage grew to 23.3 percent of all Americans in 2013, making it the most utilized of any direct and visible social policy in a given year. Medicaid benefit rates rose quickly owing to rising health care costs, from $3,101 on average in 1980 to $5,149 in 2013. As of 2015, seniors made up only 8 percent of all Medicaid beneficiaries, while children accounted for 43 percent.[63]

Coverage for low-income people under two additional policies besides Medicaid has also exceeded 15 percent of the population: the Earned Income Tax Credit (EITC) and food stamps. I discuss the EITC in the next section because its policy design, channeled through the tax code, makes it less visible to recipients than other policies considered here.

Congress enacted the Food Stamp Act in 1964, following experiments in earlier decades with federal programs to prevent hunger. Lawmakers originally combined the policy with the farm bill on the rationale that it would provide a means of utilizing U.S. crop surpluses. This arrangement facilitated the program's success because it spurred logrolling between senators and representatives from rural states and districts, both Democrats and Republicans who favored agricultural commodities and those from urban areas, typically Democrats, who favored food stamps. Thanks to such bipartisan support, food stamps became one of the more widely accepted programs for low-income people.[64]

The program, which was renamed the Supplemental Nutrition Assistance Program (SNAP) in 2008, benefited between 8 and 10 percent of the U.S. population from 1980 through 2007, as seen in figure 2.3. Its coverage increased during the Great Recession, surpassing 15 percent of the population in 2013, and has dipped slightly since then. The value of the program's in-kind benefits to prevent food insecurity hovered around $100 per month on average, in 2015 dollars, from 1980 through 2007 and increased somewhat during the recession, settling at $127 per month in 2015.[65] Today SNAP, following EITC, is the second-largest policy in the United States to alleviate poverty in families with children: it was responsible for lifting 4.7 million people, including 2.1 million children, out of poverty in 2014.[66]

Several other policies each enroll less than 5 percent of the population. Pell Grants, also shown in figure 2.3, were established in 1973 to provide financial aid to low-income college students. Although the program is small compared to those just listed, it doubled in size between 2001 and 2010, benefiting over 3 percent of the U.S. population. More than one in three college students today utilize Pell Grants.[67] Benefit rates languished in real terms during the 1980s and 1990s, falling well behind inflation and even further behind swiftly escalating tuition costs, but lawmakers boosted their coverage and generosity during the George W. Bush and Obama presidencies.[68] The average grant reached its highest rate in 2010, at $4,161 per year (in 2015 dollars).

In recent years, critics have charged that "disability is the new welfare," voicing alarm about rising coverage rates in the nation's two income support programs for the disabled and portraying recipients as swindlers, but these accusations misrepresent the programs' actual records.[69] Social Security Disability Insurance (SSDI) was enacted as an addition to OASI in 1956; passing the Senate by a single vote, it was signed into law by Eisenhower.[70] To qualify for benefits, individuals must have worked in covered employment long enough to qualify and must satisfy an earnings test. Supplemental Security Income (SSI), created in 1972 and signed into law by Nixon, is a means-tested program; the vast majority of its beneficiaries are disabled children or adults of working age, and a small portion are seniors who lack sufficient work history to qualify for OASI. For both DI and SSI, beneficiaries must prove that they are disabled according to the definition in the Social Security Act: "unable to engage in any substantial gainful activity by reason of any medically determinable physical or mental impairment which can be expected to result in death or which has lasted or can be expected to last for a continuous period of not less than twelve months."[71] Critics have charged that disability programs cover people with vague and subjective-sounding symptoms, such as psychological distress or back pain, but in fact the majority of claims are denied.[72] More than half of individuals with denied claims submit an appeal, and more than half of those who appeal eventually gain benefits.[73] Nonetheless, many fail to qualify, and as a percentage of the U.S. population, claimants remain few. SSDI coverage increased from 2.1 percent of the population in 1980 to 3.4 percent in 2015, while SSI coverage grew from 1.8 to 2.6 percent over the same period. Average annual benefits under SSDI, at $16,176 in 2015, are approximately twice as large as those for SSI, at $8,796.[74] According to the Social Security actuary, increases in SSDI coverage rates are attributable to demographic factors, including the aging of the baby boomers, the delay in the retirement age, and the recession.[75]

Unemployment Insurance (UI), established in 1935 to provide income support to the jobless, features coverage that rises and falls over time with the nation's unemployed rate. Most of those lacking jobs do not qualify for benefits, for reasons to be discussed later in this chapter. The program reached its highest rate of coverage in the postwar period in 2009, when a weekly average of 1.87 percent of the population received benefits, just slightly more than the 1.75 percent who received them in 1982. Average weekly benefits also peaked in 2009, at $341 per week in 2015 dollars, owing to increases authorized by lawmakers during the onset of the recession.

The percentage of the population using veterans' benefits, both the compensation and disability types, increased in recent years owing to the wars in Iraq and Afghanistan; these benefits are now utilized by 1.3 percent of the population annually, a rate that comes close to the high of 1.6 percent in the early 1960s, when earlier generations of veterans peaked in their usage of such benefits. The GI Bill's educational benefits, though more generous since 2008 than they had been for decades, are now utilized by less than half of 1 percent of the population annually.

In sum, these visible U.S. social policies for nonseniors have endured despite decades of vocal criticism of social programs. Some have grown considerably in the scope of their coverage, owing to both policy changes and soaring need. Several others have inched up in size but still cover a small percentage of Americans, just 1 to 3 percent. Overall, these policies do help mitigate poverty: economists estimate reductions of 60 to 70 percent.[76] That said, they do little more than provide a basic safety net and collectively have less of an impact than in prior decades. Among the policies for civilians, only Pell Grants offer a ladder to the middle class, though given soaring tuition rates, their value today is closer to that of a stepstool. Many more Americans could benefit from using these policies besides those who actually use them, a topic we probe shortly, after considering policies with more hidden designs.

The Growing Number of Policies That Submerge Government's Role

The U.S. welfare state differs from that of other nations to the extent that it features policies channeled through the tax code or through private or nonprofit organizations, making government's role in financing or subsidizing them less than apparent. The social policies in the tax code are both numerous—having increased from 81 when Reagan took office to 151 in 2010—and substantial in value, peaking at 7.9 percent of GDP in 2003 and dipping just slightly since then, to 7.4 percent of GDP (anticipated) in 2016.[77] The total amount lost in revenues from such policies surpassed $1.1 trillion in 2010.[78] From their creation as part of the Higher Education Act of 1965, student loans also functioned in a submerged manner because they operated by government providing subsidies to banks to encourage them to lend money to students. In 2010, policymakers converted them to the more visible format of direct loans from the U.S. Department of Education, though servicing arrangements are still conducted by private lenders, making them a hybrid in design.[79]

The coverage rates of particular tax expenditures wax and wane automatically, vacillating with economic trends. Like entitlement programs, once established these benefits persist, and unlike direct policies geared to working-age adults and their families, they do not require lawmakers to raise benefit levels to ensure that they keep pace with inflation. The largest tax expenditures, established in the early and mid-twentieth century, include the home mortgage interest deduction and the exclusion of employer-provided health and retirement benefits (unlike wages) from taxation. These policies contain an upwardly redistributive bias. For example, for those in the middle quintile of the income distribution in 2016, the home mortgage interest deduction was worth \$130 on average; by contrast, for those in the top 1 percent of the income distribution, it was worth \$4,930.[80]

Over recent decades, presidents of both political parties have used tax expenditures to benefit low-income Americans, particularly by expanding the EITC, which provides funds to supplement low-wage work. The Obama administration promoted the development of several other benefits to help both low- and middle-income people, including the American Opportunity Tax Credit (an expanded version of the former Hope Credit signed into law by President Bill Clinton) to defray college costs and the Making Work Pay Tax Credit to boost income during the recession for all but the highest earners, and tax subsidies for those purchasing health coverage through the Affordable Care Act.

The Earned Income Tax Credit, which began during the Nixon administration and grew slightly under Reagan, expanded further during the Clinton administration to become the nation's largest antipoverty program.[81] Its reach was enlarged further during the Obama administration. By 2013, 19 percent of all U.S. households filing income taxes claimed the EITC, as seen in figure 2.3, with an average return of \$2,395. It lifted 6.2 million people above the poverty line in 2013.[82] Although it has replaced welfare as the predominant source of income security for low-income people, it targets a somewhat different, though overlapping, group: fewer of the poorest are eligible for it because of the earnings requirement, and more qualify who have slightly higher incomes.

Still, despite the dramatic increase in the size and number of benefits in the tax code for low- and middle-income Americans, net tax expenditures continue to bestow their largest benefits on the wealthiest Americans, as seen in figure 2.4. In 2013, the most affluent fifth of all households accrued 51 percent of the dollar value of the ten largest such policies. Within that top fifth, the largest benefits were bestowed on the superrich: those in the

Figure 2.4 The Upward Redistributive Effect of Submerged Social Benefits: Shares of Selected Major Tax Expenditures, by Income Group, 2013

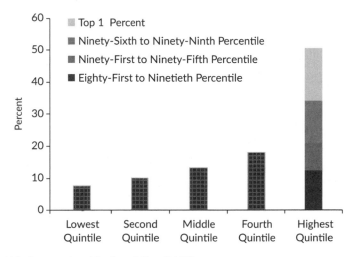

Source: U.S. Congressional Budget Office (2013).

Note: The selected major tax expenditures are the exclusion of employers' contributions for health care, health insurance premiums, and long-term-care insurance premiums; the exclusion of net pension contributions and earnings; the exclusion of capital gains on assets transferred at death; the exclusion of a portion of Social Security and railroad retirement benefits; the deduction for mortgage interest on owner-occupied residences; the deduction of nonbusiness state and local government income, sales, real estate, and personal property taxes; the deduction for charitable contributions; reduced rates on dividends and long-term capital gains; the Earned Income Tax Credit; and the child tax credit.

top 1 percent accrued 17 percent of all benefits, compared to 12 percent accruing to the eighty-first to ninetieth percentile, 9 percent to the ninety-first to ninety-fifth, and 13 percent to the ninety-sixth to ninety-ninth.[83]

Some of the personal tax expenditures included in figure 2.4 fulfill no functions related to economic security and well-being, and they are awarded on the basis of investment income rather than earned income. The preferential treatment of capital gains and dividends in the tax code benefits primarily the top 1 percent, who accrue 68 percent of the value of these provisions.[84] Wealthy individuals would owe taxes of 39.6 percent on their investment income if it were treated as ordinary income, but these tax breaks permit them to pay a tax rate of just 23.8 percent, granting them a substantial benefit in the form of reduced taxes. In the 1986 Tax Reform Act, lawmakers compromised by lowering regular income tax rates so that the highest would be just 28 percent and by fully taxing capital gains at that same rate. One year later, conservatives won an assurance that the capital gains tax would remain capped at 28 percent even if income tax rates rose. In 1997, lawmakers proceeded to lower the capital gains tax to 20 percent and decreased it further in 2003 to just 15 percent—an extraordinary benefit to wealthy Americans, particularly in the midst of the booming economy.[85] In 2012, Obama compromised with congressional Republicans to approve raising it to 23.8 percent, a level still much lower than the top marginal income tax rate.[86] The disparity is one of the major reasons why very wealthy Americans typically pay a much lower income tax rate than those with moderate incomes. In short, while the United States ties the deservingness of social benefits for low- and middle-income people quite securely to their work effort, it bestows substantial tax benefits on those whose good fortune accrues to them by virtue of their vast wealth.

So Large . . . and Yet So Small

While the U.S. welfare state has long been assumed to be smaller than that of other affluent nations, it is more accurately described simply as "different." As noted in chapter 1, if the value of tax expenditures and policies channeled through organizations are included, the size of U.S. social spending as a percentage of GDP is second-highest in the world, surpassed only by France.[87] But U.S. social policies, on net, do less to mitigate inequality and reduce poverty than those elsewhere—in part because the American welfare state redistributes substantial benefits upwards to those with higher incomes, particularly through the policies in the tax code.[88] It is also the case that many of the visible policies for low- and middle-income working-age people leave gaping holes, failing to cover many of those in need.

When critics of social provision assess changes in policies over the past few decades, they charge that benefit receipt has become much easier over time, leading the United States to become, as Nicholas Eberstadt puts it, "A Nation of Takers," or an "entitlement society."[89] It is true that the adoption of technology has in some respects simplified the application process and may have lessened some of the stigma previously attached to applying for social benefits. In the implementation of Unemployment Insurance, for example, "street-level bureaucrats" have been transformed into "screen-level bureaucrats" in the vast majority of states. Prior to the early 1990s, unemployed adults filed benefit claims by going to a public office, waiting in line, then talking in person with a frontline worker who assessed their eligibility by applying state-level rules. In 1993, Colorado was the first state to permit individuals to use an automated telephone system, which allowed them to call in to apply for benefits; forty-three states were utilizing similar systems by 2005, and by 2008 over 80 percent of both initial and continued claims nationwide were filed either by telephone or on the internet.[90] One study found that the switch to automation, by taking away some of the discretion of "rogue agents" who applied rules in a gender-biased fashion, reduced bias and boosted the percentage of female UI recipients.[91]

Food stamps (SNAP) underwent a similar change when the paper coupons that beneficiaries had been required to present to grocery store cashiers were replaced by plastic cards resembling bank or credit cards. Between the late 1980s and 2004, all states—encouraged by the federal government—adopted the Electronic Benefit Transfer (EBT) system. Nearly all states now permit residents to apply for benefits online, rather than requiring them to appear in person to do so.[92] Once an applicant's eligibility and benefit level have been determined, they are issued a card with a personal identification number (PIN) that can then be used at the point of purchase to access program benefits. Administrators electronically deposit the dollars to cover such benefits into the individual's account each month.

These procedural changes, along with the temporary increases in benefit rates and all-time highs in coverage during the recession, might lead some to assume that benefits are now attained easily and that programs have become unduly large and lenient. Yet careful studies have not found evidence that the shift to systems such as the EBT has elevated program use or diminished stigma.[93] Furthermore, despite the transition to more efficient procedures and the short-term application of more generous benefits, obstacles abound for those seeking to gain benefits. Both UI and SNAP remain targeted in ways that exclude many from qualifying for coverage, and they are still underutilized even by those who are eligible for them.

Take Unemployment Insurance: during the Great Recession, when as many as one in ten Americans found themselves jobless, the highest rate since the Great Depression, only one in three of the unemployed (32.6 percent) received unemployment benefits! The percentage of the jobless receiving benefits plummeted to the lowest point since 1980, owing to the ways in which benefit restrictions intersected with changes in the economy and the workforce.[94] To be eligible for UI, workers need to satisfy three requirements: (1) a minimum earnings threshold, which disadvantages part-time, low-paid, and young workers; (2) a qualifying reason or "good cause" for job loss, which, depending on how states define it, is problematic for those who leave a job because of their own health or that of a family member, or because they lack adequate transportation or care for their children; and (3) evidence that they are actively and continuously seeking employment, which they may be unable to provide if they left a job to care for a family member. Moreover, UI functions as fifty-one separate state systems, with state governments defining specific eligibility requirements, benefit amounts, and tax schedules, and therefore states vary considerably in their take-up rates. These problems have permeated the system since its creation in 1935, making it less valuable for less-advantaged workers, including women and minority men, than others.[95] UI's exclusivity has been exacerbated by recent trends such as the migration of workers to parts of the country, particularly the southeastern and mountain regions, that feature lower pay and lower rates of unionization.[96] As a result, among the unemployed, UI benefit receipt is strongly related to previous hours of work, level of education, and prior wages.[97] A recent study by Luke Shaefer found that the chief determinant of ineligibility was not inadequate earnings but the fact that the reason for job separation fell outside of the strict parameters permissible under the law, such that job departure was technically defined as "voluntary." In addition, Shaefer found that, among disadvantaged unemployed workers (meaning those in the largest wage quintiles as well as part-time workers who are primary wage earners), fewer than half received benefits—a much lower rate than among advantaged workers who were jobless.[98] Reform of UI is long overdue, particularly given that workers in the modern economy are more likely to endure spells of unemployment.

Eligibility for food stamps, or SNAP, is limited to poor families—those who have a gross income below 130 percent of the poverty level and few assets. Benefit amounts vary depending on earnings and expenses for basic needs such as housing and child care. Assets—the value of a home, cars, savings accounts, and so forth—were traditionally taken into account and could affect eligibility. Beneficiaries had to comply with numerous reporting requirements to remain eligible. When take-up rates declined in the late 1990s, the federal government promoted the program by creating a national hotline and an online calculator, and some states undertook outreach efforts.[99] The U.S. Department of Agriculture (USDA) also encouraged states to relax asset restrictions, for example, by reducing the limits on car ownership and by broadening eligibility through other procedural changes.[100] The majority of states now waive assets tests.[101]

Yet despite these changes, SNAP remains underutilized and inadequate.

In 2010, 25 percent of eligible individuals did not participate, among them 35 percent of the working poor.[102] Even though the program is primarily federal in its rules and procedures, states retain discretion over some decisions about eligibility and the duration of benefits, and local administrators actually run the program.[103] For these reasons, states differ starkly in the take-up rates of the benefit among their eligible populations. In 2006, for example, among those who qualified for benefits, 98 percent of those in Missouri received them, whereas in California only 50 percent did.[104] In addition, many Americans—including children—remain ineligible despite the fact that they are "food-insecure." These individuals typically live in households with incomes just above the official eligibility cutoffs for both food stamps and the school lunch program.[105] Here again, despite the program's growth, its restrictive eligibility rules and procedures and its low benefits inhibit it from achieving its larger goal of reducing hunger and malnourishment among Americans.

Similarly, the Earned Income Tax Credit has been celebrated as a policy that bestows respect and resources on low-wage workers, yet it too has limitations. By targeting the working poor, it leaves out poor people who are not employed, typically many of the same individuals who also fail to qualify for UI (for the reasons noted earlier) or for welfare (given its work requirements). Moreover, for the working poor who lack dependents, the EITC provides only the most meager benefits. In addition, EITC eligibility—like that for all means-tested benefits—phases out as individuals increase their job earnings—in effect, "taxing" them at a much higher rate as they engage in more of the very activity the policy is meant to encourage— paid employment.[106]

In one program after another, close investigation reveals that the American safety net is full of holes. A recent study by the sociologists Kathryn Edin and Luke Shaefer found that the demise of AFDC has led to considerable "deep poverty" in the United States, such that 4 percent of American households with children live on less than $2 a day per person, the World Bank metric of poverty in developing nations; this amounts to less than what many of us spend daily for coffee.[107] Andrea Campbell's book *Trapped in America's Safety Net* tells the story of her sister-in-law, who was left paralyzed after being hit by a car. As a disabled person, she could receive health coverage under California's version of Medicaid, realistically her only long-term option given her needs, yet she would qualify for it only if she and her family stayed at an income level below the poverty line and retained almost no assets, a requirement that ruled out the possibility of saving for retirement or their son's college costs.[108] Beneficiaries of this and other means-tested programs all over the United States have undergone variations on this experience. As we have seen, policies vary tremendously too, from state to state, along the vagaries of American federalism, making those in need subject to the political winds in the place where they happen to reside.[109] In sum, the nation's social programs are out of reach for many and painfully meager in benefits for those who qualify.

Several working Americans who were interviewed for this book expressed frustration that they made too much money to qualify for benefits, and yet too little to get by on. Natalie Swenson in Clinton, South Carolina, explained to me in 2015 that she had received a 10 percent pay cut at her job working for a company that had recently downsized, and as a result she was having trouble making ends meet, but government programs helped little because their eligibility rules required recipients to be "more poverty-stricken" before they qualified for aid. Previously, Swenson had qualified for the EITC; then her income rose slightly, and she lost access to the benefit. "It hurt when it stopped," she said. Donna Walker of Brooklyn, New York, concurred: she told me, in reference to the EITC and Medicaid, "If you are making just a dollar over their amount, you don't qualify."

Why do policies languish, with problems such as these going unaddressed? Policies created long ago do not necessarily continue to yield the same impact as in the past, in part because, as Jacob Hacker points out, "drift" occurs as circumstances in the external environment change; for example, new social risks may arise or economic insecurity may be heightened, yet lawmakers fail to update policies accordingly.[110] In addition, unless they regularly receive maintenance, public policies may deviate from their original purpose or level of functioning owing to the internal dynamics arising from design effects, lateral effects, or unintended consequences. The U.S. political system has shown little capacity in recent years to maintain and modernize policies as needed, or to create new ones.[111] The rise of partisan polarization has made political compromise harder to attain, and social programs for nonseniors in particular have languished.

Finally, it must be noted that policymakers embraced, from the 1970s onward, a governing logic of what Julilly Kohler-Hausmann terms "getting tough," which included both a more punitive approach to welfare and a harsher approach to criminal justice.[112]

Although this book focuses on individuals' interactions with government through policies that aim to help them and provide them with opportunities, in fact, during this same era, more and more Americans—predominantly people of color—have personally experienced the coercive power of government. Among African American men between the ages of thirty-five and forty-four in 2001, 22 percent had spent time in state or federal prison, compared to 10 percent of Hispanic males and 3.5 percent of white males in their cohort group.[113] An even higher percentage of African American men have had other encounters with the criminal justice system. As Joe Soss and Vesla Weaver observe, communities that are subjugated by race and class are governed not through the provision of rights and benefits and representation but rather through "coercion, containment, repression, surveillance, regulation, predation, discipline and voilence."[114] They quote former U.S. attorney general Loretta Lynch, who commented that in communities such as Ferguson, Missouri, police often represent "the only face of government that [residents] see."[115] These experiences are likely to have an impact on views about government and civic engagement, a theme revisited in chapters 4 and 5.

Social Provision on the Rise

Meghan Fry, who lives in Syracuse, earns minimum wage working as a manager at a retail store in a local shopping mall, and she budgets every dollar to take care of herself and her three-year-old daughter. Sometimes after she pays for rent, utilities, and gas, little remains for food, so a while back Fry herself began to skip meals. Her daughter's babysitter noticed the lack of food in their apartment and offered to help. She took Fry grocery shopping at Save-A-Lot, taught her to cook inexpensive meals, and encouraged her to apply for food stamps. Fry now receives $150 per month from the program, and though she criticizes people whom she believes abuse such benefits, she adds, "I feel like the system should help someone like me."[116]

In 2011, former House speaker Newt Gingrich referred to Barack Obama as "the most successful food stamp president in American history."[117] This tongue-in-cheek remark epitomizes the attitudes of many conservatives who worry that the nation they knew when they were younger is growing unrecognizable, not least because of increased reliance on government programs. These sentiments reflect a broader view, detected in numerous polling questions, of dissatisfaction on the part of large majorities of Americans with the direction in which the country is going.[118]

The historical shift in Americans' policy usage has occurred in the context of broad economic, social, and political transformations in the United States, and it cannot be understood in their absence. Conservatives are correct to observe that the use of social policies has been on the rise: coverage rates grew for nearly all of the twenty-one policies listed in table 2.1 between the 1980s and 2010s. Yet Americans of the mid-twentieth century had experienced upward social mobility facilitated by a growing economy and strong policies that strengthened workers' leverage and held employers accountable to them. Economic growth slowed in the 1970s, and in the decades since then, lawmakers released employers from their obligations and relaxed the tax burden on the wealthy. With ordinary Americans left to bear the brunt of change, family incomes stagnated and opportunities declined. The nation's welfare state, for all its limitations, has nonetheless provided a crucial safety net for many Americans over these decades. We will now examine how usage of its programs accumulates within individual lives and in places across the nation.

CHAPTER 3

WE ARE ALL BENEFICIARIES NOW

ALBERT CHAPPIUS, born in 1958, is a self-employed small businessman who lives in Chattanooga, Tennessee. He believes that government social programs are easily abused, "making lazy people." Food stamps particularly concern him. He recalls being in a store and seeing a woman use them to purchase soda for her two children and then pulling out her cash to buy herself beer and cigarettes. He is also troubled by Medicaid and worries that it provides benefits to "illegal aliens." By contrast, he praises benefits in the tax code, to which he attributes very different outcomes. He credits the home mortgage interest deduction with "helping inspire someone to own their own home," and the low tax on capital gains with "inspiring people to invest and help others." When I asked him in 2015 whether he would support those same policies if they were delivered differently, as checks from the government rather than as tax reductions, he replied: "No, I don't like the way the federal government handles money; we should not allow the government to take more money." He had used various tax expenditures himself and appreciated the "extra money to spend on family needs."

Rosa Smith also lives in Tennessee and is just seven years older than Chappius, but in many respects they have different circumstances, life experiences, and perspectives. He identifies as white and she as African American; he describes himself as "extremely conservative" and as a political independent, while she considers herself "moderate" and is a Democrat; he lives in a comfortable upper-middle-income home, while her family gets by on considerably less on the lower rungs of the middle class. Yet when it comes to their views of social policies, they sound remarkably alike: both draw sharp distinctions between deserving versus undeserving recipients, and both believe that policy design features influence or reward personal behavior, for good or for ill.

Smith praises the overall intention of social programs, but she feels that implementation often fails to measure up and leaves programs vulnerable to abuse. "People squander food stamps," she explains. "I can tell you who has food stamps in the grocery store by what they buy." She complains about exploitation of disability benefits by people who "claim they are bipolar when they are just lazy," and she suggests that welfare recipients should be subjected to drug testing and other requirements. Policies in the tax code, by contrast, earn her praise: "They are a service not affiliated with the government. It is the least that the government can do for those with more money. If you have more money, you spend more money and help the economy." She herself has benefited from several tax policies. Among them, she particularly lauds the EITC, noting that, "when you are 'down on your luck,' having a little bit extra goes a long way."

Throughout American history, from the poorhouses of the nineteenth century to the mothers' pensions of the early twentieth century and beyond, policymakers, frontline workers, and ordinary citizens have distinguished between deserving and undeserving beneficiaries of social policies—between those they consider to be good upstanding citizens and moochers and chiselers who abuse the system, between those they view as "people like us" and those they deem to have different values, particularly with respect to personal responsibility, including the work ethic. Time and again, these divisions have cleaved to the fault lines of race, privileging whites and marginalizing or excluding others.[1]

Since the 1970s, political leaders have invoked distinctions between deserving and undeserving citizens for broader purposes—to highlight concerns about the role of government versus markets and the value of individualism versus dependence. When Reagan in 1976 disparaged the "welfare queen"—a woman who purportedly "has used 80 names, 30 addresses, 15 telephone numbers to collect food stamps, Social Security, veterans' benefits for four nonexistent, deceased veteran husbands, as well as welfare"—in fact AFDC recipients composed only 5.2 percent of the entire population and fraud was known to be extremely rare.[2] Yet the image of a beneficiary of a public program that sanctioned nonparticipation in the workforce symbolized to many a broader threat to American values. Today, despite the fact that the successor to the program covers less than 1 percent of the population and benefits are subject to strict limitations, the force of that stereotype persists and invokes many citizens' ire, as we will see in chapter 4.

Contemporary conservatives often point to social provision to exemplify what they perceive as government's outsized role in society. Since the enactment of welfare reform in 1996, they have no longer been able to use AFDC to epitomize such claims, but some now draw attention instead to increased enrollments for other programs, such as food stamps and disability benefits.[3] Others have changed the terms of the discussion by casting the net more widely, pointing to the broader use of social provision across the population. In 2012, Republican presidential candidate Mitt Romney lambasted a near-majority of Americans when he referred to "the 47 percent . . . who are dependent on government." Donald Trump continued this approach, telling interviewer Sean Hannity in a *Fox News* interview in 2015, "The problem we have right now—we have a society that sits back and says we don't have to do anything. Eventually, the 50 percent cannot carry—and it's unfair to them—but cannot carry the other 50 percent."[4] These claims accentuate the larger theme of personal responsibility championed by conservatives, with its accompanying imperative of smaller government.[5]

Yet while the rhetoric of "us-and-them" implies that only a small minority or a particular subgroup of the population uses multiple programs while the vast majority use next to none, such claims remain unevaluated. To address how persistent and growing antipathy to social benefits and to government generally squares with Americans' experiences of such policies, first we need to specify what constitutes typical usage. What proportion of the public has ever utilized at least one such policy? What constitutes typical patterns of use of different types of policies? How does such usage vary by social group and party affiliation? While the previous chapter focused on specific programs to show changes in coverage rates over time, here we focus on individuals and examine how their policy experiences accumulate over their lifetimes.

To date, scholars have lacked data that would permit them to track individuals' social policy usage throughout their lives and how it relates to their political attitudes and rates of political participation. Ideally, we would have panel data—evidence collected from a random sample of Americans who were then reinterviewed at regular intervals over a long period of time, including at points before, during, and after program usage. This would improve on cross-sectional data, which are collected at one moment in time, by enabling us to overcome the problem of "selection bias"—the possibility that differences in program beneficiaries and nonbeneficiaries emanates from a preexisting condition rather than a program effect. Yet even existing cross-sectional surveys rarely ask about usage of social policies—with the exception of a few questions that have been posed very sporadically, just a few times, on the American National Election Studies (ANES). The Survey of Income and Program Participation (SIPP), which many experts consider the gold standard of panel data that track program usage, lacks any attention to educational benefits, health benefits, or tax expenditures, and it is silent on issues of political attitudes and participation.[6] The Panel Study of Income Dynamics (PSID) permits assessment of usage over the life course of a limited set of direct spending programs, but not tax expenditures.[7]

Fortunately, however, we can draw on a unique survey data set from the Social and Governmental Issues and Participation Study (SGIP), which was designed for the study of both Americans' experiences with social programs and their political behavior. The SGIP asked respondents, in a randomized fashion, whether they had *ever* used any of many different federal social policies over the course of their lifetimes, and it probed further about their experiences of those programs they had utilized.[8] Because the SGIP probed usage of both direct policies and those channeled through the tax code and other subsidies, some of which are means-tested and others of which are not, we can examine cumulative patterns of usage for different groups in the population.[9] As cross-sectional data, the results are subject to the limitations discussed earlier. The strength of these data is that they uniquely include both indicators of lifetime usage across a large number and diverse array of policies, many of which are typically excluded from surveys, and measures of political attitudes and participation. To complement analysis at the individual level, we also explore policy usage across place, drawing on U.S. government data that permit us to examine it at the county level, across the nation, and at different points across time.[10]

In accounting for policy usage in the SGIP data, we group the twenty-one policies into four types:[11]

1. Six direct and visible non-means-tested policies: Social Security Disability Insurance, Social Security retirement benefits, Medicare, the GI Bill, other veterans' benefits, and Unemployment Insurance
2. Seven visible means-tested policies: Head Start, Supplemental

Security Income, Medicaid, Temporary Assistance to Needy
Families (or welfare/public assistance), Pell Grants, food stamps,
and subsidized housing

3. Six non-means-tested "submerged" benefits: the home mortgage
interest deduction, employer-subsidized health insurance,
employer-subsidized retirement benefits, the Child and Dependent Care Tax Credit, 529 plans (qualified tuition programs) or
Coverdell Education Savings Accounts (education IRAs), and
student loans

4. Two means-tested submerged benefits: the Earned Income Tax
Credit and two education credits, the Hope and Lifetime Learning Tax Credits

What the evidence reveals about typical usage patterns is startling.
Nearly all Americans—all but 4 percent—report having benefited from at
least one of the twenty-one social policies, a grouping that includes both
direct payments and services from government as well as social benefits administered through the tax code. Nonbeneficiaries belong predominantly
to younger cohorts, who simply have not yet encountered or aged into the
circumstances that would make them eligible for these policies.[12] The average adult has utilized 4.47 policies over the course of his or her lifetime to
date, including, on average, 1.94 direct, visible policies and 2.53 submerged
policies.

The percentage of income flowing from social transfers has increased
across the nation, both in counties where the majority of residents typically
vote for Republicans and in those that favor Democrats, and in those where
more than 95 percent of the population identifies as white as well as in those
with higher percentages of people of color. The old dividing lines of "us"
and "them" stand in stark contradiction to Americans' actual experiences
as the beneficiaries of multiple social policies. We are nearly all beneficiaries
now, and we live in states and counties in which growing numbers of our
fellow citizens rely on government as well.

Common Experiences

The portion of the public that has ever in their lives utilized a particular
program greatly surpasses the portion that uses that same program in any
given year or in an even shorter period of some weeks or months. This is

because eligibility for social policies is conditioned on personal circumstances such as income, college attendance, and employment status, which change over the course of individuals' lives. Table 3.1 shows the percentage of respondents to the SGIP survey who indicated that they had *ever* used any of nineteen policies on the list, and who were *currently* using the other two—employer-provided health or retirement benefits. These take-up rates, in the case of the policies ever used, cannot be interpreted as precise estimates; they are probably conservative indicators given that memory constraints and in some instances perceived stigma may lead to underreporting.[13]

The table shows that the top five social policies have been experienced by large portions of the population—between one in three and one in two. The most commonly used are the three most expensive tax expenditures, starting with the tax-subsidized, employer-provided benefits—55.3 percent of Americans were currently using employee retirement benefits and 49.9 percent were using employee health benefits—followed by the home mortgage interest tax deduction, which had been utilized at some point by 45.6 percent.

Outside of the tax code, Unemployment Insurance was the most widely used social policy: 38.5 percent of Americans had received this benefit. This high rate of UI usage may appear surprising at first blush given the very low percentage of the public using the benefits at any one time, even during recessions (less than 2 percent, as we saw in chapter 2). Yet a high proportion of American adults experience job insecurity at some point in life: scholars using longitudinal data have found that 12.4 percent of Americans between the ages of twenty-five and sixty experience a spell of unemployment by the head of their household in a given year, and by age sixty, fully 66.8 will have had this experience at some point.[14] Among those using UI, furthermore, many use it briefly: 23 percent receive unemployment benefits for less than six months total across their lives, and 36 percent for less than one year in full.[15] For these reasons, the incidence of usage is high across Americans' lifetimes even though total usage at any moment in time—measured as the weekly average over the course of the year—is very low.

The frequency of UI receipt is followed by EITC usage, at 34.4 percent, indicating that one in three Americans have at some point been numbered among the working poor and thus qualified for and used the tax credit. If we consider duration of benefits, we find that 21 percent of EITC benefi-

Table 3.1 Percentage of Americans Who Report Having Ever Used Specific Social Policies

Employer-provided retirement[a]	55.3%
Employer-provided health care[a]	49.9
Home mortgage interest deduction	45.6
Unemployment Insurance	38.5
Earned Income Tax Credit	34.4
Student loans	27.4
Child and Dependent Care Tax Credit	25.7
Food stamps	25.4
Medicare	22.2
Medicaid	17.5
Pell Grants	16.0
Social Security—retirement and survivors'	15.8
Welfare/public assistance	13.9
Hope or Lifetime Learning Tax Credit	10.0
Social Security Disability Insurance	9.7
Government-subsidized housing	8.7
Supplemental Security Income	8.1
Head Start	8.0
GI Bill	5.9
529 plan or Coverdell Education Savings Account	5.1
Veterans' benefits (other than GI Bill)	4.6

Source: 2008 Social and Governmental Issues and Participation Study (SGIP).
Note: Weighted estimates. Submerged state policies shown in italics.
[a] Only current recipients of employer-provided benefits are included, not all who said that they had "ever" received such benefits.

ciaries claimed the annual credit only once and another 34 percent claimed it between two and five years.[16] These relatively short periods of program usage help illustrate that many Americans cycle in and out of usage of policies over time, a far greater proportion than utilize them at any moment in time.

Considering individuals' cumulative use of social policies, it becomes evident that such experiences are commonplace. Only 5 percent of respondents have used just one policy, while 65 percent have used four or more. Submerged policies are used more often than direct benefits: 87 percent have used at least one submerged benefit and 73 percent have used at least one direct benefit. In short, usage of social provision is widespread among Americans, occurring at several points over the course of most of their lives.

Bridging Income Disparities

Many assume that social policies exist primarily to aid the poor. To what extent have such policies been utilized by Americans across the income spectrum? In figure 3.1, we show average lifetime usage rates among individuals, by income quintile, of policies with income caps or limitations—so-called means-tested policies—versus policies that lack such features. It is important to observe that respondents' placement on the income distribution scale was based on their current household income at the time the survey was conducted, whereas policy usage rates were based on their answers to questions about having ever used particular policies in their lifetime to date. Figure 3.1 shows that accounting for individuals' combined different types of policies, the average American in the highest income group has used a total of 4.5 policies, the equivalent of those in the lowest income group. The rich and the poor differ only in the ratio of means-tested to non-means-tested policies utilized. The less well-off have used a higher proportion of means-tested than non-means-tested policies, 2.4 and 2.1 policies each, respectively, whereas those in the most affluent group had used 0.8 and 3.7 policies on average. Also remarkable is the fact that the typical person who currently lives in a middle-income household had qualified for and used a means-tested policy at some earlier point in his or her life, and it was not uncommon even among those in the highest income group to have benefited at some point from a means-tested policy, with average use just under one such policy per person. This underscores a point made by Thomas Hirschl and Mark Rank: by the time Americans reach midlife, at least half of them have experienced a spell of economic insecurity, and nearly as many have used some social safety net programs.[17] The common assumption that the welfare state serves primarily low-income people is false: its wide array of policies benefit Americans across the income spectrum, rich and poor alike, with variation occurring primarily in the type of policy design that those at different income levels typically experience.

Similarly, individuals at different income levels vary in the extent to which they have experienced visible versus submerged policies. As seen in figure 3.2, the poor have experienced 3.3 visible policies and 1.2 submerged policies, the inverse of the affluent, who have used 1.0 and 3.5 policies of both types, respectively. On net, both groups have utilized equivalent numbers of policies, but the poor have used mostly policies with designs that

Figure 3.1 Average Number of Means- and Non-Means-Tested Policies Ever Used by Americans, by Income Group

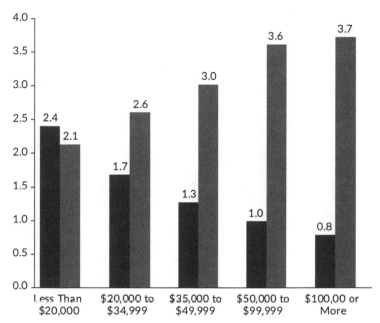

■ Average Number of Means-Tested Policies
■ Average Number of Non-Means-Tested Policies

Source: 2008 SGIP.
Note: Weighted estimates. Includes employer-provided health and retirement programs. Question wording in the SGIP necessitates that calculations combine *current* use of employer-provided retirement and health benefits with whether respondents *ever* used any of the other nineteen policies. Thus, employer-provided benefit usage is likely understated, as some respondents might have used such a benefit in the past but not presently.

make government's role most apparent, and the wealthy mostly policies with designs that obscure it. Those in the second-lowest income group have experienced slightly more visible policies than submerged ones, 2.4 and 1.9 on average, respectively, and the ratio of submerged to visible policies used grows among each subsequent income level.

The American welfare state provides plenty to those in the upper income levels, but it does so in ways that are less likely to be obvious to either the beneficiaries themselves or to other Americans. Such policies are typically fiercely defended by interest groups that benefit from them, and they avoid the annual budget battles that imperil many direct spending programs,

Figure 3.2 Average Number of Visible and Submerged Policies Ever Used by Americans, by Income Group

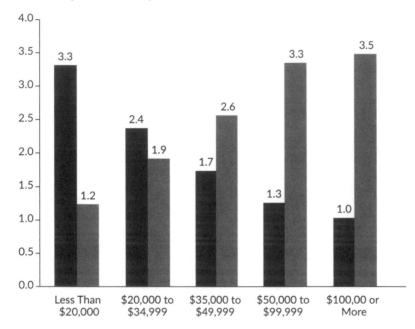

■ Average Number of Visible Policies
■ Average Number Submerged Policies

Source: 2008 SGIP.
Note: Weighted estimates. Includes employer-provided health and retirement programs. Question wording in the SGIP necessitates that calculations combine *current* use of employer-provided retirement and health benefits with whether respondents *ever* used any of the other nineteen policies. Thus, employer-provided benefit usage is likely understated, as some respondents might have used such a benefit in the past but not presently.

particularly for low-income beneficiaries. Therefore, they tend to be much safer politically and to function like entitlement programs.[18]

What is the typical "basket of policies" experienced by people at different income levels? Once people become senior citizens, the vast majority qualify for Social Security and are thus introduced to a widely shared policy experience. Here we focus instead on the policy experiences of working-age Americans, those under age sixty, among whom experiences of social policy are more likely to vary. We consider how usage of the more commonly used policies among the working-age population is distributed by income group. Figure 3.3 shows, across income levels, the usage rates of six of the seven

Figure 3.3 Percentage of Americans Under Age Sixty Who Have Ever Used the Most Commonly Used Social Policies, by Income Group

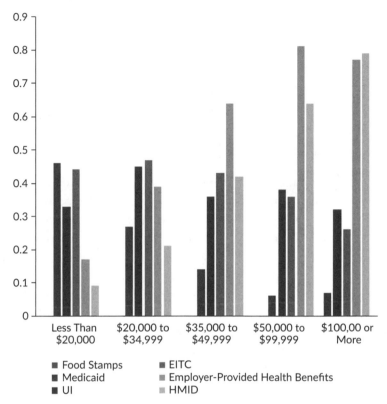

Source: 2008 SGIP.
Note: Policies shown include each of those used by at least 40 percent of individuals in at least one of the income groups, with the exception of employer-provided retirement benefits, for which usage largely overlaps with that of employer-provided health benefits.

policies utilized by at least 40 percent of individuals in at least one of the income groups.[19] It reveals that some individuals in all five income groups have used each of the six most commonly utilized policies at some juncture in their lives. For example, food stamps have been used by 59 percent of those in the lowest income group and by 6 percent of those currently in the highest income group; conversely, the home mortgage interest deduction has been used by 79 percent of the most affluent and 9 percent of those who are now poor.

Once again, this points to the fact that many Americans have experienced upward or downward mobility across their life span, so they have once used policies for which they would not qualify now. Unemployment Insurance is the most widely utilized policy across income levels, having been used by at least one in three people in each grouping, followed by the EITC, which has been used by one in three at each income level except among the most affluent. The rhetoric of recent years that has divided Americans into "makers" and "takers" misses the mark: it is more appropriate to say that Americans of all income groups have relied on social provision at various points in their lives.

Transcending the Partisan Divide

As partisan polarization has widened in the United States, no set of issues has divided public opinion as much as that concerning the social safety net, and the gaps continue to increase, as noted in chapter 1. Already in 1987, the Pew Research Center found that Democrats and Republicans were separated in their attitudes on such issues by 23 points, but by 2012 that difference had grown to a 41-point gap. The change has been driven predominantly by Republicans' growing disagreement with the statements, "It's the government's responsibility to take care of people who can't take care of themselves," "The government should help more needy people even if it means going deeper in debt," and "The government should guarantee every citizen enough to eat and a place to sleep." Democrats' views on these issues have remained quite stable over the same period.[20]

Yet, when it comes to partisans' actual usage of social policies as opposed to their attitudes about social provision, the differences are modest. Ninety-seven percent of Republicans and 98 percent of Democrats have used at least one social benefit. The vast majority of individuals who identify with either party have used at least one direct, visible social benefit, including 82 percent of Democrats and 64 percent of Republicans, and they have also used at least one submerged benefit, including 92 percent of Republicans and 86 percent of Democrats.

Americans have similar rates of overall policy usage regardless of their partisan identity. Figure 3.4 shows policy usage rates on a partisan identity scale that includes self-identified Democrats and Republicans at the two ends, those who call themselves "independent" in the middle, and those who report that they "lean toward one of the two major parties" in between. The average Democrat has used more visible direct policies than the average Republican, 2.3 compared to 1.5, and rates diminish across the scale.

Figure 3.4 Average Number of Visible and Submerged Policies Ever Used by Americans, by Partisanship

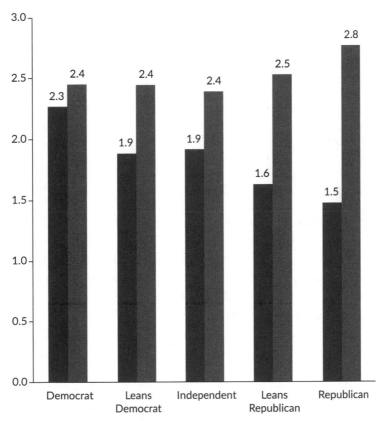

Source: 2008 SGIP.
Note: Weighted estimates. Includes employer-provided health and retirement benefits.

When it comes to submerged policies, however, the GOP supporter has a slight edge, having used 2.8 policies compared to 2.4 among Democrats, Democratic leaners, and independents. Overall, despite the gulf in rhetoric, partisans are strikingly similar in their overall rates of policy usage: the average Democrat has used a total of 4.7 policies, independents 4.3, and Republicans 4.3. Each group, moreover, has more experiences of submerged policies than visible ones. Similarly, Americans across the partisan spectrum have used more non-means-tested programs than means-tested ones, by a ratio of 3.3 to 1.0 among Republicans and 3.0 to 1.7 among Democrats.

Even when we focus on usage of specific programs, the similarities between Democrats and Republicans are more evident than the distinctions. The largest differences to be found are in the home mortgage interest deduction, which 62 percent of Republicans have used compared to only 36 percent of Democrats, and conversely, food stamps, which 31 percent of Democrats have used compared to only 15 percent of Republicans. In the case of most other policies, however, only a few percentage points separate usage rates by party. These small differences defy the growing ideological divide between the parties and the increasingly strident tone of conservative political rhetoric.

Generational Similarities and Differences

Some generational tensions have emerged in debates over the U.S. welfare state in recent years as those older Americans who happen also to be conservative have come to believe that younger generations rely more on social programs than they themselves did when they were younger. Theda Skocpol and Vanessa Williamson have found that the mostly older adults who affiliated themselves with the Tea Party held considerable disdain for what they perceived as a growing number of "freeloaders," individuals who depend on government benefits. They singled out young people, in some instances even their own grandchildren, whom they believed relied on such programs rather than earning their way through hard work, as they felt they themselves had done. With respect to the largest government programs, Social Security and Medicare, which they now utilized, they viewed their access to them as earned rights, the fruit of their work effort.[21] This perspective emerged in some interviews conducted for this book. For example, Maria McDaniels, who lives in Jackson, Mississippi, feels that government should do less overall, noting, "People have gotten in the state of mind where they think they don't have to work . . . this generation doesn't work." McDaniels herself, however, has used numerous social programs. This raises the question of how social program usage varies by age group.

Older adults, those age seventy and older, have used more social policies overall than those in the youngest group, as seen in figure 3.5.[22] Of course, this is not a surprising finding, given that we are measuring lifetime usage to date and seniors have had more time to take advantage of policies than the young. The generations differ from each other, however, in the types of policies they have used, particularly because the young have already used

Figure 3.5 Average Number of Means- and Non-Means-Tested Policies Ever Used by Americans, by Age Cohort

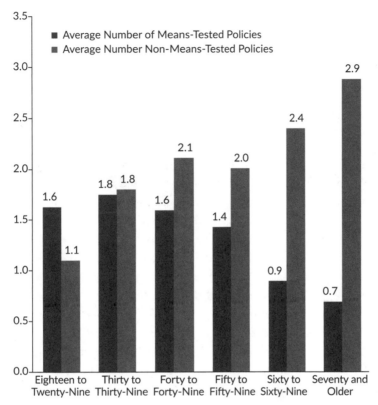

■ Average Number of Means-Tested Policies
■ Average Number Non-Means-Tested Policies

Source: 2008 SGIP.
Note: Weighted estimates. Does not include employer-provided health and retirement benefits.

more means-tested policies to date than older Americans have. That older Americans have used more non-means-tested policies makes sense, mostly because they have aged into Social Security and Medicare coverage, but also because they were more likely to have qualified for other such policies earlier in their lives: for example, most of them grew up when the draft was in place and more of them had served in the military, thus gaining access to the GI Bill and other veterans' benefits that lack income limits.[23] By contrast, individuals in the four younger and middle-aged groups have already used significantly more means-tested policies on average than those in the two eldest groups: the eighteen- to twenty-nine-year-olds, for example, have used an average of 1.6 such policies, and the thirty- to thirty-nine-year-olds have used 1.8, more than twice the rate of usage of the seventy-and-over group, whose average usage rate is 0.7 policies. This may illuminate why some older adults today feel that the young are more reliant on social provision than they themselves were at their age, and particularly why they perceive the young to be using policies for which they have less respect.

What explains the greater use of means-tested policies by younger groups compared to older groups? Those who came of age in the mid-twentieth century benefited from a robust labor market with high employment stability, prevalent employee benefits, strong labor unions, and high minimum wages, all of which enabled them to gain economic security more reliably through the workforce, with less need for social provision. Younger Americans, by contrast, reached adulthood and started families during decades when all of these conditions were deteriorating and the pay of lower- and middle-income Americans was either stagnating or, for some, falling behind. As a result, they were more likely to experience greater need as they tried to make ends meet. As well, they grew up as advanced levels of education became increasingly necessary to secure good-paying jobs with good benefits, but also as college tuition rates skyrocketed, growing much faster than inflation.[24] Furthermore, more means-tested policies have existed in recent decades than in the past (examples include the Hope and Lifetime Learning Tax Credits), and policymakers have liberalized eligibility restrictions for several of them (such as Medicaid and the EITC), making them accessible to more people.

The young have been more likely to qualify for and use a greater number of social policies earlier in their lives than older Americans. Greater economic insecurity has made them more likely to use Unemployment Insurance and other income support policies. And rising college tuition, stagnant household incomes, and higher college enrollment have prompted more of them to take advantage of Pell Grants and student loans. The generational bias in usage rates owes to these differences.

Across Race and Ethnicity

The history of the welfare state in the United States is fraught with the politics of race and ethnicity. Historically, lawmakers' reluctance to provide benefits across the "color line" hindered the creation and expansion of programs, and both policy design and implementation led to the systematic exclusion of people of color, including African Americans and Hispanics.[25]

Figure 3.6 Average Number of Visible and Submerged Policies Ever Used by Americans, by Race and Ethnicity

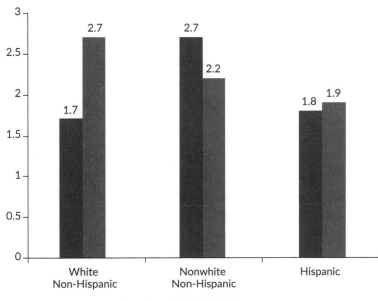

■ Average Number of Visible Policies
■ Average Number of Submerged Policies

Source: 2008 SGIP.
Note: Weighted estimates. Includes employer-provided health and retirement benefits.

Many white Americans have assumed, however, that people of color are the primary beneficiaries of social programs, and scholars have found that such perceptions have kept benefits meager and spurred the adoption of punitive provisions.[26] In fact, contemporary Americans across racial and ethnic identities have all benefited from social policies across their lifetimes. These groups differ little in overall usage rates; variation exists primarily in the types of policies they have experienced.

As shown in figure 3.6, whites have benefited disproportionately from submerged policies, having used 2.7 on average, compared to 2.2 among nonwhite non-Hispanics and 1.9 among those who identify as Hispanic.[27] By contrast, when it comes to visible programs, nonwhite non-Hispanics have benefited from more of them, 2.7 on average—notably, the same number as the number of submerged policies utilized by the typical white non-Hispanic. Overall, the latter have used nearly identical numbers of visible social policies as Hispanics, 1.7 and 1.8 on average, respectively. To the ex-

tent that white non-Hispanics perceive nonwhites as using more social policies than themselves, that view emanates more from differences in policy
visibility than actual differences in usage rates.

If we probe distinctions in usage of means-tested versus non-means-
tested programs, similar disparities emerge. White non-Hispanics have used
the smallest number of means-tested policies on average—1.1 versus 2.3
among nonwhites and 1.5 among Hispanics—but the reverse case holds for
non-means-tested policies, of which whites have used 3.2 on average compared to 2.7 among nonwhites and 2.2 among Hispanics. In sum, the policy
designs most commonly experienced by those who identify with different
groups vary, but overall usage of programs is quite uniformly widespread.

This overview of social policy usage patterns across individuals' lives makes
evident various patterns. It confirms that older Americans are correct to
infer that the young have used more means-tested programs than they
themselves have used, and that wealthier Americans would be correct to
observe that the least-advantaged have used more visible policies than they
have. Yet our inquiry reveals that notwithstanding these differences, most
of which are modest, social provision has actually benefited Americans
across the divides of income, party, generation, and race and ethnicity. Use
of social policy is quite ubiquitous, and social groups are distinguished less
by their rate of usage than by the types of policies that benefit them—for
example, with submerged policies typically helping the affluent more and
visible policies helping the less well-off.

From the Redwood Forest to the Gulf Stream Waters

Now we consider changes in reliance on social provision across time and
place, throughout the United States. We live our lives not as isolated individuals but as members of communities, as inhabitants of places. Presumably the extent to which others in our local areas benefit from government
transfers may influence how we ourselves perceive the role and value of
government. Here again we examine data from the U.S. Bureau of Economic Analysis, which tracks over forty different programs. (As noted earlier, these data—unlike the data examined so far in this chapter—do not
account for tax expenditures except for the EITC, child tax credits, and a
few smaller ones.)

Throughout the nation, in counties that have long suffered from high poverty rates, in those that enjoy affluence, and in all others in between, the amount of social provision flowing to residents from the federal government has grown substantially over the past thirty-five years. This is evident in figures 3.7 and 3.8, which show the mean percentage of personal income of county residents that came from federal transfers in 1979 and 2014, respectively. Overall, the percentage of personal income flowing from federal transfers in the median county increased from 12.69 percent in 1979 to 22.70 percent in 2014, a 79 percent increase. The mean value of transfers allocated to Americans grew from $3,236 in 1979 to $7,729 in 2014 over the same period (in 2014 dollars).

Generally, the counties in which residents depended the most on federal aid in 1979—a group that included many counties throughout the southeastern states, particularly in Appalachia and the Mississippi Delta, and in northern Michigan and Wisconsin—remain among the most-aided today, but the degree of their reliance has increased substantially, typically doubling. Among the ten counties in which residents receive the highest average percentage of income from federal transfers, at rates ranging from 48 to 61 percent, nine are located in Kentucky, a traditionally poor state where the long-term decline of the coal industry has left many worse off than before. In Owsley County, which heads the list, already in 1979 residents gained 39 percent of their income from federal transfers; by 2014, that figure had exploded to 61 percent. The one county among the top ten located outside of Kentucky is Holmes County, Mississippi, which has the lowest life expectancy rate in the nation.[28]

Overall, however, the comparison of the maps from 1979 and 2014 reveals the immense transformation in usage rates that occurred in more typical counties everywhere. Nationwide, as the middle class struggled, need increased and federal transfers became more commonplace. Today, in 44 percent of all counties in the nation, in far-flung areas, residents receive on average more than 24 percent of their income from federal transfers. This generalization applies not only to pockets of the country long associated with poverty but also to counties surrounding deindustrialized cities such as Cleveland and Pittsburgh and rural counties in Oregon, Washington State, Idaho, Montana, and elsewhere. Overall, the majority of states include some counties in the most-aided category shown on the map—those in which at least 36 percent of residents' personal income on average comes from government transfers. Nearly all states include some counties in which at least 24 percent of residents' income comes from those sources. Even the

Figure 3.7 Federal Government Social Transfers as a Percentage of Personal Income, by County, 1979

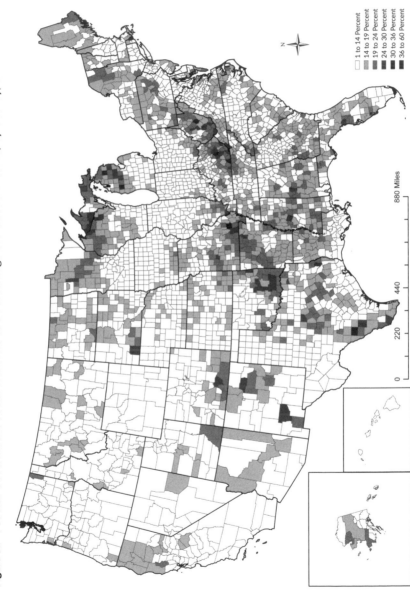

1 to 14 Percent
14 to 19 Percent
19 to 24 Percent
24 to 30 Percent
30 to 36 Percent
36 to 60 Percent

0   220   440   880 Miles

Source: Government transfer data from U.S. Bureau of Economic Analysis (2016).

Figure 3.8 Federal Government Social Transfers as a Percentage of Personal Income, by County, 2014

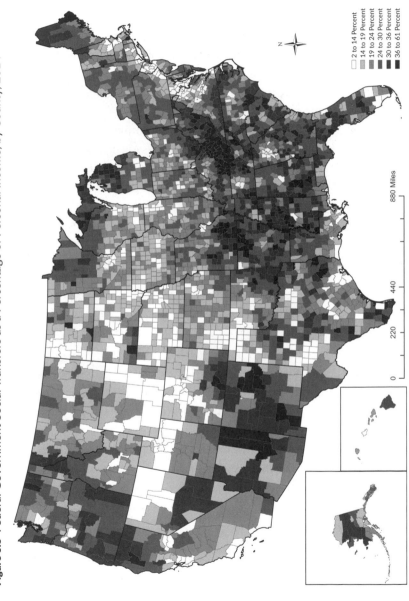

2 to 14 Percent
14 to 19 Percent
19 to 24 Percent
24 to 30 Percent
30 to 36 Percent
36 to 61 Percent

0   220   440   880 Miles

Source: Government transfer data from U.S. Bureau of Economic Analysis (2016).

very wealthiest counties in the nation have seen increases in government support: in Nassau County, New York, for instance, transfers grew from 8 to 12 percent of income, and in Douglas County, Colorado, they increased from 3 to 7 percent.[29]

Federal government transfers transcend demographic differences across counties. We can consider the composition of the population within counties according to residents' self-identified race or ethnicity, distinguishing between white and several categories grouped together here as "nonwhite," including black, American Indian or Alaska Native, Asian or Pacific Islander, or two or more other categories. Not surprisingly, given the greater prevalence of poverty and lower incomes among nonwhite Americans, there is a perceptible tilt toward a greater percentage of federal dollars in counties that have a higher percentage of nonwhite residents, but it is very slight.[30] The populations of counties in the most-aided category in figure 3.8 are, on average, 83 percent white, just barely lower than the nationwide rate of 85 percent white. In fact, very homogenous counties—those populated nearly entirely by whites—proliferate among those that use the highest rates of government transfers. Among the fifty counties in the nation with the very highest rates of social transfers, thirty-eight have populations in which 90 percent or more of residents identify as white. The county with the highest share of personal income coming from transfers in the nation, Kentucky's Owsley County, has a 98 percent white population. While several others in the top group are also located in Appalachia, examples outside of that region include Roscommon County in Michigan, which ranks nineteenth in the nation in transfer receipt and where the population is 97 percent white, and Sharp County, Arkansas, which is 96 percent white and ranked twenty-second.

Regions of the United States differ somewhat from each other in the average percentage of residents' income that flows from social policies, but strikingly, all areas experienced marked increases between 1979 and 2014. In 1979, the Middle Atlantic states led the nation in reliance on federal transfers, followed by New England.[31] Although other regions have surpassed them on that measure, these states continued to net the greatest dollar amounts per capita, at $8,766 and $8,538 per capita, respectively. By 2014, federal transfers accounted for the greatest percentage of income in the southeastern region of the nation, where they grew from 11.46 to 19.34 percent. The Great Lakes region of the Midwest ranked second, at 18.08 percent in 2014, up from 10.45 percent in 1979. Even the Rocky Mountain region, which in 2014 had the lowest average rates in the nation at 13.77 percent, had experienced a 65 percent increase. In sum, in counties across the nation and across multiple divides, Americans have become much more likely to benefit from government social policies than in the past.

We Are Nearly All Contributors as Well

If Americans across the board are utilizing government benefits, who is paying for them? When Romney spoke of the "47 percent" who expect government to "care for them," he added, "These are people who pay no income tax."[32] Congressman Paul Ryan elaborated on the implications of this idea, predicting ominously, echoing the language of the libertarian thinker Ayn Rand: "So we're going to a majority of takers versus makers in America and that will be tough to come back from that. They'll be dependent on the government for their livelihoods [rather] than themselves."[33] Is it really the case that the United States is becoming a society in which most people only benefit from government and just a few, by contrast, contribute to it? To address this question, here we consider the revenue side of the ledger.

Since the United States adopted the federal income tax in 1913, following the ratification of the Sixteenth Amendment, it has embraced a progressive approach in which those who receive greater "market incomes," meaning earnings prior to government transfers, contribute a larger percentage of their income.[34] In short, it collects taxes based on people's ability to pay, and it helps slightly to mitigate inequality.[35] Today a substantial percentage of Americans do not have federal income tax liability, owing to changes in the federal tax code that President Reagan signed into law in 1988 and that have been expanded since then, in policies approved by presidents of both parties.[36] As of 2016, 44 percent of Americans paid no income taxes, down from the 50 percent peak during the Great Recession, when lower earnings moved more people below the threshold of tax liability.[37]

But although a sizable share of Americans do not pay federal income taxes, all who participate in the workforce and earn wages "above the table" contribute payroll taxes, which pay for the Social Security and Medicare benefits of current retirees and others eligible for benefits.[38] This system of taxation now collects 34 percent of all federal revenues, functioning as a respectable junior partner to the federal income tax system, which generates 46 percent. (Of the remainder, corporate income taxes account for 12 percent, and excise, estate, and gift taxes and other miscellaneous taxes each make up the remaining smaller portions.)[39] The payroll tax system is regressive, given that all employees, regardless of income, pay at the same rate of 7.65 percent as of 2016, up from 6.13 percent in 1980. This tax, furthermore, is only applied to the first $118,500 of an individual's earnings in a given year, beyond which earnings are tax-free, further underscoring the extra burden it imposes on ordinary Americans compared to the affluent. As a result of these features, the majority of Americans, fully 65 percent, pay a larger sum in payroll taxes than they pay in income taxes.[40]

President Franklin D. Roosevelt, who promoted Social Security and signed it into law in 1935, believed strongly in the necessity of a system to which future beneficiaries themselves contributed. This design, he argued, ensured that the benefits would be perceived as "earned," with eligibility established through years of participation in covered employment or marriage to someone with such a record. "With those taxes in there, no damn politician can ever scrap my social security program," he said.[41] In actuality, the system currently operates through a "pay-as-you-go" arrangement, in which current earners' payroll taxes finance the benefits of current retirees. It also functions as a system of social insurance in the case of unexpected events, providing survivors' benefits and disability benefits. These arrangements underscore the mutual obligations of all Americans to one another. Public opinion polls show that the program enjoys support across income and age groups.[42]

Accounting for both of these major types of federal taxes as well as government transfers, how much do Americans of different income levels contribute to and receive from the federal government? The answers lie in table 3.2, compiled by the Congressional Budget Office. The top row shows market incomes across income quintiles in 2011, highlighting the high degree of economic inequality. The second row lists average amounts of government transfers received from all levels of government. The sum of market income and government transfers is equivalent to before-tax income, shown in the third row. Notably, those in the lowest quintile received the least in actual dollars from government transfers, though such transfers made up a more substantial percentage of their before-tax income (37 percent) than for those in any other quintile. The fourth row lists average federal taxes, including income and payroll taxes, as well as corporate and excise taxes. (State and local taxes, property taxes, and sales taxes are not included here.) It should be noted that federal taxes implicitly take into account most tax expenditures, as such policies lower the tax liability of households, although

Table 3.2 Average Household Income, Transfers, and Taxes, by Before-Tax Income Group, 2011

	LOWEST QUINTILE	SECOND QUINTILE	MIDDLE QUINTILE	FOURTH QUINTILE	HIGHEST QUINTILE	ALL HOUSE-HOLDS
Market income	$15,500	$29,600	$49,800	$83,300	$234,700	$80,600
Government transfers (federal, state, and local)	9,100	15,700	16,500	14,100	11,000	13,300
Before-tax income	24,600	45,300	66,400	97,500	245,700	93,900
Federal taxes[a]	500	3,200	7,400	14,800	57,500	16,600
After-tax income	24,100	42,100	59,000	82,600	188,200	77,300

Source: U.S. Congressional Budget Office (2014), 2.
[a] Federal taxes includes individual income taxes, payroll taxes, corporate income taxes, and excise taxes.

the two largest—the excludability of health and retirement benefits—are not accounted for in such calculations, so this table underestimates the benefits for those in the higher income groups.

As table 3.2 makes evident, Americans across income groups both contribute to and benefit from federal government. The average household in each quintile paid some federal taxes. Any American who has participated in the paid workforce at some juncture in his or her life has contributed, and most of those who are not already retired do so presently. Households in the lower three quintiles paid less in taxes than they received in transfers; for those in the fourth quintile, the two amounts were nearly equivalent. Those in the top quintile gained by far the greatest benefits through the tax code, through policies whose presence, though invisible in this table, is shown in figure 2.4.

F. Scott Fitzgerald once began a short story by writing, "Let me tell you about the very rich. They are different from you and me."[43] Ernest Hemingway later famously recalled Fitzgerald's remark in a story of his own, with the mocking retort, "Yes, they have more money."[44] The wealthy are taxed more precisely because they have more money. In the United States, however, these same individuals gain extensive benefits through the same process.

When it comes to federal taxes and benefits, we are all makers and we are all takers. Put differently, we are a political community of shared sacrifice and mutual interdependence.

One Nation Indivisible

Sheila Turner, who was born in 1973, is a self-described "stay-at-home mom" who lives in Dallas, Texas, in a middle-income household. She considers herself to be extremely conservative on politics and identifies with the Republican Party. When asked what she thinks of when she hears the term "government social programs," she says, "Giving money to those who don't want to work." Her views of such programs are "mostly negative," she reports, because they provide support for "people who don't prioritize their budgets and pay for their [own] bills." She believes that "government does a poor job of managing things," and that "people should provide for themselves."

Yet Turner readily acknowledges that her family has used several specific policies. Her daughter used financial aid to attend college, both Pell Grants and student loans. Her husband used Unemployment Insurance for several months while unemployed, about which she comments, "Every little bit helps when you have no income." She and her family have also utilized several features of the tax code, including the EITC, the home mortgage interest deduction, and the tax-free status of employer-provided health and retirement benefits. She does not view these tax expenditures as government social benefits, but rather as incentives for making certain decisions, explaining, "They give people a reward for using their money the right way."

American rhetoric about government benefits implies that we are a deeply divided nation of "us" and "them," the deserving and the undeserving. Yet the evidence tells a different story. When we consider individual Americans across different incomes, parties, and ages, nearly all have used social benefits, and although usage patterns vary, particularly with respect to policy types, the commonalities loom larger than the differences. Similarly, when we consider Americans with respect to the communities across the country where they live, whether rich or poor, they are far more likely to use more such benefits today than Americans did thirty-five years ago. We nearly all benefit from the federal government's social policies, and we nearly all contribute to those policies, whether through payroll taxes, income taxes, or both. The question is, how does such usage affect our overarching views of government? We now turn to examine that puzzle.

CHAPTER 4

DIFFERENT LENSES

ALICE GINGOLD, born in 1979 and a self-described ideologically conservative Democrat, lives in Boise, Idaho, in a lower-middle-income family. She credits several policies with helping her at various points in her life, including the Special Supplemental Nutrition Program for Women, Infants, and Children (WIC), Medicaid, Unemployment Insurance, and some tax code policies. She particularly appreciates Medicaid, which covered her when, as a single parent, she gave birth to her daughter, and which also covered the infant's first month of life, spent in a neonatal intensive care unit. Yet overall, Gingold remains highly skeptical of government. She feels that it "shouldn't really be involved in health care" because it "oversteps and hinders progress." For her, the term "government social programs" brings to mind "socialism" and "creating an entitlement generation, not a generation of workers." She feels that government is taking away "families' rights to their own beliefs," citing recent controversies over the Confederate flag (which had been taken down at the South Carolina statehouse not long before our interview in 2015) and taxpayer funds going to Planned Parenthood.

In Fort Collins, Colorado, George Porter, though twenty-two years older than Gingold and a self-described "extremely conservative" Republican, has some experiences and viewpoints in common with her. He explains that his family has "less than we ever have had," noting that it is "hard to find good-paying work and decent benefits and wages and a full-time position." In particular, he emphasizes the cost of health care. Over the course of his life, Porter has benefited from numerous policies, including SSI, Medicaid, welfare, food stamps, and the EITC. Yet overall, he says, government has been

of "little help" and it "makes things more expensive and harder for the average blue-collar family." Like Gingold, he also associates "government social programs" with "socialism" and criticizes them for not providing sufficient incentives for people to work. He hopes that government will do
more to help Americans find jobs, raise their wages, and provide economic
security. "I pray for this United States to exist how we know it should be,"
he concludes.

The mystery deepens: if so many people in all corners of the nation rely
on U.S. social policies, how could government itself at the same time be so
unpopular, even despised, by so many? It would seem that as more people
benefit from such policies, appreciation for government would grow. To the
contrary, its reputation could hardly be worse.

Certainly some Americans do connect their appreciation for public benefits with government itself. Linda Nichols, in Florida, states forthrightly
that government has helped her in her own life, providing assistance that
she "never would have thought she would need" when she was younger.
When the economy slowed in her area, starting around 2005 and worsening considerably in 2008, she and her family relied on government benefits.
Jack Hamilton, in Kansas City, Missouri, deeply values the ways in which
government has assisted his grown children in moving toward financial independence by helping them pay for their college educations and providing
them with access to health coverage through the Affordable Care Act. He
believes that, for the country as a whole, "the distribution of wealth is getting out of hand," and that government should reduce inequality through
more generous benefits and expanded coverage in social programs, as well
as by raising the minimum wage and taking other actions to boost the value
of work. Several other interview respondents echoed similar themes.

The variation in Americans' views about government, even among those
who themselves have benefited from numerous social programs, raises a
question: What explains these differences? Nearly all who have used such
policies speak positively about their experiences, yet that does not restrain
some of them from expressing general disapproval of government, if not
outright contempt, while for others, policy experiences appear to have bolstered their appreciation of government and conviction that it should do
more to assist other Americans. Now that more Americans rely on public
social provision than ever before *and* antigovernment sentiments abound
and continue to intensify, this mysterious divide has become increasingly
puzzling and consequential for U.S. politics.

Although scholars have examined Americans' attitudes about government in some depth, we know surprisingly little about how personal experiences of social policies—particularly as they accumulate in individuals' lives—relate to those attitudes. Existing studies of the determinants of attitudes about government focus primarily on individuals' social characteristics, partisanship, and political ideology.[1] To the extent that scholars assess the role of public policies, they explore how individuals perceive specific groups of policy beneficiaries, such as welfare recipients.[2] The question remains how actual policy usage, particularly repeated experiences of it, might affect attitudes about government generally, and how the impact might vary with the types of policies that individuals most frequently encounter.

Another limitation of our existing knowledge of the determinants of Americans' attitudes toward government is the exclusive focus of analysis to date on one or two manifestations of such views. Typically, scholars explore variation in political trust, drawn from the classic survey question: "How much of the time do you think you can trust the government in Washington to do what is right—just about always, most of the time, or only some of the time?" Sometimes, too, they consider responses to another question: "Would you say the government is pretty much run by a few big interests looking out for themselves or that it is run for the benefit of all the people?"[3] Yet little attention is given to the standard measures of political efficacy, on which citizens' views have also worsened dramatically over time; these include levels of agreement with the statements that "public officials don't care much what people like me think" and "I have no say in what government does."

To better understand Americans' attitudes about government, we should consider a greater variety of forms and recognize that individuals' assessments may vary depending on the specific object or activity being investigated. Margaret Levi and Laura Stoker have argued that besides generalized political trust, attitudes toward specific administrative agencies or political actors may also be politically consequential and worthy of study.[4] Moreover, individuals may feel positively about some aspects of their relationship to government but not others, and they may consider government to function well in some respects but not in others. It makes sense to probe multiple dimensions of citizens' perceptions of government.

In this chapter, we delve further into the survey data to examine how Americans' perceptions of government might be related to their personal history of social policy usage as well as several other factors. We consider how lifetime histories of policy usage are associated with subsequent views of political efficacy and other attitudes about government. Also, to understand the underlying mechanisms, we examine particular cases, first comparing the EITC and public assistance and then a few higher education policies. As noted in chapter 1, the SGIP survey design permits this kind of analysis but does not allow us to rule out the possibility that attitudes may have predated policy usage or been influenced by other factors not measured by the instrument. Also, it should be noted that while earlier chapters have pointed to the geographic manifestations of the government-citizen disconnect, illuminated by the maps in chapters 1 and 3, explaining the underpinnings of that disconnect lies beyond this project, as the national survey data used here do not permit it.[5]

As we shall see, most Americans rate their own experiences of social policies quite positively. Policy design and delivery make a difference in shaping broader attitudes about government to the extent that some accumulated and specific experiences of direct, visible policies generate more positive attitudes, but this happens only in some instances. Social identities and group affiliations often override the impact of personal policy experiences. In some instances, policies play an indirect role, as inherited perceptions of them are channeled through social identities and shared experiences that influence views of government. The most consistent influence on citizens' assessments of government emanates from their unfavorable perceptions of welfare, views which are themselves shaped by social identities. As a result, in spite of the frequency and near ubiquity of citizens' policy experiences, the government-citizen disconnect prevails.

Evaluating Policy Experiences

Given the widespread usage of social policies, we might wonder whether policy experiences themselves are somehow causing hostility to government. This concern would be warranted if such experiences were largely negative and conveyed harmful messages to recipients. Several case studies do suggest that low-income and disabled Americans in particular encounter numerous obstacles when they seek coverage for particular policies, through processes that can be stigmatizing or disempowering.[6] Such dynamics may be exacerbated by the trend in some policies toward more restrictive rules or lower benefits, as discussed in chapter 2.

Overall, however, Americans appreciate the specific policies they person-

Figure 4.1 Beneficiaries' Assessments of Their Experiences of Social Policies

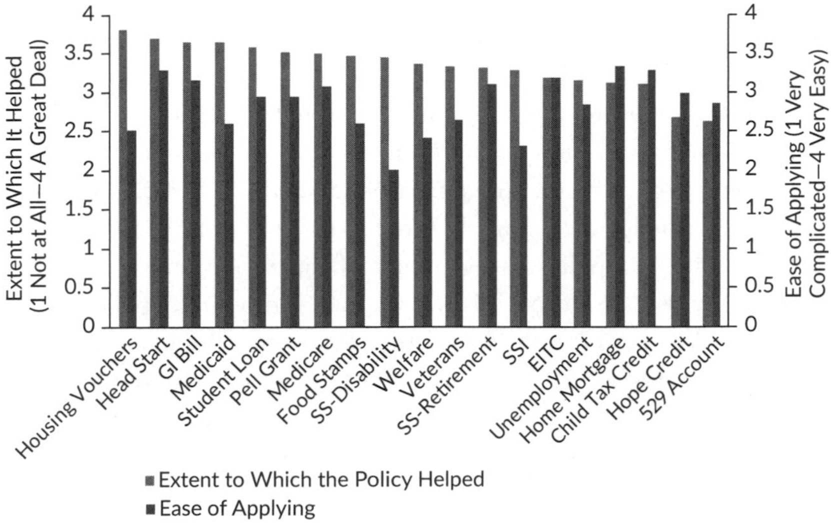

■ Extent to Which the Policy Helped
■ Ease of Applying

Source: 2008 SGIP.

ally have used and give them fairly high marks. After a survey respondent reported that she or he had used a particular policy, interviewers asked several follow-up questions, including, "To what extent did [the policy] help you: a great deal, to some extent, a little, or not at all?" Most policies, as shown by the light gray bars in figure 4.1, enjoyed favorable average ratings, ranging from "to some extent" to "a great deal." Direct, visible policies scored particularly high, most notably several that extend health care or education—namely, Head Start, the GI Bill, Medicaid, student loans, Pell Grants, and Medicare. The lowest assessments were earned by tax expenditures, which seem to have left less of an impression on recipients. For example, although the home mortgage interest deduction is generally lauded by policymakers, more so than housing vouchers, among beneficiaries the housing voucher program received higher evaluations for the help it offered.[7]

Another survey question inquired, "When people apply for government benefits, sometimes they find that the process is easy while on other occasions it is complicated. In your experiences with [the policy], would you say that qualifying for benefits was easy or complicated, or don't you remember?" As shown by the dark gray bars in figure 4.1, the policies in the tax code received strong assessments, equaling or surpassing other policies, for the ease of applying for them. The process of determining eligibility for tax expenditures differs markedly from that for other policies, owing to the lack of involvement by public officials and the absence of personal scrutiny. As Patricia Strach has observed, in order to claim tax benefits, individuals themselves do the work of ascertaining eligibility, perhaps with the aid of an accountant or volunteer tax preparer.[8] By contrast, personnel in government agencies must typically determine whether direct benefits are appropriate. These policies, particularly those that require more intensive personal scrutiny of applicants by public officials to establish eligibility, garnered lower assessments. This was the case for disability policies, both SSDI and SSI, as well as for some other means-tested income assistance policies, such as Medicaid and welfare. Yet such evaluations were not ubiquitous: notably, Pell Grants and the EITC, though both means-tested, earned praise for the ease of application that applicants experienced. For the EITC, the assistance received by many beneficiaries from a tax preparer or volunteer may have aided in generating such reactions.

Some policies excelled in one dimension while faring less well in another. Beneficiaries of housing vouchers found them to be quite complicated to attain, yet they earned greater accolades than any other policies for the help they offered. Tax expenditures, by contrast, received praise for the ease of attainment, yet beneficiaries gave them relatively little credit for making a difference in their lives. Overall, however, Americans value their social benefits quite highly.

Seeing Government Through Different Lenses

Scholarship on policy feedback suggests that policies themselves may serve as sites of political learning for beneficiaries, offering experiences that affect their general attitudes about government and their own status as citizens. Policy design and delivery perform these roles by imparting cognitive messages to beneficiaries or bestowing resources on them.[9] Many empirical studies have examined such policy effects, usually by examining one policy at a time, or a small number of policies. The data utilized here, by contrast, permit us to explore how individuals' accumulated usage of multiple social policies with distinct designs and delivery types may influence their perceptions of government.

To develop a richer understanding of citizens' attitudes toward government, we can evaluate several indicators of such views. We consider some assessments that directly involve social welfare functions, namely, the extent to which individuals believe that government helped them in times of need or provided opportunities to improve their standard of living. As more general indicators, we consider individuals' sense of external political efficacy, meaning their perception of government's responsiveness to "people like them." We explore citizens' views of how well democracy is functioning presently and whether they enjoy the status of rights-bearing members of the political community on par with others. Finally, as a measure of views of civic obligations, we examine citizens' perceptions of their tax burden and whether they consider it fair.

The Effects of Policy Experiences

To probe how prior policy experiences might influence individuals' attitudes about government, we consider the impact of policy design and delivery. It is reasonable to assume that *visibility* matters—that policies that convey perceptible effects and make government's role more traceable to beneficiaries generate a greater impact on attitudes than those that obscure government's role.[10] Some policies issue resources in a manner that makes their value fairly obvious, as in the case of Social Security, a benefit delivered to recipients in the form of direct deposits of funds into their bank accounts.[11] Others, such as those that simply reduce what individuals owe in taxes, make the actual value of resources less explicit.[12] Some policies feature administrative arrangements that make government's part in providing benefits plainly manifest, as did the original GI Bill education and training benefits. By contrast, other policies camouflage government's activity, such as public subsidies that support employer-provided health and retirement benefits or arrangements that charge private actors for service provision, as in the case of Medicare.[13] We would expect that policies with more direct and visible designs and delivery of benefits might heighten individuals' perception of their value and make it more apparent that government is the source, whereas those with more submerged designs might fail to engender such effects.

We might also expect that the distinction between whether policies are *targeted to low-income people or applied to citizens generally* will influence the perceptions of government that these policies generate.[14] Scholars have argued that eligibility rules featuring income ceilings, otherwise known as "means-testing," treat individuals in a manner that is demeaning and stigmatizing and therefore are likely to foster social stratification or "second-class citizenship." By contrast, policies that encompass broad swathes of the population through more universalistic eligibility criteria may bestow dignity and respect on beneficiaries, incorporating them as honored members of the political community.[15] Some scholars suggest that policies that aid the poor need not necessarily induce stigma and that stigma may result instead from the specific way that policies are designed. Social Security, for instance, as Theda Skocpol has pointed out, features "targeting within universalism," an approach that incorporates the less well-off into the same programs as others but does more to boost their incomes.[16] Another means-tested policy, Head Start, includes mechanisms that foster democratic inclusion, as Joe Soss has demonstrated.[17] An in-depth study of the EITC has revealed that, by contrast to TANF, the tax credit helps beneficiaries experience a sense of social inclusion by regarding them as reputable taxpayers.[18] Therefore, although it is reasonable to expect that some means-tested policies may inculcate more negative attitudes about government than non-means-tested policies, variation in policy design is also likely to affect attitudes toward government.

The dynamics described here rely on individualistic notions of political experience, reasoning, and behavior, the presumption being that people operate independently as they receive and process information and make judgments about the political world and their place in it. Yet social identities and shared ideas and values play a powerful role in shaping how people perceive and interpret social and political phenomena. Christopher Achen and Larry Bartels, in their book *Democracy for Realists*, argue that group affiliations play a powerful role in motivating political viewpoints, often greater than that of rational deliberation. They explain that people may share with others of the same race, gender, religion, or place a sense of "linked fate," viewing themselves as faring similarly in society and having common interests or a similar role.[19] Accordingly citizens formulate their political perspectives in the context of such groups.[20] In our analysis here, we need to consider how these identities and affiliations, relative to public policies and in conjunction with them, influence perceptions of government.

Partisan Affiliation and Ideas About Welfare

Political parties, as organizations, attempt to offer citizens coherent views about how society should operate and the appropriate role that government should play. While the parties have long diverged on their stances on multiple issues, the gaps in partisans' views have widened in recent decades, as polarization and "teamsmanship" among elected officials have increased.[21] It is reasonable to expect, therefore, that individuals' partisan identity will be related to their views about government.

Scholars diverge in their assessments of the sources of partisanship. Achen and Bartels argue that party affiliation is less an active choice than it is the product of political socialization or joining together with those with whom one shares a common sense of identity.[22] Other scholars stress the role of ideas in generating individuals' partisanship, and perceive individuals as making deliberate choices in the matter.[23] It is outside the scope of this project to sort out these chicken-and-egg questions; in either case, or through a complex blend of both dynamics, partisanship is like to be associated with how individuals perceive government.

In addition to the general ideas encapsulated by partisanship, individuals' specific ideas about social provision may affect their overall assessments of government, and these may also emanate from social contexts. It is well documented that although Americans support social provision generally, and majorities support expanded aid to poor people in particular, many express strong opposition to programs they view as undermining the work ethic.[24] This theme permeated the open-ended interviews conducted for this study. A constructive version of it stresses that public assistance programs are not well run and should be adjusted to function more effectively. Such a view is articulated by Lydia Perry of North Carolina, who adds: "All programs should be about getting you on your feet, not to keep you where you're at." A harsher variant is epitomized by the views of Pete Hunter of Louisiana, who lambasts "free handouts" and says that beneficiaries should have to show proof of looking for work before receiving aid, that their benefits should decline in value with time spent in the program, and that they should be subjected to drug testing.

Social identities and shared experiences may influence these views of public assistance. For one thing, it is often assumed that hostility to welfare might run highest for those with incomes just above the fiscal cliff, the threshold for eligibility for means-tested benefits.[25] Scholars have also found evidence that such views can be strongly racialized. As Martin Gilens observes, "Welfare itself remains the most talked about and least liked of America's social policies. The public's opposition to welfare is fed by the potent combination of racial stereotypes and misinformation about the true nature of America's poor."[26] Yet, while racial dynamics are likely to influence views about welfare, it is reasonable to expect variation in whether they do so and that other factors may also fuel dislike for the policy. Katherine Cramer notes that when she heard rural whites in Wisconsin criticizing welfare recipients, "they were talking about their white neighbors, not people of color in the cities."[27]

We can examine the SGIP data to probe the determinants of perceptions of welfare, drawn from a question about respondents' "view of that program," measured on a 4-point scale from "very unfavorable" (1) to "very favorable" (4). Overall, more Americans expressed favorable views toward welfare (56 percent) than unfavorable views (24 percent), but still one in five reported having "very unfavorable views."[28] To understand who is most likely to hold unfavorable attitudes, I conducted an analysis that allowed me to control for several factors, including education, income, gender, and race or ethnicity.[29] Full results of a logistic regression analysis are shown in appendix E, table E.1.[30]

Striking results pertain to income level. Those in the $20-35,000 income bracket do not differ significantly in their views from those in the lowest income category, nor do those in the highest income category, $100,000 and above, but within the three middle income groups, from $35,000 up through $99,000, individuals are significantly more likely to disapprove of welfare.[31] These results suggest that it is not only the working poor, those just above the "fiscal cliff," who harbor antipathy toward welfare; rather, this hostility pervades the middle class generally—people who may feel that life has been difficult in recent decades, as their incomes have stagnated or grown only a little, even while their families have increased their participation in the labor market.

The results also reveal a significant racial bias in welfare attitudes. At each income level, whites are significantly more likely to disapprove of welfare than African Americans as well as Asians and Pacific Islanders.[32] The long legacy of racial politics triggered by debates over social provision, particularly in distinctions about the deserving versus the undeserving poor, appears to be manifest in this result, channeling racial resentment.[33]

Figure 4.2 illustrates these relationships, showing the probability of having a favorable attitude toward welfare, across income levels and by race. (Asian and Pacific Islanders are not shown due to the small number of cases in some subgroups.) African Americans' and whites' views, though they differ, for the most part parallel each other across income levels, indicating

Figure 4.2 Predicted Favorability Toward Welfare Among Whites and African Americans, by Income Group

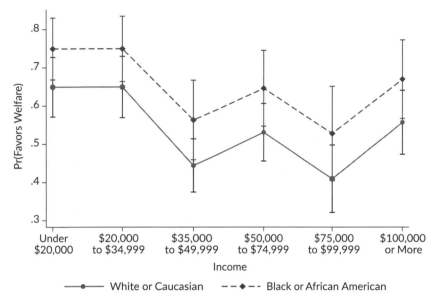

Source: 2008 SGIP.

the significance of both race and income in shaping views.[34] Individuals from households with incomes below $35,000 per year are all quite likely to favor welfare, with blacks more likely than whites to do so (75 percent compared to 65 percent.) Welfare favorability drops, however, for those in middle income groups, where blacks are only between 53 and 65 percent likely to favor it, while whites are only between 41 and 53 percent likely to do so. Among the highest income groups, welfare favorability is higher: blacks have a 70 percent likelihood of favoring it and whites a 55 percent likelihood of favoring welfare. In short, welfare favorability varies by both income and race; it is not driven solely by one dynamic or the other.

In turn, perceptions of welfare, because they touch "on the central values that animate public life," may influence attitudes about government generally.[35] Individuals may think of welfare as a demonstration of "government in action" and conclude that it wastes money, undermines laudable values, and demeans those whom it aims to assist. Arlie Hochschild, in her conversations with conservatives in Louisiana, detected a narrative underlying their stories: they felt that they had long been waiting in line for the American Dream, exercising patience and working hard, but that the federal government was increasingly enabling others—who claimed to be victims—to cut in line ahead of them. They perceived that, "over their heads, the federal government was taking money from the workers and giving it to the idle. It was taking from people of good character and giving to people of bad character. No mention was made of social class and enormous care was given to speak delicately and indirectly of blacks, although fear-tinged talk of Muslims was blunt. If the flashpoint between these groups had a location, it might be in the welfare offices that gave federal money to beneficiaries."[36] Individuals' hostility to welfare may also render their own usage of social programs a source of shame, which may dampen the impact of such experiences. For any of these reasons, those who dislike welfare might extrapolate from that attitude toward a more negative view of government generally, and vice versa.

Social Identities, Policy Legacies, and Shared Experiences

Individuals may adopt general orientations toward government from a social group with which they identify or with whom they share experiences and make sense of them together, as Achen and Bartels have argued.[37] Yet scholarship on how social identities matter in politics often misses a crucial factor: how public policies themselves can create shared experiences among group members, and can shape, give meaning to, or even create their identities, in ways that influence their perceptions of and orientations to government. Group identities may subsequently carry with them political meaning.

Over time, political identities may be passed down, such that latter-day affiliates inherit orientations toward government that were shaped by the public policy experiences of their predecessors. Put differently, such affinities may convey a legacy of perceptions of government that is rooted in the group's historic experiences of public policy. Alternatively, they may reflect group members' widely held current assessments of the general relationship between themselves and government, perhaps reflecting experiences of policies other than social benefits. Of course, identities are multiple and fluid; a single individual may identify with various different groups, and the extent to which one identity or another influences her political behavior may depend on the circumstances, point in time, or other factors.[38] These complexities lie beyond the scope of what can be examined further here, given the scope of the argument and data limitations, but they await further development by other scholars.[39]

American government has long conveyed to white men, for example, that it is highly relevant to their lives, both their identity and their well-being, whereas for women and men of color, such recognition has occurred more recently and less completely. By the 1830s, white men in the United States enjoyed political rights well in advance of those of citizens of other nations, where such status was still tied to property ownership. They also acquired civic obligations, particularly those of citizen soldiers; as such, they might be called upon to sacrifice their personal safety and even their lives for the nation. That status also endowed them with respect, representation, and rights. The earliest social benefits in the United States were bestowed on male veterans to honor their military service.[40] In the 1930s, white men gained privileged treatment in the nationally run social and labor policies of the New Deal, while women and minority men were relegated to state-run policies characterized by greater variation and more particularistic requirements on beneficiaries.[41] The GI Bill, established in 1944 for returning World War II veterans, granted new access to education to men across the economic spectrum.[42] These policies conveyed, particularly to white men, that government was an entity oriented to serving them and responding to their needs. The message to women was articulated by one female veteran, speaking of the GI Bill: "Oh, I think we viewed it as a policy for the men. I mean, they really created it with the men in mind, didn't they?"[43]

Although social policies today no longer include such overtly discriminatory features, gender roles in politics remain rooted in the legacy of the policy history that induced males to identify more closely with government than women. Policies have probably long conveyed to women that, as Nancy Burns, Kay Schlozman, and Sidney Verba put it, "politics is not my world."[44] This view may remain integral to women's gender identity today, affecting their views about government. This would explain why, compared to men, women still tend to have lower levels of interest in politics, less political knowledge, and, aside from voting, lower rates of political participation.[45] Women also remain less likely to run for political office, and still today the U.S. Congress is only 19.4 percent female.[46] The underrepresentation of women in political leadership perpetuates the gender divide, given that when women see elected officials, they literally do not see people who look like themselves to the extent that men do.[47] Of course, women may also be less inclined to view government as being on their side given the continuing discrimination they experience in realms beyond social policy, as evidenced by the recent revelation of widespread sexual harassment in several areas of employment. For each of these reasons, it is reasonable to expect, therefore, that men may hold more positive view of government than women.

The United States, throughout much of its history, has also treated residents differently on the basis of their race and ethnicity, incorporating those of European descent earlier and more fully into core policies while excluding or marginalizing those of African, Latin American, or Asian descent, as discussed in chapter 2. The U.S. Constitution legitimized slavery until it was outlawed by the Thirteenth Amendment, ratified during the Civil War, in 1865. During Reconstruction, black adult males gained voting rights, their rates of participation soared from 1 to 80 percent, and robust biracial party competition emerged, ushering in public education in the South, integrated police forces, rapid improvement in literacy rates among African Americans, and numerous other changes.[48] Yet by the late nineteenth and early twentieth centuries, those reforms had been rolled back as the states and the federal government sanctioned racial segregation over the next several decades.[49] Today, more than a half-century after the nation once again adopted civil rights reforms in the 1950s and 1960s, blacks experience inequality in myriad venues, not least the criminal justice system.[50] Latinos, both immigrants and those born in the United States, encounter discriminatory treatment that remains sanctioned by political discourse.[51] Communities of low-income people of color are disadvantaged not only by insufficient governmental attention in some domains, such as social policy, but also, as Joe Soss and Vesla Weaver point out, from "*too much* governmental oversight, interference, and predation."[52] Blacks, Latinos, and other people of color, therefore, are likely to have more negative attitudes about government than those of European descent. It should be noted that these shared views may emanate not only from historical experiences but also from present-day ones, in policy domains besides social policy.

Older generations of Americans are likely to have more positive attitudes about government than younger Americans. Those who experienced political socialization during the middle years of the twentieth century experienced government functioning relatively well. In the post–World War II decades, government facilitated strong economic growth and its widespread distribution across the income spectrum in a manner that mitigated inequality and built a middle class.[53] Educational attainment soared during these decades as public policies enabled more and more Americans to become the first in their families to attend college and enjoy greater opportunities as a result.[54] Americans who came of age in that era witnessed the federal government achieving such feats as the building of the interstate highway system and sending the first mission to the moon. Younger Americans, by contrast, experienced political socialization as economic growth slowed down, budget deficits constrained new programs, and partisan polarization grew, making the governing process far more contentious and prone to gridlock than before. In recent decades, the welfare state remained generous and inclusive for older Americans, as we saw in chapter 2, while several policies for those of working age deteriorated in value. It is reasonable to expect, therefore, that older Americans will have more positive attitudes about government than those in younger generations.

Americans who have encountered an abundance of economic opportunities, many of them facilitated by government, are likely to have acquired different perceptions of government than those who have experienced downward mobility or persistent poverty. Scholars know that higher levels of socioeconomic status, such as higher levels of education, are associated with greater political participation. The prevailing explanation is that highly educated individuals possess the requisite resources, skills, social networks, and flexibility with their time to get involved in politics.[55] The process of becoming educated also bestows lessons about civic engagement and its value.[56] And as several studies have found, more affluent individuals can also witness government working on their behalf, representing their views more consistently and reliably in the policy process than it does for those with lower incomes.[57] It is likely, therefore, that highly educated or higher-income people have more positive views of government than those with less education or income.

In sum, Americans are likely to vary in terms of the lenses through which they see government: some may wear "rose-colored glasses," viewing it more positively, while others see government more negatively, and still others may have their vision obscured altogether, such that they barely notice government's role in their lives. Besides policy design and implementation, many aspects of individuals' shared identities may influence these perceptions. For some, their own personal accumulated experiences of public policy may affect their views of government, whereas for others, the impact of those experiences may be overwhelmed by other factors.

Analyzing the Determinants of Views of Government

Now we turn to specific survey questions that will permit us to examine empirically the relationships discussed here. We can consider several manifestations of people's attitudes about government. The first two would appear to relate most directly to social policy usage: the level of agreement—on a 4-point scale from "disagree strongly" (1) to "agree strongly" (4)—with the statements "Government social programs have helped me in times of need" and "Government has given me opportunities to improve my standard of living."[58] While those two measures are related to what government bestows on citizens, a third relates to what it extracts through taxation: assessing a sense of civic obligation. Given the saliency of taxation to views about government in recent decades, we probe answers to the question, "When it comes to paying federal income taxes, do you feel you are asked to pay your fair share, more than your fair share, or less than your fair share?" (with "less than" as the highest value). Collectively, these first three measures formulate what can be called the "social contract" dimension of attitudes about government. It is reasonable to expect that these measures, which are most closely related to government's role in providing social benefits (as well as extracting resources), may be most likely to be associated with higher rates of policy usage, with the first two more related to visible policies and the latter to those in the tax code.[59]

A different set of measures belong to what could be termed the "democratic" dimension. Two of them are standard measures of what political scientists call "external political efficacy," or individuals' sense of government responsiveness to them: "Public officials don't care much what people like me think," and "People like me don't have any say about what the government does." These questions use the same scale as the one discussed earlier (and another discussed later), but it should be noted that strong agreement in these particular instances indicates negative views about government whereas in the case of the other measures it indicates positive views.[60] The next two indicators probe individuals' assessments of the health of democracy and whether they themselves are fully included in its promises. The first evaluates respondents' level of agreement with the statement, "Generally, I feel like a full and equal citizen in this country with all the rights and protections that other people have," and the second offers an answer to the question, "On the whole, are you very satisfied, somewhat satisfied, somewhat dissatisfied, or very dissatisfied with the way democracy works in the United States?" (with "very satisfied" as the highest value). Prior scholarship has found instances of a means-tested visible policy—namely, AFDC—being associated with lower political efficacy and a visible non-means-tested policy—namely, the GI Bill—being associated with views akin to full inclusion as citizens. Scholars have yet to assess, however, how accumulated policy usage may relate to these measures.[61]

We evaluate several potential determinants of these attitudes about government, beginning with accumulated personal experience of policies with particular design features. As measures, we include the sum of individuals' usage of each of four policy types, distinguishing between whether their design is visible or submerged, and whether it is means-tested or not. (The policies in each category are listed in chapter 3.) The submerged means-tested category includes only two policies, the EITC and the Hope and Lifetime Learning Tax Credits. Therefore, later in the chapter we also subject the EITC to a case study analysis, probing further to compare beneficiaries with similarly situated individuals who have used policies with different features.

Individuals' ideas about government can be assessed through the inclusion of two variables. Partisanship is measured on a 5-point scale from "Republican" (1) to "Democrat" (5).[62] Attitudes about welfare support are indicated as discussed previously.

We can explore how social identities relate to views of government by including several additional variables. Gender is indicated by those who identify as male compared to female; race is indicated by "nonwhite," a category including those who identify as black/African American, American Indian, Aleut, or Eskimo, Asian or Pacific Islander, or some other ethnicity, as compared with those who identify as white or Caucasian; and ethnicity is indicated by "Hispanic origin or descent," with "other" as the missing or reference category. Age is measured on a scale from eighteen to ninety-two, with older individuals receiving higher values.[63] Three educational levels are assessed, including a high school degree or less (which is the missing reference category), some post–high school education or training (which includes associate's degrees, attendance at trade schools, and coursework), and a four-year college degree (BA or BS) or higher, including graduate school or an advanced degree. Finally, total household income is measured on a 6-point ascending scale, from under $20,000 (0) to $100,000 or more (6).[64]

The analyses are conducted using logistic regression; full results are shown in appendix E, table E.2. There they are presented as coefficients and as marginal effects, which allows us to assess the statistical and substantive significance of each variable. Here I summarize the main findings and provide visual results from two of the seven analyses that are illustrative of the general patterns that emerged throughout.

Policy Experiences and Attitudes About Government

We begin by considering the direct impact of individuals' personal experiences of public policies, across their lifetimes, on their attitudes about government. The key finding here is that having used a greater number of visible means-tested policies is associated with a more positive view of government on one indicator: with respect to government social programs having helped "in times of need." For each additional such policy an individual has ever used, holding all other factors we are controlling for at their mean, the likelihood of agreeing that government has helped increases by an average of 12 percent. The graph on the left in figure 4.3 depicts how the probability of agreeing with the statement changes as individuals' policy usage rates changes.[65] It reveals that a person who has used no means-tested visible policies has about a 41 percent probability of agreeing that government has helped in times of need, and that increases to 55 percent for those who have used one such policy, 79 percent for those who have used three such policies, and close to 100 percent for those who have used six or more such policies. Despite the scrutiny that usage of such policies may impose on recipients, those who have utilized them appreciate them and recognize government's role in providing them.

Yet, aside from this result, repeated usage of visible policies was not associated with any other enhanced views of government among the seven indicators probed here. Extensive usage of non-means-tested visible policies shows no relationship to any broader evaluations of government. It would have seemed reasonable for recipients of such policies to be more likely to think that government had provided opportunities to improve their standard of living, for example, but this was not the case. Similarly, we might expect that those who regularly relied on visible government largesse, whether means-tested or not, would be more likely to feel that public officials are responsive to people like them, that they have a say in what government does, that they are treated as full and equal citizens, that democracy is operating well, or that they are taxed fairly. Yet even multiple experiences of such policies did not appear to influence such views.[66]

Figure 4.3 Factors Associated with Greater Agreement That "Government Social Programs Have Helped Me in Times of Need"

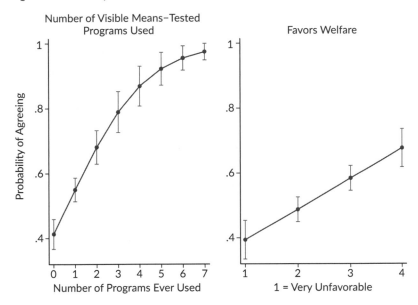

Source: 2008 SGIP.

Neither did usage of the non-means-tested submerged policies exert any bearing on recipients' broader views about government. Policymakers have explicitly justified the existence of several non-means-tested submerged policies, such as the home mortgage interest deduction, on the basis that they provide opportunities for Americans to make themselves better off, yet recipients seem not to perceive this impact. Nor did repeated usage of such policies relate to their attitudes about the fairness of their taxes—an ironic result given that such policies reduce what households owe in taxes, for example, by favoring those paying mortgages over those who rent their homes, those saving for college over those who cannot afford to save, and so forth. The submerged designs of these policies, however, made these results unsurprising.

A striking finding emerges, however, in the case of submerged means-tested policies: on several dimensions, usage of more of these is associated with significantly more *negative* views of government. There is one exception, and it was in keeping with expectations: recipients of these policies are significantly more likely to feel that they are taxed fairly, or even pay less than their fair share in taxes, rather than more. The substantive impact is large: for each additional such policy a person has used, all else equal, the recipient is 36 percent more likely to think that the amount of taxes he or she pays is fair. Aside from this, however, those who have benefited from more such policies are significantly more likely to *disagree* that government has provided them with opportunities (by about 6 percent), more likely to *agree* that public officials do not care what people like them think and that they have no say in what government does (by 7 and 6 percent, respectively), and more likely to *disagree* that they feel "like a full and equal citizen with all of the rights and protections that other people have" (by 5 percent). In figure 4.4, the graph in the upper-left corner indicates that people who have used no submerged means-tested policies have a 47 percent chance of agreeing that they "don't have any say about what the government does," whereas that probability increases to 59 percent for those who have used two such policies.

It is unlikely that policy experiences of means-tested submerged policies themselves cause individuals to develop worse attitudes about government; rather, it is more likely the case that those who qualify for these policies already possess negative views about government, and the policies fail to mitigate them. These recipients—the working poor, who make just enough not to qualify for visible means-tested policies—are individuals who have been living in the crosshairs of the economic and political changes of the last several decades that have diminished their opportunities to attain good-paying jobs. Their negative attitudes about government suggest that they feel like the dispossessed of contemporary American society. We probe these striking results more thoroughly in the focused analysis of the EITC in the next section.

Overall, these results offer some evidence that the government-citizen disconnect emanates in part from policy design. Ironically, the policies associated with some impact on broader views about government are those that tend to be the most stigmatized and in which government's role as a provider may be most evident—the visible means-tested policies. Repeated usage of these policies conveyed to recipients that government made a positive difference in their lives. Yet, beyond that, multiple uses of neither visible nor submerged policies appeared to have any bearing on enhanced attitudes about government. In the case of the means-tested variant of submerged policies, moreover, accumulated usage failed to mitigate more negative views of government, leaving recipients more resentful than others and assured only that they pay a fair amount of taxes. In sum, despite the

Figure 4.4 Factors Associated with Agreement That "People Like Me Don't Have Any Say About What Government Does"

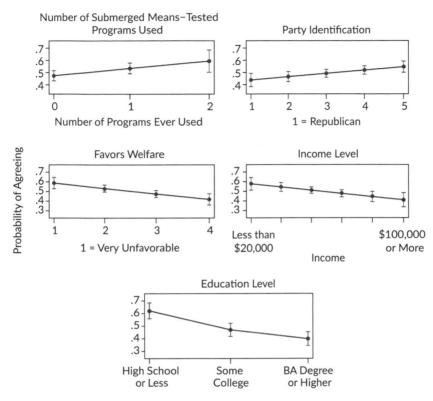

Source: 2008 SGIP.

considerable resources committed to each of these policy types, with modest exceptions, the impact of policy usage on citizens' perceptions appears to evaporate, at least over the long term. Specific policies may make a difference in attitudes, as some studies have shown, but accumulated memories of policy usage seem to exert little bearing on broad attitudes about government.

Extrapolating from Welfare to Government

More than any of the variables measuring personal experiences of government in action, individuals' abstract views about public policy and their partisan affiliations emerge as highly influential in shaping views about government. Attitudes about welfare, unlike other factors, yield highly significant and consistent associations with every general view toward government explored here. Those who have more favorable views of welfare consistently express more positive outlooks on government generally, and those with strong disdain for welfare hold more negative views. No other indicator bears such a persistent relationship to attitudes about government.[67]

Those with very unfavorable views of welfare, holding all else equal, including rates of policy usage, are on average 27 percent less likely than those with very favorable views of welfare to think that government social programs have helped them in times of need. The graph on the right in figure 4.3 shows that individuals who have very unfavorable views about welfare have a probability of acknowledging that government has helped them in a time of need of about 40 percent, compared to 68 percent among those with strongly favorable views toward welfare. Those who hold unfavorable views about welfare are about 12 percent less likely to acknowledge that government has provided them with opportunities than those with more favorable views, even when they have the same overall policy usage rates.

Negative attitudes about welfare are also associated with low political efficacy. Individuals with these views are 7 percent more likely to agree that public officials do not care what they think and 6 percent more likely to think that people like them have no say in what government does. This latter attitude is depicted in figure 4.4, in the graph on the lower left, showing that those with strongly unfavorable views of welfare have nearly a 60 percent probability of agreeing that people like them have no say in what government does compared to a 42 percent probability among those with strongly favorable views toward welfare. Those who feel very unfavorably toward welfare, compared to those who feel very favorably, are about 15 percent less likely to feel like full and equal citizens and 21 percent less likely to feel satisfied with the way democracy is working in the United States. They are also significantly less likely to think that the taxes they pay are fair.

Those holding unfavorable attitudes toward welfare appear to regard the program as a microcosm of how government operates, and extrapolate from it to government generally. They voice disapproval of government and a sense of alienation from it, on all counts. This antipathy toward government may stem predominantly from a view of TANF, a policy that covers less than 1 percent of the population presently, or possibly individuals holding this view may associate "welfare" with a broader set of means-tested programs; unfortunately, we lack evidence that would permit us to specify the reference points they use. These findings bring to mind Hochschild's understanding that those who are angry at the government share an interpretation of contemporary life that features people like themselves who feel that they have worked hard and waited patiently for the American Dream, while undeserving others have "cut in line" ahead of them—and government policies have enabled them to do so.[68] "Welfare" epitomizes their perception of such unfairness being facilitated by government.

When it comes to partisan affiliation, the results reflect the highly polarized contemporary polity in which partisan identity plays such a major role in providing cues to individuals and in which debates over the role of government loom large. We begin with a striking exception to the rule: once we control for the numerous other factors discussed here, partisans are *not* divided over whether government has helped them in times of need, the question that most directly taps into social provision. On each of the other indicators, however, significant differences emerged between partisans. Interestingly, Republicans held more positive views than Democrats in all respects: they were significantly more likely than Democrats to say that government provides opportunities that have improved their standard of living, public officials care what they think and they have a say about what the government does, they are treated as full and equal citizens, and democracy is functioning well. In figure 4.4, the upper-right-hand graph shows that as an individual moved up the partisan scale from being a strong Republican to a strong Democrat, the probability of agreeing that one had "no say about what the government does" increased from 44 percent to 55 percent.[69] These results, drawn from survey data during the final months of the George W. Bush presidency, might be attributable to a phenomenon that Marc Hetherington and Thomas Rudolph have observed: that as partisan polarization has increased, trust in government has vacillated with the party in power.[70] Perhaps political efficacy operates similarly. Alternatively, the indicators here may tap into aspects of government on which Republicans generally feel more favorably. This question deserves further exploration by future investigators.

Social Groups Convey Policy Legacies

Individuals' shared identities and common experiences with others are associated with several different dimensions of their views about government. In nearly all instances, the results, as anticipated, show that those belonging to social groups that have historically enjoyed greater privileges provided by public policies are more likely to have positive perceptions of government. Conversely, those who shared experiences or identified with those who have been excluded from, neglected by, or marginalized by public policy are more likely to have negative attitudes.

Historically, U.S. social welfare policies have advantaged particular groups, a legacy that may have generated long-term effects on perceptions.[71] Nonwhites are about 12 percent less likely than whites to agree that government has helped in times of need.[72] Nonwhites are also 14 percent less likely than whites to feel that they are full and equal citizens, and they have 54 percent lower odds of feeling that they are taxed fairly. Similarly, people who are older are more likely to feel that they are treated as full and equal citizens who enjoy all of the rights and protections enjoyed by others; these respondents came of age in an era when markets and government worked effectively in tandem to foster opportunity and curtail inequality. Men are 1.9 times as likely as women to feel that they are taxed fairly.

Americans who have attained higher levels of schooling or who earn larger paychecks hold considerably more positive views about government than those who have less. Those with four-year college degrees or higher are 9 percent more likely than those with high school degrees or less to agree that government has provided them with opportunities to improve their standard of living. This view makes sense, given the federal financial aid and state-level support available to college students. The highly educated also hold much greater confidence in government's responsiveness to people like them. Those with college degrees are 11 percent more likely than high school graduates to feel that government officials care what they think. Asked whether they agree that "people like me don't have any say in what the government does," college graduates are 22 percent more likely to disagree, and those with some college 15 percent more likely to disagree, than the least-educated group. The bottom graph in figure 4.4 shows that the probability of agreeing with this statement decreases most sharply between high school graduates and those with some college, from 62 to 47 percent. Income matters as well: as seen in the lower-right graph of figure 4.4, the probability of agreeing is 57 percent for those in the lowest income category, then diminishes steadily to 41 percent, for the highest income group.[73] This finding is consistent with research by Martin Gilens, Larry Bartels, and Benjamin Page, who show that lawmakers respond little to the preferences of less-advantaged Americans relative to how they respond to those who are better off.[74] The highly educated and those with higher incomes diverge only in their view about taxes: those with a college degree are about 72 percent more likely than those with just a high school degree to feel that they are taxed fairly, whereas those with higher incomes are 11 percent less likely to think so than those with lower incomes.

These results admittedly involve simplifications of social reality; the relatively small size of the data set does not permit us to examine more fine-tuned variation in identity or to grapple with intersectionality.[75] Nonetheless, what becomes apparent is that people hold orientations to government that reflect how those in the social groupings to which they belong or with whom they identify have experienced it historically through public policy experiences.[76]

The Limits of Personal Experiences of Public Policies

In its strictest interpretation, policy feedback refers to how policies may shape recipients' own support for (or opposition to) those same policies, and their likelihood of taking political action to support (or oppose) them. This investigation, by contrast, has considered a broader question: whether individuals' cumulative past experiences of public policy influence their general views of government. The results here, so far, suggest that such capacity is fairly limited, at least in the contemporary political context. It is noteworthy that usage of more visible means-tested policies generates any greater appreciation of government, given that some such policies are stigmatized and the individuals they help are likely to possess other identities that predispose them against feeling incorporated as first-class citizens. More striking, however, is the rarity of discernible positive effects by the non-means-tested visible policies or their submerged counterparts. Perhaps the most important finding here is that those who receive means-tested submerged benefits retain negative attitudes about government, remaining more likely than others to feel, for example, that government officials do not care about them. This result is relevant to the 2016 election results to the extent that some white working-class voters, expressing resentment about government's lack of responsiveness to them, helped swing the outcome: many of these individuals and their families are likely to have benefited from the EITC and other social policies.[77]

If accumulated personal experiences of policies do so little to improve recipients' views of government, what does influence their thinking? It appears that citizens draw on several other sources that overshadow their own personal experiences of social provision. It is not that government policies do not matter at all, but rather that their impact is channeled less often through direct personal experiences than through indirect means, such as the perceptions of policies individuals adopt from the social groups with which they identify or share experiences based, for example, on their race, socioeconomic status, or age group. The impact of these factors pales, furthermore, compared to the role of individuals' views about welfare. Antipathy to welfare policy derails many from adopting more salutary views about government; indeed, although "welfare as we know it" was eradicated two decades ago and fewer than 1 percent of Americans now benefit from this program, its image lives on and continues to operate as a major force in driving hostility not only toward social provision but also toward government generally.

Although our examination of policies so far has attempted to disentangle the impact of the accumulated usage of policies based on their degree of visibility and whether they are means-tested, questions remain. Particular policies target differently situated individuals through their terms of eligibility, and such differences—some of which we were not able to measure or control for in the previous analysis—may themselves drive distinctions in attitudes about government. To consider similar individuals who use policies with different designs, we now focus on two cases.

The EITC Versus AFDC/TANF

No public policy has received more accolades for its role in reducing poverty in the past two decades than the Earned Income Tax Credit (EITC). Recently, a superb in-depth study of the EITC by a group of sociologists found that its positive impact extends beyond economic well-being to social inclusion. After conducting extensive and in-depth interviews with beneficiaries, the authors conclude, "Through the EITC and the other refundable credits that have followed in its path, America has brought at least a portion of the poor into mainstream society in a way that has seldom been done before by an antipoverty policy."[78] These findings by Sarah Halpern-Meekin, Kathryn Edin, Laura Tach, and Jennifer Sykes suggest that the EITC conveys very different messages to citizens than the nation's more traditional income support policy for low-income Americans with children, namely, Temporary Assistance to Needy Families (TANF), otherwise known as "welfare."

Prior research has shown that obtaining welfare has, at best, failed to incorporate the poor as citizens and, at worst, has discouraged their civic engagement.[79] Joe Soss has demonstrated that TANF's predecessor, Aid to Families with Dependent Children (AFDC), lowered beneficiaries' sense of external efficacy and of governmental responsiveness, because they found welfare offices to be unresponsive to their claims and they extrapolated from that experience to draw similar conclusions about government generally.[80] Once lawmakers created TANF in 1996, according to Soss and his collaborators Richard Fording and Sanford Schram, a new "poverty governance" emerged that is characterized by punitive supervision of the poor, involving a "paternalistic" disciplinary approach. The procedures and rules the states adopt vary in harshness, and the frontline caseworkers implementing those rules and procedures vary in how they use their discretion to decide when and how severely to impose sanctions. Proponents of the approach claim that it advances the civic incorporation of the poor, but Soss, Fording, and Schram find that experiences of the stricter versions significantly deter such engagement.[81]

In explaining why the EITC and welfare diverge so sharply in their effects on social inclusion, Halpern-Meekin and her collaborators point to policy delivery, particularly its features that beneficiaries themselves highlighted in interviews. To apply for TANF, individuals must travel to what is typically a dark and dreary welfare office, usually in a building that connotes "stigma and shame."[82] Former beneficiaries reported that the treatment they receive at the hands of caseworkers is impersonal at best and often rude and demeaning. As Angelica Rivera remembered, "It was horrible. . . . They give you miserable money and then you have [them] on your case all the time. . . . I think [the caseworkers] look at you like you're no good because you're on assistance. . . . I don't think she respected me . . . they were making me look like a liar." Bryn Gamble, who applied for welfare after her daughter was born, felt that caseworkers failed to acknowledge her work history, treating her instead as if she were someone who would abuse the system. She explained her reaction, "Are you kidding me? I paid my taxes! Do you want to see my résumé? Do you want to see my paycheck stubs? I was so mad. It was disgusting. . . . It was just so degrading and it was just so disrespectful."[83] Another interview subject said, "They treat you like an animal just because you need a little help getting back on your feet."[84] Consistently, former beneficiaries reported that they resorted to welfare only out of dire necessity, when they had no other options, and that receiving it bestowed on them an intense sense of shame.[85]

The experience of claiming the EITC could hardly offer a greater contrast. Claimants, rather than going to a decaying government office building to apply for benefits, apply for them privately, either by completing the paperwork on their own or by seeking help from a nonprofit agency or, more typically, a for-profit agency that seeks such business. Beneficiaries reported to Halpern-Meekin and her collaborators that at the bright and "neat as a pin" offices of H&R Block, friendly and professional staff members treated them as valued customers.[86] Instead of asking clients intrusive personal questions that threatened to disqualify them from benefits, staff gathered basic information about their earnings and then entered it in the tax software they used to get customers as high a credit as possible.[87] Like other taxpayers, EITC claimants paid H&R Block to process their forms; once they were informed of the amount of their return, they were offered the opportunity to receive it on the spot, for an extra fee. Unlike TANF, which imposed a sense of stigma, EITC offered claimants a "veritable certificate of deservedness."[88] The authors sum up the differences: "No welfare bureaucrats are controlling their lives. The working poor can exercise autonomy and spend that gloriously large lump sum however they please . . . their status as beneficiaries of a cash assistance program is invisible. They . . . filed their taxes just like every other hardworking American."[89] Whereas other forms of direct social provision tend to be underutilized, EITC now has a high take-up rate ranging between 77 and 81 percent, presumably for reasons related to its design and delivery.[90]

Given the EITC's capacity to foster social inclusion, Halpern-Meekin and her coauthors pose the question whether it might also foster a sense of political inclusion and civic engagement. This compelling question lay beyond the scope of their study, but it is central to the focus here, and the EITC's unique policy design makes it a particularly valuable case to examine. By probing individuals' responses to these two means-tested policies, we can examine the impact of the visible versus submerged designs on attitudes about government. Making this distinction is possible because the EITC, unlike most other policies limited to Americans with lower incomes, is embedded in the tax code, and yet unlike most tax expenditures, it channels funds to the working poor rather than the affluent. By contrast to the expectations of Halpern-Meekin and her collaborators, findings earlier in this chapter indicate that submerged means-tested policies fail to leave recipients with the impression that government social programs helped them in times of need, whereas visible means-tested policies did generate such an effect. However, the EITC's bestowal on individuals with little or no tax liability of a lump sum of money in an amount that makes a substantive difference in their lives may make government's impact more visible and foster positive effects on this view or other attitudes about government. The data examined here permit us to distinguish between the attitudes of those who had used the EITC, those who had used TANF or AFDC, those who had used both, and those who had used neither.

Here we conduct the same basic type of analysis as in the previous section, but for the policy variables we drop the four sums of different types and substitute ever having used the EITC, ever having used AFDC or TANF, or ever having used both; the use of neither policy serves as the missing reference category.[91] In addition, we aim to account for government's growing levels of surveillance and coercion, particularly in low-income communities, through policing and other aspects of the criminal justice system. Over the past forty years, for example, incarceration rates have skyrocketed, with particularly high rates among men of color and with consequences that are concentrated among low-income people. It makes sense to account for this in our analysis given that scholars have found that interactions with the criminal justice system yield deleterious consequences for civic engagement, including attitudes about government.[92] The data set permits us to control for whether an individual has ever been convicted of a felony. The results are presented in the appendix in table E.3 and summarized here.

Those who have benefited from use of AFDC or TANF, controlling for age, income, education, race, ethnicity, gender, party, and a felony conviction, are 23 percent more likely than nonbeneficiaries of these policies to say that government social programs have helped them in times of need. Those who have received both AFDC or TANF and the EITC are 38 percent more likely to say that government has helped them. By contrast, those who have used just the EITC do not differ significantly in their attitudes on this measure from nonbeneficiaries. Although EITC recipients seemed to welcome the funds they have received through the policy, they appear not to think of it as help provided to them from government to assist them in a time of need. When asked whether government had provided opportunities to improve their standard of living, it was only the EITC beneficiaries whose answers differ significantly from those of nonbeneficiaries of

Figure 4.5 Predicted Probability of Agreement by Users of EITC and AFDC/TANF That Government Helped in Times of Need or Provided Opportunities, by Income Group

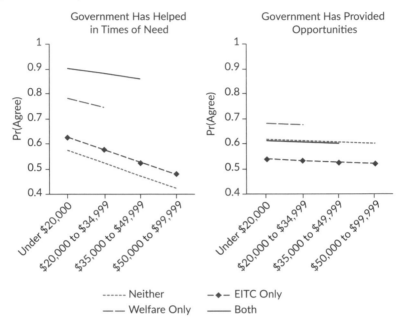

Source: 2008 SGIP.

either policy, but surprisingly, they are 8 percent more likely to disagree with the statement. In this instance, it seems that EITC beneficiaries probably held negative attitudes even before policy receipt, and the experience did little or nothing to mitigate those attitudes. As members of the working poor, they may feel that the American economy has passed them by and that public policies have done little to transform their circumstances. Alternatively, they may associate government assistance and provision of opportunities with dependence and feel that they have transcended such dependence through employment.[93]

Figure 4.5 shows the predicted probability, by policy receipt and across income levels, that an individual would express awareness of government's role in helping them in times of need or in providing opportunities. Individuals at higher incomes are less likely to believe that government has aided them, but those who have at some point utilized AFDC/TANF or utilized both one of those and EITC remain more likely than nonbeneficiaries or EITC beneficiaries to perceive government as having assisted them or provided opportunities to improve their standard of living.[94]

In some ways, recipients' reactions to the EITC are surprising, given that it is an unrestricted cash credit more generous than any other policy for low-income people, it has been explicitly rationalized by policymakers as a means for recipients to gain opportunities to improve their standard of living, and scholars have documented that it does indeed lift people above the poverty line. Nonetheless, the EITC's design (being embedded in the tax code), combined with its delivery mechanism (typically claimed with the help of private tax preparers rather than government officials), probably obscures government's role in actively enhancing beneficiaries' lives.

When it comes to political efficacy, EITC recipients voice significantly more negative assessments than nonbeneficiaries of either policy, being 7 percent more likely to agree that public officials do not care about people like them and 8 percent more likely to think that they have no say in what government does. Other results resemble those in earlier models, but unsurprisingly, the newly included variable—having had a felony conviction—bears a significant relationship to the view that one has no say in what public officials do: those with such a record are 19 percent more likely to concur with that negative assessment of government.

The relationships between policy receipt and income on these political efficacy attitudes are shown in figure 4.6. People at higher incomes express greater confidence that public officials care about them and that they have a voice in politics, compared to those at lower incomes. As a general assessment by low-income people, such reactions are reasonable given the results of Martin Gilens's research, which shows how little representation they actually receive.[95] What is striking here, however, is that it is those who have ever received EITC who are most likely to express low political efficacy: they are more convinced that government is unresponsive to people like them than are beneficiaries of TANF/AFDC or both or neither policy.

These are ironic results given that over the past quarter-century public officials have purposefully directed large sums of money to EITC beneficiaries through this policy. Here again, however, the delivery mechanism may interfere with beneficiaries' capacity to recognize that it is government that is responsive to them; rather, they may be more likely to credit whichever business, organization, or individuals assisted them in filing their tax forms.

Finally, we consider individuals' views about whether they pay their fair share in taxes. This is the one attitude on which EITC beneficiaries articu-

Figure 4.6 Predicted Probability of Agreement by EITC and AFDC/TANF Users That "Public Officials Don't Care Much" and "People Like Me Don't Have Any Say," by Income Group

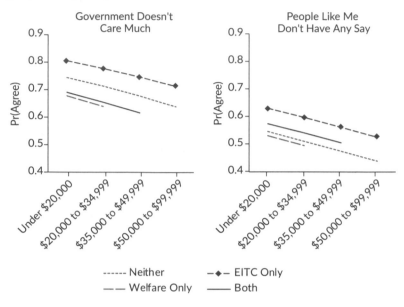

Source: 2008 SGIP.

lated more positive views than nonbeneficiaries: they were 50 percent more likely than nonbeneficiaries to feel that they pay the right amount or less than their fair share, an acknowledgment of their special tax status.[96]

In other respects, however, while EITC usage may have resulted in a greater sense of social inclusion, it did not appear to do much to convince recipients that it was government that was enabling them to improve their lives or that it was responsive to them. This is an ironic result that highlights the invisibility of benefits, or at least their failure to engender much appreciation of government's role in individuals' lives. In the next chapter, we probe the relationship these between benefits and political participation. Meanwhile, we turn to another case: higher education policies.

Higher Education Policies

The U.S. federal government, since the mid-twentieth century, has played a major role in helping college students afford tuition. The array of policies that offer such assistance comprise several variants of policy design, both means-tested and non-means-tested and visible versus submerged. Pell Grants and tax credits for tuition (called Hope and Lifetime Learning Credits at the time survey data were collected, the predecessors to the American Opportunity Tax Credit) both tie eligibility to income limits, but they differ in that the grants make government's role relatively visible while the tax credits do not. Several other policies are available to college students regardless of income, but among them only the GI Bill features a visible design. By contrast, qualified tuition programs ("529s") and the Coverdell Education Savings Account are firmly ensconced in the tax code. Student loans had hybrid characteristics when the survey was conducted, as most students borrowing to pay tuition had government-subsidized loans from private banks or Sallie Mae (SLM Corporation), while a few had direct loans from the U.S. Department of Education.[97]

As figure 4.1 shows, beneficiaries of the higher education policies—the GI Bill, Pell Grants, and student loans—ranked them quite positively in terms of the difference they made in their lives, compared to the assessments offered by beneficiaries of several other policies. Recipients may have placed a particularly high value on programs that finance college, given that the experience could significantly alter their life trajectories, both by providing the opportunity to improve their standard of living and in numerous other less tangible ways.[98] Notably, however, the two types of tax expenditures for higher education costs ranked at the very bottom of the entire list of programs, suggesting that their impact barely registered in recipients' minds.

This variation in assessments by beneficiaries of different higher education policies is repeated in figure 4.7, which shows how they evaluated the impact on their lives of the policies they used. Overall, the two policies that make government's role most visible gain the highest recognition, while the two that most submerge it receive the least recognition, and the policy with the hybrid design—student loans—falls midway between the others. Over 65 percent of the recipients of the visible policies and student loans feel that they "helped a great deal" compared to 30 percent of those using the tax policies, and the former beneficiaries are also more likely to say that they "could not have afforded education without" those policies and that they "would not have considered education" without them. Recipients assigned these rankings notwithstanding the variation in obligations imposed by the benefits: the GI Bill requires the highest price of all, putting oneself in harm's way through military service, and student loans must be repaid,

Figure 4.7 Beneficiaries' Perceptions of Higher Education Policies

■ Helped a Great Deal
■ Could Not Have Afforded Education Without
■ Would Not Have Considered Education Without

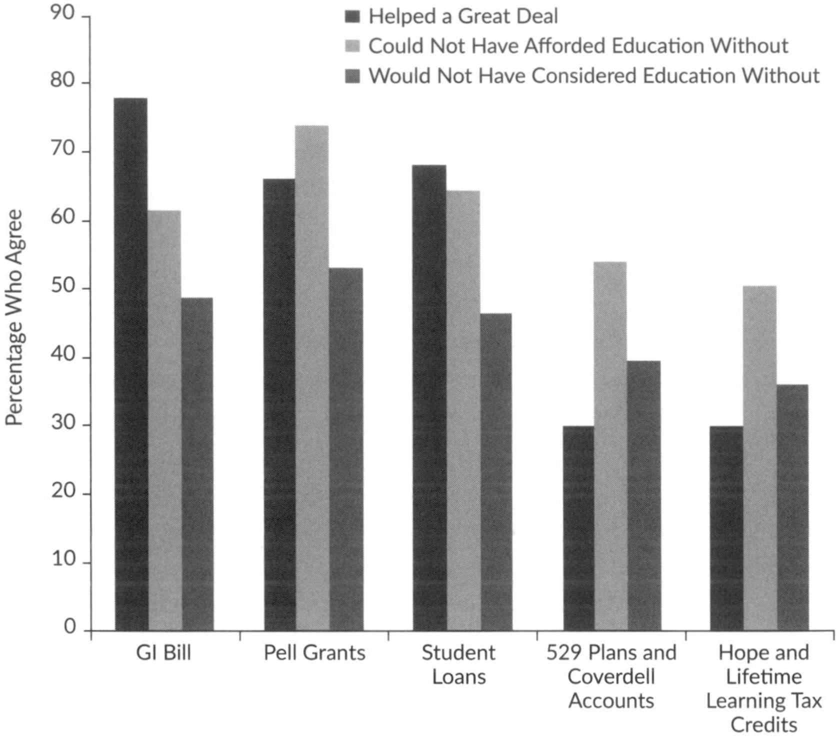

Source: 2008 SGIP.

while the policies in the tax code require no such burdens. Neither do recipients' assessments appear to be associated with the degree to which policies responded to economic need, given that the means-tested Hope and Lifetime Learning Tax Credits received less recognition than student loans, for example. Rather, beneficiaries' level of appreciation appears to be related to differences in policy visibility, as those who more clearly saw policies making a real difference in their lives held them in higher esteem.[99]

Now we can assess how individuals' experiences of these higher education policies subsequently influence an attitude about government that would seem pertinent: the extent of their agreement that government has provided them with opportunities to improve their standard of living. We control for the same variables as in previous analyses, but include only those who attended at least some college and therefore had the opportunity to use these policies. The coefficients for the higher education policy usage variable in each model are shown in figure 4.8; full results are shown in ap-

Figure 4.8 Impact of Higher Education Policy Usage on View That Government Provided Opportunities to Improve Standard of Living

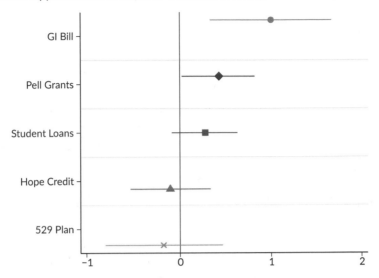

Source: 2008 SGIP.
Note: Analysis includes only those with some college or more education.

pendix table E.4. The two policies with visible designs, the GI Bill and Pell Grants, are positively related to respondents agreeing that government provided them with opportunities. The GI Bill beneficiaries, compared to non-beneficiaries and controlling for other factors, are 23 percent more likely to agree that government provided them with opportunities, and Pell Grant recipients are 10 percent more likely to agree. No significant relationships with policy usage emerges in other analyses.[100] Once again, it appears that policy visibility influences whether beneficiaries are likely to acknowledge government's positive role in their lives. In other respects, attitudes about welfare act as the only consistently significant indicator of views, as those who feel less favorably toward the policy are less likely to acknowledge that government has provided them with opportunities, all else equal.

Different Lenses

Americans are united in their usage of social provision but divided by their perceptions of government. Many citizens do not draw connections between the social benefits they have utilized and their general assessments of government. In part, the failure of policy experiences to influence perceptions of government owes to policy design. Those with accumulated or particular experiences of visible policies are more likely to perceive that government has helped them in times of need or provided opportunities. By contrast, submerged policies fail to register such an impact.

Perceptions of government are more typically driven by sources other than personal experiences of policies. For those who harbor highly negative views about welfare, typically middle-income people and whites, it serves as a microcosm of government generally, informing their view of it and fueling their hostility to it. These attitudes exert an influence that overwhelms even repeated firsthand experiences of policy receipt. Shared group identities and experiences, which themselves may channel historic experiences of public policies among predecessors, also influence orientations to government. Each of these dynamics overpowers policy feedback effects, leaving citizens oblivious to the role government plays in their lives.

In sum, when Americans think about government, only in some instances does their memory of the social policies they have benefited from hover at the top of their minds. As a result, the strong antigovernment attitudes that prevail in the United States today can be found even among many people who themselves have benefited a great deal from social policies. These views may attract Americans to candidates and organizations that articulate such views, even if they hold positions that threaten the very policies from which individuals have benefited.

And yet another puzzle remains. If some individuals who benefit from large numbers of mostly visible policies do indeed adopt more positive views of government, then why are their voices not heard in American politics? We now turn to face that conundrum.

CHAPTER 5

UNEQUAL VOICE

IN 2016, the candidacy of Donald Trump energized white working-class voters in rural areas and small towns, and their heightened mobilization, particularly in Rust Belt states, helped tip the Electoral College vote in his favor. Americans simultaneously gave the Republicans the majority of seats in both chambers of the U.S. Congress. The election results awarded the GOP the opportunity to pursue the policy goals it has long articulated, including repeal of the Affordable Care Act, which had expanded the ranks of those with health coverage by 20 million; restructuring and scaling back Medicare and Medicaid; privatizing Social Security; and placing greater restrictions on the use of SNAP, or food stamps. This raises the question of how Americans, given their widespread reliance on social policies, could put in office a government run by public officials who have voiced the explicit intention to scale back several of those very policies.

Not only voting patterns but other forms of political participation as well present a puzzle: Why is contemporary American politics not more animated by efforts to protect, preserve, and expand existing social policies? Many pundits and scholars assume that self-interest drives politics, and that therefore we might expect to see beneficiaries of social policies highly mobilized to defend and bolster them. Certainly there are important examples of such activity from the American past, such as welfare activists in the 1960s marching for program improvements, and Social Security beneficiaries in the 1980s defending their program against threatened cuts. Yet the years leading up to the 2016 election saw very little issue-driven activity by those who benefit from social policies. Instead, the voices of policy critics grew the most pronounced, and they became highly mobilized through organizations such as the Tea Party and Americans for Prosperity.[1]

Variants of these questions have been raised often in recent decades as journalists and pundits have sought to explain phenomena ranging from the "Reagan Democrats" to the voters who supported Obama in 2012 but then switched sides to vote for Trump in 2016. Some observers have argued that Americans vote against their own economic self-interest because they put greater priority on cultural or social issues; they imply that voters either suffer from "false consciousness" or are duped.[2] Political scientists have found little evidence of such dynamics, and they describe instead a more complex reality in which most people vote consistently with the party with which they identify, often on the basis of the social groups to which they belong, and some choose allegiances depending on their issue priorities.[3] Katherine Cramer finds that place matters: people living in rural and small-town Wisconsin resent urban-dwellers, who they believe pay fewer tax dollars than they do while receiving more in government services, such as spending on schools and infrastructure. They are also under the impression that urbanites do not work as hard as they do and that they are either coddled public-sector employees or wealthy elites. These beliefs predispose rural and small-town residents toward a party that aims for a smaller government.[4] But none of these explanations consider how individuals' own usage of social policy relates to their efforts to raise their voices in politics.

By taking policy usage into account, this book proposes a two-pronged explanation. In part, as we saw in chapter 4, despite people's appreciation of social policies, those policies play only a limited role in their assessment of government generally. Rather, other considerations typically predominate and spur antigovernment attitudes even among those who have utilized numerous public policies, making them amenable to political mobilization by candidates, groups, and parties that appeal to such views. In addition, the political playing field may be tilted in a manner that advantages those who are less cognizant of government's role in their lives and who are less supportive of expanded social provision. It is this latter possibility that we examine in this chapter.

Here we consider how the articulation of political voice relates to individuals' own usage of social policies by examining who takes part in various kinds of political participation, distinguishing between individuals who have used different types of social policies. We begin by investigating how

Americans' attitudes about social spending vary with the extent of their experiences of different policies. As we will see, those who have used more visible social programs themselves tend to support social policies more strongly, whereas the use of a greater number of submerged policies does not influence recipients' attitudes.

Next, we examine the extent to which beneficiaries of different programs get involved in political activities. It should be noted that the data used here do not permit us to assess cause and effect because we cannot carefully distinguish between the time of policy usage and the time of participation. Rather, we are looking at relationships in a descriptive fashion, examining the different rates at which people with different policy experiences participate in political activities. This analysis reveals that those who have little awareness of how government has helped them personally tend to participate at the highest levels, making their voices heard by elected officials. By contrast, those who are most appreciative of government's role and most supportive of expansive policies are more often missing in action when it comes to civic engagement. Their voices are much less likely to be exercised in elections and in politics generally. Not surprisingly, therefore, they often go unheard and unheeded in the political process.

From Policy Usage to Program Support

How do people's own experiences of social provision relate to their views about such policies? Do the number and type of policies they have utilized bear any relationship to their views about spending on social provision and whether government's role in it should be enlarged or contracted? To examine these questions, we begin by considering respondents' current attitudes as indicated by several questions following this prompt: "We are faced with many problems in this country, none of which can be solved easily or inexpensively. I'm going to name some of these programs, and for each one, I'd like you to tell me whether you think we're spending too much money on it, too little money, or about the right amount." In nearly all cases, Americans across the board support spending increases, but typically those who have themselves benefited from the policy in question at some point in their lives offer stronger support than others. In figure 5.1, "aid to the unemployed" offers an illustrative example that is typical of most policies: beneficiaries and nonbeneficiaries both support greater spending, but the beneficiaries do so more strongly. Welfare is an outlier in that nonbenefi-

Figure 5.1 Views That the United States Spends Too Little Versus Too Much on Specific Policies, by Beneficiary Status

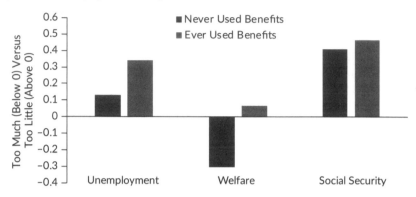

Source: 2008 SGIP.
Note: Weighted estimates.

ciaries believe that too *much* is spent on the program, and even beneficiaries themselves offer only tepid agreement that it is underfunded. Social Security is also unique, but in this case because no significant difference separates beneficiaries and nonbeneficiaries, both of whom are strongly supportive.

Of course, policy beneficiaries and nonbeneficiaries often differ markedly from one another in many other ways besides policy receipt, so next we will conduct an analysis in which we can hold such factors constant. It is reasonable to expect that those who have experienced government in action in their own lives through usage of several visible policies would be more supportive of greater spending and a stronger role for government in policy delivery, while repeated use of submerged policies might fail to register such effects. We might also expect that enhanced social provision would be favored by those with greater need, namely, those with less income, the young, women, minorities, and those with less education. We would also expect that Democrats and those who favor welfare would be more predisposed to expanded public social provision.

Now we examine two models of support for social provision. In the first, we consider the determinants of overall support for social spending, indicated by the sum of answers to eight of the questions that ask whether "we're spending too much money on it, too little money, or about the right amount." The specific items include "housing for the poor," "Social Security," "welfare," "aid for poor people," "aid for college students," "health care," "assistance for child care," and "aid for the unemployed." Each reply that the government is spending "too much" loses one point and each that it is spending "too little" gains a point, producing a scale ranging from –8 to 8, from spending conservatives to spending liberals. In a second model, we examine a question about health coverage, asking, "All in all, do you favor or oppose the United States government guaranteeing health insurance for all citizens, even if it means raising taxes?" Responses range from "opposes strongly" (1) to "favors strongly" (4). The full results are shown in appendix E, table E.5.

The examination of social spending support shows that greater use of visible policies bears a significant relationship to thinking more should be spent on policies generally. Those who have used more visible means-tested policies are 20 percent more likely to support greater spending, and those who have used more visible non-means-tested policies are 30 percent more likely to do so.[5] As expected, no significant relationship exists between using a higher number of submerged policies of either type and spending attitudes. In other respects, the model mirrors expectations, with significantly stronger support for more spending among those who are younger, nonwhite, and Democrats and who favor welfare. In terms of educational levels, those who have attended some college or attained some post–high school education or training are significantly more likely to have conservative views about spending than those with only a high school degree or less education, whereas those with at least a bachelor's degree or more education are indistinguishable in their views from their high school–educated counterparts.

The magnitude of some of the key determinants of support for social spending is shown in figure 5.2. As accumulated experiences of visible means-tested policies increase from zero to four, support for spending increases from 5.5 to 7 on the 8-point scale; the same shift occurs as usage of visible non-means-tested policies grows from zero to three. Strong Republicans register a 4 on the scale, with policy liberalism increasing gradually up through strong Democrats, who register near 7.5. Similarly, those who most disapprove of welfare offer support for spending around the midpoint of 4.5, and as welfare favorability increases, spending support grows up to 7.5 among those who view it most positively.

Turning to analysis of who supports a guarantee of health coverage for all citizens, even if it means raising taxes, those who used a greater number of visible means-tested policies were 34 percent more likely to favor such coverage. No other significant results emerged based on type of policy

Figure 5.2 Factors Associated with Support for Greater Social Spending, Selected Variables

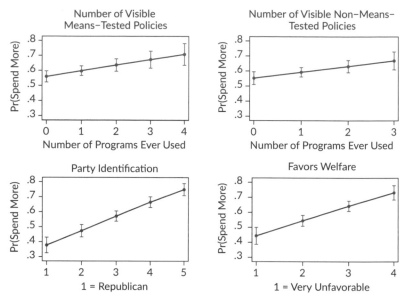

Source: 2008 SGIP.

usage. Young people, Democrats, and those who favor welfare were also significantly more likely to favor guaranteed coverage. Figure 5.3 shows key relationships substantively.

In sum, personal experiences of different kinds of policies are associated with very different views about what government should do in the realm of social provision. Individuals who have repeatedly witnessed government aiding them through visible social policies are significantly more likely to favor an expanded role for government and increased funding. Experiencing a greater number of submerged policies, by contrast, appears to bear little or no relationship to such views. The next question, then, is: How are different types of policy usage related to the exercise of political voice? Do those with policy experiences that showcase government's role make their voices heard as much as others?

The Policy-Participation Disconnect

Given that individuals who have used more visible policies, especially means-tested ones, are more cognizant of government's role in their lives

Figure 5.3 Factors Associated with Support for the U.S. Government Guaranteeing Health Insurance for All Citizens, Even if It Means Raising Taxes, Selected Variables

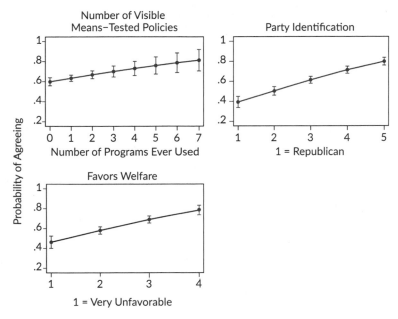

Source: 2008 SGIP.

and more supportive of expanded social provision than others, to what extent do they take action to make their views known through political participation? How much do those who have used a greater number of policies with submerged designs participate? We now turn to address these questions with respect to voting and other forms of political participation. We also consider the extent to which those with different policy experiences are mobilized by candidates or political parties and other groups.

Voting

Election analysis in the media tends to revolve around the choices made by voters, despite the fact that most voters opt routinely for candidates of the same party they have favored throughout their lives.[6] Much less attention is given to who actually shows up to vote versus who stays away, and how it matters.[7] This question is crucial, because rates of nonvoting are high. Voter turnout in the United States in recent presidential elections has ranged from a nadir of 48 percent of the voting-eligible population in 1996, when Bill Clinton was reelected, to a peak of 57 percent in 2008, when Barack Obama was first elected.[8] Put differently, typically a greater percentage of Americans do not vote at all in a presidential election than the percentage that votes for either major candidate.[9]

A small shift in the enthusiasm and mobilization of one set of voters and a dampening of interest among others can make an immense difference for the outcome. In 2016, among eligible voters, approximately 28.4 percent cast their votes for Hillary Clinton—who won the popular vote—27.2 percent for Trump, and 3.4 percent for third-party candidates. The plurality of eligible voters—the remaining 41 percent of the electorate—stayed away from the polls entirely.[10] On the one hand, the ranks of actual voters appeared to be substantially consistent with 2012, with Trump's victory owing to his ability to pick up a small margin of voters who had supported Obama that year.[11] Yet, if in key states, as many additional voters had been mobilized, the outcome might have been quite different.

Low voter turnout among the voting-eligible population in the United States is nothing new: after voting rates soared throughout the late nineteenth century, often reaching 80 percent, they fell in the early twentieth century and never recovered. Contemporary turnout levels put the United States far behind most affluent nations: it ranks thirty-first among thirty-five nations in the Organization for Economic Cooperation and Development (OECD).[12] Political scientists have done much to explain the differences, pointing to the frequency of American elections, the institutional hurdles that range from being required to register to vote long before Election Day in most states to the recent emergence of voter identification laws in many states, and the lack of a penalty for not voting, unlike other nations that impose small fines on those who fail to show up.[13]

All of this means that analyzing the composition of the actual voting public is crucially important for evaluating how well representative democracy is working. If the composition of nonvoters mirrors the composition of voters, turnout rates will not matter for representation, because nonvoters can be effectively represented by the choices of their voting compatriots. Scholars know that if an individual performs just one political activity, it is most likely to be voting, which is by far the most common activity in which people participate, and it is therefore expected to be less biased by socioeconomic status than others.[14] Yet it is also clear that turnout is skewed toward those who have higher incomes and who have more conservative policy views.[15] This raises the further question: How does voter turnout relate to individuals' policy experiences?

When we consider voting rates among beneficiaries of different policies, considerable disparities emerge. Overall, only 82.4 percent of those who have ever used visible means-tested policies report that they are currently registered to vote compared to 89.4 percent of those who have used submerged non-means-tested policies—a 7 percent difference. Among those who are registered, we can consider the percentage who report that they have voted in all elections since they became old enough to vote—on a scale from "never voted" (1) to "voted in all" (5). The results for presidential elections accentuate the voices of beneficiaries of submerged non-means-tested policies, among whom 59.1 percent say they vote in all elections versus 52.5 percent of those who are beneficiaries of visible means-tested policies—a 6.6 percent difference. In nonpresidential elections, turnout plummets among Americans across the board, but it is those who have used more visible non-means-tested policies, a predominantly older group, who take part the most, with 28.4 percent voting in all such elections versus only 23.1 percent of those who have used visible means-tested policies—a 5.3 percent difference.

Beneficiaries of different policies are registered and actually vote at different rates from one another, in both presidential and nonpresidential elections, as shown in figure 5.4. Those who derive social benefits from the tax code vote at high rates, with recipients of several such policies heading the list, while those who use visible means-tested policies tend to be clustered at the bottom. For example, 66 percent of those who have used the tax benefits of personal saving for college tuition, the 529 plans, or Coverdell Education Savings Accounts, vote "always" a rate that is more than double that of welfare (AFDC/TANF) beneficiaries, at 29 percent. Those who use visible non-means-tested policies also vote more often than fellow citizens who have used means-tested visible policies. In nonpresidential elections, for instance, those who have used veterans' benefits vote at twice the rate of food stamp beneficiaries, 28 percent compared to 14 percent.

What difference could disparities in turnout rates make for electoral outcomes and political representation? The 2010 midterm election offers a case in point. In March 2010, President Barack Obama signed into law the Affordable Care Act, accomplishing a goal that Democrats had pursued for the seventy years since Harry S. Truman occupied the White House: the expansion of health care coverage to working-age adults. Already as the

Figure 5.4 Percentage of Beneficiaries Who Are Registered to Vote and Report Voting Regularly

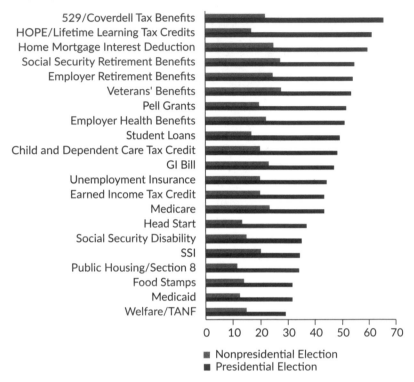

Source: 2008 SGIP.

controversial law was making its way through Congress, it sparked opposition by a nascent grassroots organization, the Tea Party. This insurgent conservative group acted strategically, recruiting candidates to run in the 2010 midterm election and mobilizing voters to support them.

The midterm election presented an excellent opportunity for the Tea Party to exert an impact. Voter participation in midterms has been declining for decades and has become skewed to older and white voters, who favor conservative candidates, while young people and members of minority groups are increasingly underrepresented. In 2010, turnout reached 41.9 percent, its lowest point since the U.S. Census began keeping track in 1978.[16] The Tea Party's extra efforts to energize conservative voters in that election brought it considerable success.[17] Not only did the Republican Party regain the House by a large majority, but it also managed to replace moderates with conservatives, effectively shifting the party much further to the right. Hostility to social provision, along with opposition to taxes and immigration, marked the top priorities of the energized body.[18]

Once the newly elected members took office, they benefited from the perks of incumbency, and most managed to hold on to their seats in subsequent elections. The reconstituted membership of Congress voted repeatedly to repeal the Affordable Care Act, a policy that stood to benefit those who were less likely to have cast votes in 2010. In short, Congress effectively represented those who were most likely to show up and vote, while the priorities of those who stayed away—to the extent that they diverged—were largely ignored.

In 2016, a mere 80,000 votes in the states of Wisconsin, Michigan, and Pennsylvania enabled Trump to seize the Electoral College victory.[19] With such razor-thin margins, the composition of the electorate can have immense consequences. Contrary to the media's portrayal of Trump as the champion of working-class voters, support for him was highest among middle- and upper-income groups—those with incomes above $50,000— while Americans with lower incomes favored Hillary Clinton by large margins.[20] Higher-income people routinely vote at higher rates than low-income people.[21] Put differently, participation by those who have more typically used non-means-tested submerged benefits outpaces that of beneficiaries of visible means-tested policies. The 2016 election led to victories, moreover, by public officials who actively campaigned for both tax cuts, which would benefit predominantly high-income people, and reductions to social policy, which would disadvantage particularly those who were less likely to have voted.

Beyond Voting: Other Forms of Political Participation

Inequality in political voice, though evident and consequential in voting, looms even larger in other political activities, as Sidney Verba, Kay Schlozman, and Henry Brady have shown, and therefore we must broaden our consideration of how policy receipt is related to participation.[22] Figure 5.5 shows, among individuals who have ever benefited from particular types of social policies, the percentage of those who have ever taken part in any of five different forms of political activity: working on a volunteer basis for a candidate running for national, state, or local office; contributing money to a candidate, party group, political action committee, or other organization supporting candidates; serving in a voluntary capacity on any

Figure 5.5 Average Rate of Political Participation Among Beneficiaries of Social Policies, by Type of Policy

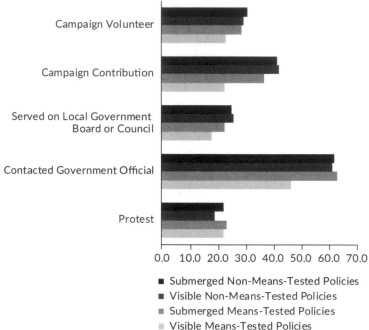

Source: 2008 SGIP.
Note: Includes those who have ever received any of the benefits in each policy type.

local government board, council, committee, or group dealing with community problems or issues; and contacting a government official or someone on the staff of such an official about problems or issues of concern. In four of the five activities—all but protest—individuals who have used visible means-tested policies participated the least. Not surprisingly, the gap is the largest when it comes to making financial contributions, reflecting the fact that those with higher incomes can afford to give more money, while activities that involve the contribution of time are less skewed in the participatory bias.[23]

Protest stands alone as the one activity in which those who most value government's role in social provision participate, on average, at comparable rates to others. Marching in demonstrations is typically thought of as a "weapon of the weak," as something that those who lack resources and status in society might be most likely to engage in. As it turns out, however, it is actually the one activity with a more level playing field, the one in which beneficiaries of different types of policies participate at similar rates. Still, it is the least common of the political activities examined: approximately one in five people in each group of beneficiaries have ever been involved in protest.[24]

The survey data used for these analyses do not permit us to sort out cause and effect; we cannot specify whether particular policy usage experiences themselves deterred subsequent political participation, given our inability to distinguish between the timing of policy receipt and different types of political participation. Case studies of policy feedback have found evidence of such a connection, showing that beneficiaries of Social Security and GI Bill education and training benefits take part in political activity more than their other characteristics would suggest, while welfare beneficiaries participate less.[25] The aim here, rather, is simply to describe the relationships between these phenomena. Given the well-established correlation between socioeconomic status and political participation, it is not surprising that those who qualified for policies based on level of need are least likely to participate in politics.

The most striking finding is that Americans who are most aware of government making a difference in their lives and who are most likely to support expanded social provision are the least likely to take part in politics. This pattern replicates itself in one domain of political activity after another. Generally speaking, those who are less cognizant that government has mattered in their lives speak with an outsized voice in politics. The political realm is dominated, in short, by those who are least aware or appreciative of the difference that government has made for them personally.

Mobilization

Low participation rates by those who use visible policies are not an inevitable outcome. Scholars know that although individuals with higher socioeconomic status enjoy many advantages that make them more likely to participate in political activity, these patterns can be mitigated and on occasion disrupted if political actors make a greater effort to engage the less well-off. In some periods, such as during the 1960s and 1970s in the United States and in the 2008 election, candidates and political parties and other organizations have more intensely mobilized less-advantaged groups, and

Figure 5.6 Percentage of Beneficiaries of Social Policies Who Report Having Been Contacted by a Group or Candidate and Asked to Participate in Politics in the Past Five Years

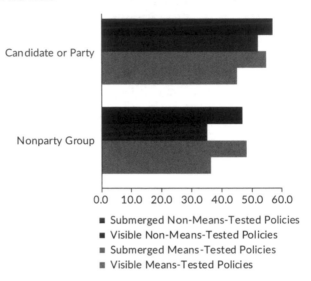

Source: 2008 SGIP.

their participation rates grew.[26] This is the exception, however, not the rule.

The frequency of mobilization by individuals with different types of policy experiences is shown in figure 5.6. Those who have used visible means-tested policies are the least likely to have been contacted in the past five years by political candidates or political parties encouraging them to vote or take part in the political process. They have also been contacted at low rates by groups other than political parties, in this case at rates comparable to those for beneficiaries of visible non-means-tested policies. By contrast, on both measures those who have used submerged policies, whether means-tested or not, are much more likely to have been invited to participate in politics.

The policy-participation disconnect need not be so prevalent, but the lack of efforts by parties and groups to mobilize those who use more visible benefits makes it so. As a result, individuals who are less likely to perceive government as making a difference in their lives are mobilized more by candidates, parties, and other groups. This boosts their participatory advantage and strengthens their political voice.

Comparing Political Participation by EITC and Welfare Recipients

Now we will consider how the political participation of individuals compares if they have similar socioeconomic status but have benefited from policies with different types of designs and delivery. Specifically, we can compare recipients of the EITC and welfare or AFDC/TANF, as we did in the previous chapter. Among EITC beneficiaries, 44 percent report that they are registered to vote and typically vote in presidential elections, compared to just 29 percent of AFDC or TANF beneficiaries; in nonpresidential elections, the rates are 20 percent and 15 percent, respectively. Although both policies are directed to low-income people, the beneficiaries may differ in some important respects that also affect political participation. To probe further, we consider how such policy experiences (either one separately or both in combination) are related to political involvement of four types: being registered to vote, voting in presidential elections, voting in other elections, and the sum of the five activities examined in figure 5.5. We control for several factors known to be related to political participation, including income, education, age, party, gender, race or ethnicity, and interaction with the criminal justice system, as indicated by whether an individual has ever been convicted of a felony.

In three out of four indicators, EITC beneficiaries are more likely than others to participate (as seen in appendix table E.6). As we control for numerous characteristics, they are significantly more likely to be registered to vote, to vote in nonpresidential elections, and to participate in a greater number of political activities. Only in presidential elections is their voter turnout indistinguishable from that of others with similar characteristics. Neither those who have used only AFDC or TANF nor those who have benefited from both one of those programs and the EITC differ significantly in participation from those who have used neither. In other respects, the determinants of voting resemble well-established findings: those who are older, have higher incomes, have more education, are not Hispanic, and do not have a felony record generally take part at higher rates.[27] Women are significantly more likely to be registered and to vote in presidential elections, and men to participate in the other political activities, also consistent with scholarly findings.[28]

Figure 5.7 shows the probability of being registered to vote for those who have received either the EITC or AFDC/TANF, both, or neither, by income, and figure 5.8 shows the same relationships for voting in nonpresi-

Figure 5.7 Probability of Being Registered to Vote, by Program Receipt, Across Income Groups

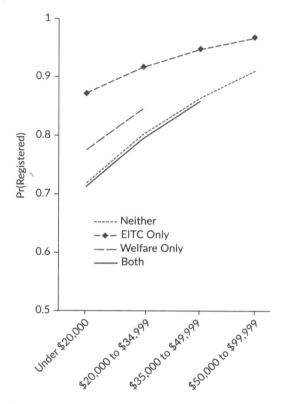

Source: 2008 SGIP.

dential elections. Increased income, as expected, is associated with a higher likelihood of both types of electoral involvement. The magnitude of the relationship varies, however, with policy experiences. Those who have utilized EITC are considerably more likely to be registered, with a probability of nearly 90 percent even at the lowest income level and rising to nearly 100 percent at the highest incomes. Similarly, they are much more likely than the other groups to vote in nonpresidential elections, at each income level.

We are left with paradoxical findings. EITC beneficiaries, relative to others of comparable socioeconomic status, are significantly more engaged in politics. Ironically, however, as we saw in chapter 4, they are more likely to enter the political sphere holding more negative views of government. Although they are the beneficiaries of social policy that has grown more generous in recent decades, they largely view government as unresponsive to them and are more certain than others that it has not provided them with

Figure 5.8 Probability of Voting in Nonpresidential Elections, by Program Receipt, Across Income Groups

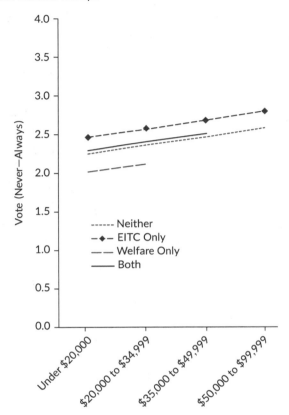

Source: 2008 SGIP.

opportunities to improve their standard of living. It is not enhanced political efficacy that explains the higher political participation of EITC beneficiaries; they may be mobilized by the sense of "social inclusion" that Halpern-Meekin and her collaborators identified or by their antipathy to government. Conversely, welfare recipients tend to be more cognizant and appreciative of government's role, but they participate considerably less in the politics, such that their voices are largely inaudible in the political process.

In short, use of a policy with a submerged design fails to direct beneficiaries' attention to the role that government plays in their lives through that policy, leaving their antigovernment views unmitigated. Yet these same individuals are particularly inclined to make their voices heard, loud and clear, in American politics.

Changing Times in Kentucky

As of 2015, the state of Kentucky, one of the poorest in the nation, show-cased the successes of the Affordable Care Act (ACA). Under Democratic governor Steve Beshear, the state had created the Kentucky Health Benefit Exchange, a health insurance marketplace otherwise known as Kynect, and used the expanded eligibility provisions of the ACA to enroll 428,000 adults in Medicaid. As a result, the ranks of the uninsured among working-age adults with incomes below the cap of 138 percent of the poverty line fell from 40.2 percent in 2013 to 23.6 percent in 2014. Kentuckians were enjoy-ing greater access to care and enhanced ability to pay for it, as a result, and the percentage of uninsured hospital stays plummeted.[29] Yet, that same year, the state's voters elected Republican governor Matt Bevin, a million-aire backed by the Tea Party, who ran for office on the promise that he would terminate the state's participation in expanded Medicaid under the ACA.

The developments around the ACA in Kentucky provided a microcosm of broader trends in the state. Federal social benefits, not including the larg-est tax expenditures, had grown steadily in recent decades, from 12.74 per-cent of all income in Kentucky in 1979 to 23.70 percent in 2014.[30] Over the same period, as we saw in chapter 1, the state shifted from sending moderate Democrats to Congress to sending moderate Republicans, and then gradu-ally replaced them with increasingly conservative members of the GOP, those supported by the Tea Party. In short, the state epitomizes the growing government-citizen disconnect. What can explain it?

These developments in Kentucky relate to what we have been seeing in this chapter and in chapter 4: that when many Americans assess govern-ment and participate in politics, they are not thinking about their own ex-periences of social benefits, particularly if those policies were designed in ways that obscure government's role. Public opinion and voter choices are shaped through the interplay between ordinary Americans' responses to circumstances and elections, on the one hand, and the articulation and framing of issues and choices by political elites and the media, on the other.

To gauge how this process may be operating in Kentucky, we need to consider the state's particular economic and political circumstances and how they relate to broader national developments. Coal-related employ-ment peaked in the late 1940s, after which the number of jobs in the in-dustry began to decline, and those numbers have plummeted further in recent decades, from over 47,000 in 1979 to fewer than 6,500 in 2016.[31]

Technological advances over this period reduced the need for workers and employment declined, even though coal production remained stable until the mid-1990s.[32] Subsequently, factors such as competition from western coal-producing states and abroad and new environmental standards introduced by the Clean Air Act and Kyoto Protocol lessened demand for Kentucky coal. More recently, the abundance of cheap natural gas has reduced coal production and employment even further.[33]

Political transformation followed in the wake of economic shifts, as Republicans gradually won elections and replaced Democrats. Republicans placed the blame for the loss of coal mining jobs on environmental regulations and cast the Democratic Party as responsible. These claims lacked credence on two counts. First, the loss of jobs in the industry long predated the regulations and owed to a variety of factors, as noted earlier. Second, laws such as the Clean Air Act enjoyed bipartisan backing. Nonetheless, Republicans succeeded in pinning the blame for the industry's demise on Democrats. The Democratic Party's embrace of gay rights and other issues, moreover, made it seem increasingly out of step in this socially conservative state.[34] Similarly, the divide over gun rights probably drew many Kentuckians toward the GOP. Political scandals involving Democrats also aided the Republicans' rise.[35] In combination, these factors shifted the state's partisan allegiances.

Subsequently, the state's Republican delegation changed as officials either grew increasingly conservative themselves or faced primary challenges from the right—or both, as happened with Senate majority leader Mitch McConnell. As a county executive in Louisville in the late 1970s, McConnell was known as a moderate who squelched anti-abortion bills, supported unions, and was pro–civil rights. When he ran for the U.S. Senate in 1984, however, he won by merely five thousand votes. This close finish prompted him to take stock of changes in the GOP, the South, and Kentucky and to move to the right.[36] The strategy succeeded for McConnell, and in turn, he promoted it among other Republicans who sought to win in the state as well. Under McConnell's leadership, the state's public officials shifted from mostly Democrats to mostly Republicans, and he landed the Senate's top position.[37] Meanwhile, however, the Tea Party was mobilizing in the state and promoting still more conservative Republicans to run for office. McConnell himself had to ward off a primary challenge in 2014, though he emerged unscathed.[38] Increasingly, political momentum in the state turned further and further to the right.

The confluence of these factors may be leading some Kentuckians, though they use and appreciate social benefits, to downplay their significance. They may view benefits as a reminder of the state's economic downturn and the loss of job opportunities and accept the charge of state officials that the Democratic Party is to blame. The value put on self-reliance in Appalachian culture may lead many to disapprove of welfare benefits even if they or their family members have themselves utilized some form of means-tested social provision.[39] As we have seen, this attitude fuels greater disdain for government. These abstract views about government and policy probably obscure the role of personal experience of social benefits as an indicator of government effectiveness and beneficence.

Still, these public opinion dynamics leave much of the Kentucky mystery unresolved, given the particularly high rate of usage of highly visible transfer programs by the state's residents. It is reasonable to expect that Kentuckians who have used numerous visible means-tested policies would be more cognizant and supportive of government's role, like similar individuals elsewhere, so we might expect them to participate in politics with an eye toward protecting and expanding social provision. Yet, in fact, as we have seen earlier in this chapter, such individuals are less likely to participate in politics. While we lack individual-level data about Kentuckians that would permit us to specify such voting rates, we can get a sense of these patterns by examining the state's voter turnout by county in recent elections. The scatterplot of "All Voters, 2012" in the upper-left-hand corner of figure 5.9 shows the percentage of registered voters in each Kentucky county who turned out to vote in the 2012 presidential election in the state. The percentage of registered voters in each Kentucky county who turned out to vote is strongly and negatively related to government transfers as a percentage of personal income in that county (see results of t-tests in appendix E.) As seen in the two lower figures on the left side, this relationship held among both Democratic and Republican voters, but it was more extreme among the Democrats, who voted at particularly low levels in those counties where residents most rely on transfers. As a result, an election in which 60 percent of Kentucky voters favored Mitt Romney, the candidate who had dismissed those who were "dependent upon government," residents of counties in which social benefits accounted for a higher percentage of income were significantly less likely to participate.

The right-hand side of figure 5.9 shows voter turnout at the county level in the 2014 midterm election, relative to transfer receipt. In that year, voters in high-transfer-receipt counties were as likely to vote as those in low-

Figure 5.9 Federal Government Social Transfers and Voter Turnout in Kentucky Counties, 2012–2014

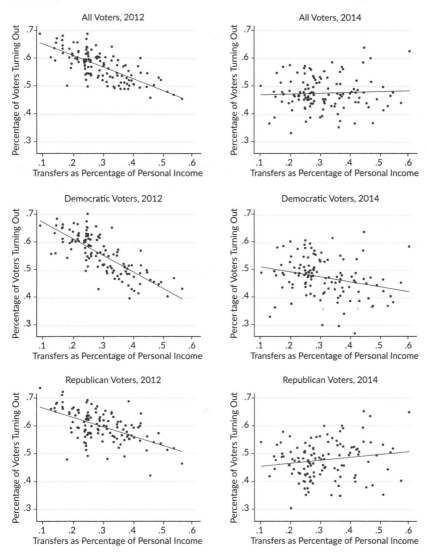

Source: County-level turnout data are available from Commonwealth of Kentucky, State Board of Elections, "Turnout Statistics," http://elect.ky.gov/statistics/Pages/turnoutstatistics.aspx (accessed February 15, 2018). Government transfer data are from BEA (2016). BEA data include all transfers to individuals from governments: retirement and disability insurance benefits, medical benefits, income maintenance benefits, unemployment insurance compensation, veterans' benefits, education and training assistance, and other transfer receipts. These data are available in table CA35 of the (regional) local area and personal income and employment data. Averages are computed using population and income figures from table CA1.

transfer-receipt counties, with no significant difference between them in turnout rates. Put differently, midterms are low-participation events that draw out only more regular voters, particularly older Americans, who are typically beneficiaries of Social Security and Medicare. That year, Republicans in high-transfer-receipt counties were significantly *more* likely to turn out than those in low-transfer-receipt counties, perhaps indicating successful attempts to mobilize them. Meanwhile, Democrats held to the same pattern as in 2012, voting less in high-transfer-receipt counties. Such differential turnout helped, for instance, the Tea Party–supported candidate, Representative Thomas Massie, secure reelection when only 35.3 percent of the electorate of his native Lewis County participated, including 38.4 percent of Republicans and 29.8 percent of Democrats.[40] In 2015, just 30.6 percent of the state's electorate voted in the gubernatorial election, and 52.5 percent of them—only 16 percent of the state's voters—elected Bevin, who promised to do away with ACA-funded health care in the state.[41] In short, who shows up to vote—versus who stays away from the polls—may go far to explain election results in Kentucky.

Numerous factors are likely to coalesce to influence voters' preferences and attract some to the polls while deterring others. Kentucky's politics has been transformed over the past thirty-five years by the rightward shift of the Republican Party, the mobilization of voters toward it, and the disproportionate nonparticipation by residents—sometimes particularly Democrats—who live in areas that most depend on government benefits. So it is that one of the poorest states in the nation, one that especially benefits from social transfers, has increasingly sent to Washington, D.C., public officials who are determined to undermine the very programs on which their constituents so greatly depend.

Once Election Day came in 2016, Trump won Kentucky handily, netting 62 percent of all votes. The victory was remarkable given that the majority of voters in the state, 51 percent, are registered Democrats and even more so given Trump's promise to sign a repeal of the ACA, which had so greatly expanded coverage in the state.[42] Yet it is in keeping with election results over the past two decades as the state has increasingly favored the GOP; in fact, a Democratic candidate for the presidency has not claimed Kentucky's electoral votes since Bill Clinton did so in 1996. Similarly paradoxical, the state's congressional delegation, along with its governor, aims to scale back social benefits—in a state in which nearly one in four dollars of personal income comes from federal social transfers. Yet only 59 percent of eligible voters in the state voted, and Republicans turned out at a higher rate than Democrats—63 percent compared to 58 percent. Moreover, only 45 percent of those with no partisan affiliation showed up. The electorate seems to have overrepresented citizens who are less aware of the value of social benefits and underrepresented those who appreciate and wish to expand them.[43]

The Participatory Tilt

How is it that the nation has shifted to electing more officials who want to undermine social policies at the very same time as citizens depend on them more than before? The answer is in part for reasons we saw in chapter 4, that many Americans use benefits that make government's role less than apparent, and that when they evaluate government, other considerations and affiliations loom more heavily in their minds than their social policy experiences. But it is also a matter of who shows up to participate in political activity. Those who have benefited from more visible government programs are both more aware of the role that government has played in their lives and more supportive of social spending. Yet they tend to participate less than other Americans, for reasons related to their socioeconomic status and also because candidates, parties, and groups do less to mobilize them and involve them. As a result, their voices are less likely to be heard in the political process, which meanwhile overrepresents those who are less aware that government has made a difference for them. The American polity is skewed by a participatory tilt that exaggerates the views of those who remain incognizant of government's role in their lives and drowns out those of others. But it does not have to be this way.

CHAPTER 6

RECONNECTING CITIZENS AND GOVERNMENT

REVOLUTIONS ARE NEVER TIDY and predictable affairs: sometimes the intended targets in the existing regime survive relatively unscathed, while other features are unintentionally torn asunder. When American conservatives grew newly empowered forty years ago, they stormed the barricades to scale back the size and scope of the federal government, and social policies loomed prominently in their sights. Yet, as the decades passed, nearly all of these policies endured; moreover, policymakers expanded the coverage of several of them. As a result, today citizens of all stripes use social policies at various junctures across their lifetimes. They rate their experiences of them quite positively across the board and typically support increased spending for them.

In the meantime, however, the antigovernment sentiments unleashed by these decades of discord have continued to mount, coalescing to threaten fundamental and long-established aspects of representative government and liberal democracy in the United States. In what may be an extreme instance of unintended consequences, contemporary conservatism has proven largely ineffective in blunting policy feedback effects that maintain support for specific social policies, but powerfully effective in undermining confidence in American government itself. Americans' deteriorating faith in the foundational principles and core institutions of U.S. government now imperils the fragile norms on which the system rests.

The years of mounting antigovernment politics came to fruition in 2016 when a candidate with no experience in government or politics secured the nomination of one of the two major parties. Throughout the campaign, Donald Trump and those who advocated for him called for a "revolution," one that would "get rid of the status quo."[1] Trump himself repeatedly repudiated or ignored principles enshrined in the Constitution, as well as the legitimacy of political opposition and a free press, the integrity of the electoral process, and long-standing norms of civil discourse.[2] Yet he soared to victory in the Electoral College, his rise fueled by those who had grown especially hostile toward government. Voters who supported Trump, controlling for other factors such as partisanship, education, and race, were especially likely to exhibit low levels of confidence in government, as measured by both trust in government and agreement that "politicians don't care about people like me."[3] Extreme frustration with government figured prominently among the sources propelling the ascent of an unprecedented candidate.

Widely shared among Trump's supporters was the view that the nation's circumstances were so desperate that radical change was necessary even if it entailed risk. A Pew study conducted just before the election found that when it came to solving the major problems facing the country, 84 percent of those who favored Clinton preferred "proven approaches that solve problems gradually, even if change may take a while," whereas the majority of those behind Trump, 53 percent, opted for "new approaches that may solve problems quickly, but also risk making things worse."[4] In Paris, Kentucky, local shopkeeper and Trump supporter Cindy Hedges explained that since coal mining collapsed, her business had been slow, her husband had lost his job, and they were struggling to afford health coverage. She felt that the country needed "somebody spectacular to set us straight." Though she voted for Obama in 2008, she said, "I love Trump. He shoots from the hip." Asked whether that might be dangerous, she replied, "I don't care. After all we've been through, I just don't care."[5]

Yet it was not clear that Trump's supporters actually favored some of the proposals he had in mind, such as the repeal of the Affordable Care Act. Many expressed worry after the election about what would become of their health coverage if Republicans followed through on their plans to dismantle the law. In Whitley County, Kentucky, 82 percent of voters supported Trump, despite the fact that when the ACA was rolled out, the uninsured rate had fallen from 25 percent in 2013 to 10 percent in 2016. A reporter who spoke to many residents of the county the week after the election found that they "did hear the promise of repeal but simply felt Trump couldn't repeal a law that had done so much good for them." One woman, Kathy Oller, who herself had signed up many people for the ACA but voted for Trump, said of the ACA, "We all need it. You can't get rid of it." Said Debbie Mills, another beneficiary of the law who had voted for Trump, "I guess I thought that, you know, he would not do this, he would not take health insurance away knowing it would affect so many people's lives. I mean, what are you to do then if you cannot pay for insurance?" Many people said that they hoped that Medicaid would be expanded further, to cover yet more of the working poor.[6] Focus groups conducted in Rust Belt states at the same time by the Kaiser Family Foundation came to similar conclusions and suggested that Trump supporters did not favor the solutions being discussed by Republicans in Congress, which they feared would make matters worse. Their predominant concerns revolved around rising health care costs, including out-of-pocket fees, deductibles, and prescription prices.[7] In actuality, they did not want the ACA to be repealed, but rather to be improved and made more generous. One year into Trump's presidency, the ACA remains in place, though his administration has sought to weaken it by reducing the enrollment period and permitting state waivers, one of which permits Kentucky to make Medicaid receipt subject to work requirements.

Most Americans today rely on the availability of social benefits and appreciate them. The fact that such widespread usage is rarely acknowledged in public life, however, feeds the antigovernment discourse. As a result, the policy process has become increasingly dysfunctional and incapable of reforming and updating policies or creating new ones to respond effectively to social and economic problems. This government-citizen disconnect has permitted, moreover, the fraying of Americans' respect for and confidence in their political institutions, making norms and principles that have long undergirded the system appear vulnerable. This final chapter reflects on how circumstances evolved to this point, how these developments matter for the future of representative government, and what strategies might be useful for restoring the connection with citizens so that democracy can be preserved and strengthened for future generations.

Paradoxes of Contemporary Politics

The story of the American welfare state's persistence and growth during a long period of growing antipathy to government is one of multiple paradoxes. It begins with the fact that even as the war on social policies raged over the past forty years, most such policies actually persisted and several were expanded in their coverage. Some were enlarged because more people qualified for them, as in the case of Social Security and Medicare, and others were expanded because lawmakers extended their reach, as in the case of Medicaid and the Earned Income Tax Credit. This is not to say that these policies adequately meet the country's needs: to the contrary, stringent eligibility rules prevent many people from qualifying for coverage by policies ostensibly targeted at them, as in the case of Unemployment Insurance and disability benefits, and benefit rates for many policies are desperately low, as in the case of food stamps. Neither do I mean to suggest that existing policies do as much as they could to mitigate soaring economic inequality. Indeed, despite the much-touted virtues of the market, many lower- and middle-income Americans, particularly those with low or moderate amounts of education, have experienced stagnating wages, deteriorating benefits, and diminished opportunities for decades. The United States is unique in the extent to which its social policies bestow benefits on affluent people, particularly the policies ensconced in the tax code, which have for the most part persisted, with few alterations, during this period.[8] In short, even as the market has become less reliable as the source of income and benefits, the American welfare state, complete with its particularities and shortcomings, has prevailed over time.

Most Americans, moreover, over the course of their lives, have occasion to use several different social policies. Policy usage experiences span all sorts of differences in American society, including income, generation, race and ethnicity, and partisanship. Divided though Americans appear to be in their views about the welfare state, nearly all share the experience of having benefited from it at least at some juncture in their lives. Americans rely on government not only if they fall into poverty but also, more typically, when they seek assistance to afford health coverage, pay for advanced education, acquire housing, save for retirement, or acquire income if they lose their job. Government aids people in each of these common experiences so that they do not risk economic insecurity as they fulfill basic needs or pursue educational opportunity.

Yet Americans' cumulative usage of social policies and their appreciation of most such policies do surprisingly little to mitigate their increasing hostility toward government generally. These personal, direct experiences of government, even if repeated multiple times, yield little impact on beneficiaries' overall views about government.

In theory, policies convey information about government to citizens via their design and implementation.[9] After World War II, the GI Bill's education and training benefits, for example, conveyed to beneficiaries that government mattered for their lives in positive ways, and that it was for and about people like them.[10] Policies with ostensibly visible designs do have a salutary impact on general views in some instances. Many other policies today do little to reveal to Americans government's role in their lives. High rates of usage of policies embedded in the tax code yield no such effect, even though such benefits can be quite generous. For Americans who have used means-tested submerged benefits, the generosity of those benefits fails to mitigate their typically highly negative views of government. In short, when it comes to the impact of accumulated social policy usage on several general views about government we have assessed in this book, policy feedback effects, more often than not, are conspicuous by their absence. Their information-providing role largely fails to materialize.

In the absence of information, social identities and group affiliations fill the void, shaping individuals' perception of government, even when it runs contrary to their personal experience of social policies. Perhaps most strikingly, disapproval of "welfare" translates into scorn for government generally, as those who evaluate it most harshly perceive government as unresponsive to people like themselves, no matter how many social policies they have utilized. Since TANF covers so few people today, "welfare" appears to have taken on outsized symbolic importance. Perhaps to some it serves as a synonym for any form of social provision they regard as "unearned." Most important, for those who despise it, "welfare" has come to epitomize government in action generally, in ways that generate strong disapproval. In addition, other manifestations of ideology and shared identities shape citizens' views of government, overriding the impact of information gleaned from actual policy experiences.

The final paradox emanating from the government-citizen disconnect is that those who have used more visible policies and are thus more likely to credit government and to be more supportive of more generous social provision are less likely than others to raise their political voices: they are less likely to participate in nearly all political activities. Conversely, those who are the least aware of the difference that government makes in their lives and who are less supportive of expanded benefits are far more likely to make their views known in politics and to elect officials to represent them. This participatory tilt amplifies the voices of those who disparage government, ensuring repeated threats to social provision, the perpetuation of inequality, and, most problematic, the undermining of Americans' primary means of working together across differences to address any problems addressing society. But before elaborating on these consequences, we need to consider the mechanisms that have produced these paradoxical politics.

The Rise of a Political Economy Hostile to Government

To sum up, we have arrived at a political moment when Americans' assessments of government generally are out of sync with their own direct, personal lived experiences of it, and when the voices of those who do appreciate its role in their lives remain largely unheard. It has not always been like this. Many who came of age with the Great Depression and World War II remembered, decades later, the difference that government had made in their lives and their families' lives, in policies ranging from New Deal relief to the GI Bill. During the middle of the twentieth century, they and their compatriots gave government high marks, registering much greater trust and a stronger sense of political efficacy than Americans do today.

This raises the question: What dynamics led the United States to develop the government-citizen disconnect? Put differently, did changes in public opinion among ordinary Americans bubble up from below, or were they responsive to elite-led shifts in American politics? Drawing on literatures in political science, history, and sociology, it appears that over the past forty years several developments have transformed the relationship between political elites and ordinary citizens. Whereas in the past, public officials, the media, and civic organizations each did more to make government's role evident to Americans, their capacity to perform that role has become frayed or distorted, permitting antigovernment attitudes to flourish or even fostering them.

Groups, organizations, and other institutions can mediate the relationship between government and citizens. If these institutions are functioning well, they can help citizens interpret their experiences of policies, "connecting the dots" to understand the role that government plays in their lives. Alternatively, these institutions may lose such capacity if they grow weaker—as have labor unions over the past four decades, for example. Some groups may emerge, furthermore, that purposefully obfuscate the salutary role that government plays in Americans' lives and aim to transform the image of government into a hostile entity. These latter developments have characterized the past several decades of American political development.

Already by the 1970s, political elites in the Republican Party actually promoted an antigovernment orientation as a political strategy to help aid their electoral fortunes. Some newly elected conservative Republicans in Congress at the time began to strategize about how the party could shed its minority status. Seeking to distinguish the GOP further from the Democrats as a means of pursuing electoral advantages, they proceeded to run more resolutely against government, aiming to scale back taxes, social provision, and regulations.[11] Certainly some changes were already under way at the state and local levels—for example, in antitax and anticrime campaigns.[12] The new stance of conservatives in Washington, D.C., gave fuel to the fire. As political competition grew between the parties in their quest to control each chamber of Congress and the presidency, government itself became the focal point that Republicans used to rally their base.

Meanwhile, rank-and-file partisans began to diverge ideologically to a greater extent than had been the case previously. As economic development proceeded after World War II, and in the wake of the civil rights era, white southerners—long a solid Democratic constituency—gradually shifted to the Republican Party.[13] At the same time, liberals in the North and West increasingly affiliated with the Democratic Party.[14] These changes occurred in part because some people actually shifted their allegiances, but also because many younger Americans joined different parties than their parents. In addition, those who had aligned themselves with a party because of a single issue or because people with whom they identified belonged to it gradually adopted the broader set of issue positions associated with the party.[15]

Republican Party elites seized on the insurgent mobilization of the grass roots and directed it toward an aggressive antigovernment political agenda, particularly after the party won control of both chambers in 1994. That victory strengthened their resolve and laid the groundwork for more victories over the next decade. Democrats managed to regain both chambers of Congress in 2006 and the White House in 2008. Yet, in 2009, conservatives came roaring back by organizing the Tea Party, a network of groups that attacked moderates in their own party and supported conservative challengers to them in primary elections. By 2010, and in subsequent years, the Tea Party succeeded in sending to Congress a large number of right-wing firebrands who thumbed their noses at party leaders and eschewed compromise.[16] Still, the GOP lacked the capacity to achieve some of its central policy goals, failing in repeated votes up through 2016 to repeal the Affordable Care Act, and this further fueled the anger of its base and led to its support for political outsider Donald Trump.

Although the Republican Party carried the flag for the repudiation of government, the basic message resonated with many Americans across the political spectrum, even among those who did not connect with the GOP's policy agenda. Several developments in addition to partisan shifts probably also undercut the authority and legitimacy that government had held for an earlier generation of Americans. For example, transformations in the media reduced its capacity to engage citizens in the political process and to communicate to them effectively about politics. The emergence of far more partisan forms of media than had existed forty years ago encouraged some citizens to become more extreme, angry, or outraged about politics, while prompting others—particularly those lacking strong positions on issues—to disengage from the political process altogether.[17] In addition, media coverage of the poor shifted over time: after portraying the poor in the 1960s as "victims of an economic system that had no place for them," the media were depicting them by the 1970s as "cheaters, as lazy or unwilling to work," and highlighting "the dysfunctions of government efforts to help them."[18]

Federated civic organizations, which had enjoyed high memberships through much of American history and as recently as the mid-twentieth century, grew severely atrophied. When they were strong, such organizations helped ordinary citizens acquire skills that they could transfer to the political realm; they connected elites and less affluent Americans for a common purpose; some—namely, labor unions—directly empowered less-affluent Americans; and in some instances, they directly coordinated efforts by their members to promote policy goals. In all of these ways, civic organizations made government's relevance and purpose evident to citizens, "connecting the dots" between citizens' lives and government activity. The demise of these organizations has deprived ordinary people of the skills and means to connect to the political realm and, conversely, closed off an avenue by which political leaders can reach citizens. Antigovernment attitudes thrive more easily in their absence.[19]

Last but not least, the United States has witnessed the rise of money in politics over the past quarter-century. The amount invested in political campaigns has grown much more quickly than family income or spending on numerous sectors of the economy. Moreover, conservative political organizations have mobilized support for an antigovernment agenda, as demonstrated by the Tea Party and the activities of donors such as the Koch brothers and the Mercer family, who aim to shift the GOP to the right.[20]

Corporate interests have ratcheted up the amount they devote to lobbying, in both dollars and professionalization.[21] Political scientists tend to be somewhat skeptical of the extent to which money in politics matters, finding little evidence that it actually changes votes, though they acknowledge a more compelling case that it shapes the political agenda.[22] Yet the most powerful impact of money in politics may be on citizens themselves, who have increasingly adopted the widespread conviction—felt across the political spectrum from left to right—that government is "rigged." Indeed, ordinary people detect that government is run largely by elites whose backgrounds are very different from their own and who are not often responsive to them. Some scholarly research suggests that, on both counts, they are correct.[23]

In sum, as Americans have evaluated government in recent decades, they have done so in a transformed political economic context in which organizations, groups, and institutions that previously helped citizens understand government's role and their interests have lost capacity, while others have adopted a hostile, antigovernment agenda. Those shifts have largely undermined the informational role of public policy, leaving people to fall back on viewpoints emerging from social identities as they assess government.

Throughout the middle of the twentieth century, Americans across the party divide were united in antipathy to communism, while generally affirming of their own government. Since the Berlin Wall came down and the Soviet Union was dismantled, that source of societal unity has evaporated. Ironically, antigovernment attitudes toward Americans' own government have emerged in its place. These attitudes serve in effect as the broad public philosophy of the modern era—an inherently antipublic era. Despite sharp partisan polarization, antigovernment attitudes animate many Americans across the political spectrum.

The Threat to Democracy

Why does it matter if we as Americans have become more disdainful of our own government? Government embodies our shared capacity to accomplish anything as a society; it encompasses the institutional arrangements and political processes to which we all have a collective claim for attempting any goal that surpasses the reach of families, neighborhoods, civic organizations, and businesses. It permits us to work together, across our many differences, to find ways to protect our individual rights and collective security, promote a vibrant economy, and foster opportunity. Government gives us a means to confront vast problems ranging from the warming of the planet to inequality and poverty, the employment losses caused by technological change, the quest for cures to disease, and myriad others.

The chief principle underlying American government is that it derives its legitimacy from the consent of the governed, that its power flows from "we the people." Established in a radical break from rule by the British monarchy, it rests on principles of republicanism, with authority flowing from ordinary citizens through their elected representatives. For nearly its first century in existence, the nation's bold experiment in disowning an aristocracy was undercut by its sanction of the institution of slavery. It would be yet another century before civil rights were guaranteed to all citizens. Even now, the legacy of white supremacy persists in residential segregation and educational inequality, and racial inequality has reemerged in new forms, owing particularly to the criminal justice system. Yet despite the slow development of democracy and indeed, of backsliding from it, the U.S. political system has shown itself to be capable of change and renewal, as Richard Valelly demonstrated in his book on the "two reconstructions."[24]

The American political system does tend to operate slowly. Its eighteenth-century institutional forms, epitomized by the separation of powers, present numerous hurdles and obstacles to decision-making and make governing more complicated than in parliamentary systems. The Constitution also fragments authority through federalism, as only a few other affluent nations do, and the U.S. version is more decentralized than the others.[25] Nonetheless, the U.S. government, as it evolved into the later twentieth century, appeared slowly to be becoming more representative of the diversity of American society. At its best, the political system functioned by requiring political actors to find ways to work across their differences and to navigate the complexities of institutional arrangements, through compromise and negotiation. In so doing, on occasion they accomplished broad goals sought by the American people.

Thus, if we turn against our own government, we turn against ourselves, in an act of collective self-destruction. What is the alternative? It is not rule by the people. Rather, anger at our collective forms of self-government appears to be leading our society toward something antithetical to the founding ideals of the nation: greater comfort with concentrating power in strong leaders, presidents with increasing degrees of authority to act on their own. In addition, antigovernment attitudes are permitting the flourishing of oligarchy—a cadre of wealthy business elites whose interests are furthered by such a system. These developments undermine the possibility for collective action based on democratic principles.

For ordinary Americans to respect government, they need to know that it is operating on behalf of the good of the nation, in the words of the U.S. Constitution, "to establish justice, insure domestic tranquility, provide for the common defense, promote the general welfare, and secure the blessings of liberty." But what if government *is* actually performing many of those functions but citizens cannot see its role in them, or do not recognize them as government in action? If that is the case, faith in democracy may dissipate unnecessarily. That is where we find ourselves today in the United States.

Certainly it is the case that the U.S. government could have done more in recent decades to enable citizens to adjust to changing economic circumstances and to mitigate growing disparities. Other nations have faced the same trends of globalization, but those with stronger labor protections have witnessed less of an increase in economic inequality.[26] The United States used to be a world leader in providing advanced education to citizens—the key criterion for success in the modern economy—but in recent decades other nations have surpassed it, while it has done only a little better than standing still.[27] The nation has been most responsive to those who already benefit from the modern political economy, and much less so to those who have been left behind.[28] Some U.S. policies created in the past, furthermore, channel ample benefits to private-sector interests and make it difficult for policymakers to create new and improved policies without building on the existing foundation they provide. Public officials forged the Affordable Care Act, for instance, atop the existing structure of U.S. health coverage, which supports the health insurance industry—an approach that is necessarily complicated and deprives government of much leverage to control costs, and yet, without taking this approach, reform would probably have proven impossible.[29]

Although the United States has nevertheless increased the extent to which it provides economic security and educational opportunity to citizens, many Americans who are beneficiaries of these policies do not perceive government to be responsive to them. This conundrum amounts to a government-citizen disconnect. With the relationship between government and citizens strained to the breaking point, many Americans are now willing to risk endangering the political system in pursuit of fundamental change. Democratic governance itself is at stake.

How Can Citizens Reconnect to Government?

For many years in teaching undergraduate courses on American government, I have assigned students a homework task of interviewing a family member about a public policy that has affected his or her life. I encourage students to speak to their oldest living relative in the United States, typically over the phone. For international students or recent immigrants, I connect them with an adult on campus or in the community who is willing to have such a conversation. I instruct students to ask their interview subjects why they chose a particular policy to talk about and what difference they believe it made in their lives, whether positively or negatively. Students summarize the discussion in writing and then reflect on it themselves.

They routinely report back that they learned something they did not know previously about their family regarding how government had mattered for them in some personal way. They often discover that a grandparent or parent would not have acquired an education were it not for the GI Bill, or student loans, or Pell Grants, and they hear that person reflect on how that affected their children's and grandchildren's opportunities. Many come to realize how much their older relatives value Social Security and Medicare. Not all of the policies mentioned are social provisions; some relatives describe the impact on their lives of the draft, civil rights laws, or immigration policies. Some relatives tell of their role in actively resisting laws or mobilizing for policy change. Students are struck by the meaningful, tangible role of policies in the lives of their own families and often sense the implications for their own life stories.

The United States embraces the ideal of the self-made individual, of dreamers and strivers who, with courage, talent, and hard work, fulfill their ambitions, whatever they may be. We cherish the heroic stories told by those seeking public office and depicted on the screen in box-office hits of those who come from humble backgrounds, overcome obstacles, and ascend to success. These narratives infuse our culture and influence what we tell ourselves about our own lives and the lives of our family members. Many would acknowledge that successful individuals have often been aided by family members who are also hardworking and who have made sacrifices on their behalf. But even that slightly wider view of how an individual succeeds in life is likely to leave out some other crucial sources of support along the way.[30]

We routinely understate the significant role that government plays in our lives in providing opportunities, financial security, and a safety net. Americans who were among the first to receive new forms of social provision may have been less likely to take such effects for granted. Several years ago, I conducted interviews with over thirty veterans of World War II, and before I raised specific questions about public policy, I posed this question to them: "As you look back over the course of your life, certain events or opportunities may stand out as highly significant or as turning points. What might these be?" Many people mentioned growing up during the Depression, their service in World War II, or meeting a person who became a mentor or their spouse. But a large number also mentioned a public policy—the GI Bill—as a crucial turning point. Survey data bore this out. One respondent wrote that the GI Bill "gave our family a 'boost' that has allowed us to help our children go to college more than I had expected, i.e. GI Bill benefits have been passed to a second generation!"[31]

Most contemporary college students who do not need financial aid themselves have parents, grandparents, or great-grandparents who were the first in their family to go to college and who managed to do so because public universities and colleges, federal student aid, or both made it affordable. Those with family savings for college may be aided, too, by their grandparents' access to Social Security or Medicare, which spares their family from needing to devote resources to the basic needs and health care of the older generation.

A fuller accounting of an individual's success might include an inventory of their own usage of any of the twenty-one policies investigated in this book, as well as an examination of how such policies affected those in their extended family. Unemployment Insurance, for example, may have enabled a parent to get through a period between jobs, preventing a plunge into more dire straits and forestalling a need for various forms of public assistance. For many families, tax benefits such as the home mortgage interest deduction or those accrued by receiving government-subsidized employer-provided retirement benefits translate into more disposable income. Those who have suffered from a disability or serious health condition may perceive more readily than others how unfortunate circumstances beyond one's control can alter a life story, and how invaluable social provision may be.

Taking such inventories and learning how government has mattered in our families' lives, we could begin to make its role more visible. Government itself could facilitate this process by making available to citizens a "taxpayer receipt" that details the value of the benefits they receive through the tax code, including subsidies for employer-provided benefits, and ideally by also indicating the value of direct social benefits, including social insurance.

Yet as we have seen, information alone may be insufficient. Policy designs do not speak for themselves in communicating the value of government. Even if appealing internet tools and other procedures help citizens make sense of how government has helped them and their families over time, the impact on assessments of government may still be minimal. In our highly polarized polity, where organizational linkages that connect citizens and government have frayed and some groups beat the antigovernment drum, more is needed. Organizations that seek to strengthen democracy must step up to play these roles, making connections for citizens and drawing them into politics when the fate of policies is at stake. They can do so effectively by developing activists, including individuals from communities that are usually excluded from civic engagement.[32] In the process, they can help people see how government matters in their lives—through social policies like those examined here as well as through others—and spur their involvement in the political process.

The Way Forward

For those who want government to be smaller and who disapprove of social policy, knowing that they benefit from it themselves may be unlikely to change their outlook. Partisan polarization reflects growing difference in orientations toward government among Americans, and this gap shows little sign of abating. Probing more deeply, moreover, reveals that the narrative and priorities offered by both Democrats and Republicans suffer from the lack of a vision of how the United States can remain true to its ideals of freedom, equality, and opportunity while navigating a dramatically changing economy and labor market.

To many Americans, the understanding that others in their communities and they themselves have benefited from social policies may be of little consolation if they despair of jobs lost in their communities and the sense that opportunities are on the wane. They may be painfully aware of the abundance of underemployed family members, whether twenty-somethings struggling to find a foothold in the labor market or those in late middle age who find themselves downsized out of a good-paying job and unable to find another that offers anywhere near comparable pay and benefits. Some may be saddened by the decay of residences and shuttering of businesses in the small towns or Rust Belt cities where they reside. Others may harbor a sense of shame over their own use of social policies, wishing instead for job opportunities that would fortify their sense of self-worth in a society that champions the ideal of self-reliance.

How can we move forward together? For decades, policymakers have promoted free trade and the shift toward technology, with the promise that those left behind by this approach would be compensated. Some might argue that rising social spending over time, particularly on policies such as the EITC, functions as just such a form of compensation. But by themselves, such policies are insufficient. Not only are they too meager to permit a decent standard of living, but more importantly, they cannot by themselves satisfy a nation that places immense value on hard work and individual initiative as essential to sustaining freedom, facilitating innovation, and being able to support our families. For Americans who are already in midlife and lack sufficient employment, and for communities with deteriorating economies, innovative approaches are required. Certainly there is no one-size-fits-all approach; economic development strategies and support for individuals hoping to enter the job market or find better opportunities can be usefully tailored at the regional, state, and local levels.

At the same time, the most effective way for public policies to promote opportunity for younger generations of Americans is through making advanced education affordable. Since its very beginnings, the United States—both at the federal and state levels—has embraced public policies to promote higher education. These policies deteriorated in the 1980s through 2006, leaving the college graduation rates stagnating and student loan debt growing at the same time that job opportunities for those with less than a college degree disappeared. Since 2007, federal policymakers have redoubled the nation's commitment to financial aid, but public universities and colleges continue to face budget shortfalls as states struggle to afford other priorities instead. This leaves college completion out of reach for many qualified students.

Meanwhile, the United States has failed to provide adequate, affordable vocational training for those who seek a different path beyond high school.

Instead, those students have been largely relegated to a for-profit sector that is costly to the nation and serves students poorly, often leaving them worse off than if they had never aspired to improve their lives. On both counts, reform is necessary, at both the national and state levels, to enhance opportunities for the next generation.[33]

As Americans face the future, far more unites us than divides us. We are not a nation of moochers and takers. Rather, we are a political community, one built on respect for the ideas that all are created equal and that "we the people" can govern ourselves. We can advance by honoring our reciprocal obligations to each other through the bonds of citizenship. By reaffirming that quest, we can carry on together, as citizens of a democracy.

APPENDIX A

DESIGN AND PROCEDURES FOR THE SOCIAL AND GOVERNMENTAL ISSUES AND PARTICIPATION STUDY

The Social and Governmental Issues and Participation Study (SGIP) was designed to examine Americans' usage of and experiences with social policies in relation to their participation in politics and their attitudes about government and policy. Very few surveys include questions about both policy experiences and political attitudes and behavior, and the few that do generally ask about only a small number of policies.

In designing the survey, I used existing survey questions to the extent possible. I generally drew on the American National Election Studies (ANES) and the American Citizen Participation Study for questions about political attitudes and participation and about demographics. For policy usage questions, I used (or adapted) wording from questions asked earlier in surveys, including some I had written for a survey conducted by the Maxwell School in 2005, the Maxwell Poll on Citizenship and Inequality.

To manage concerns about feasibility and reliability, I consulted with survey design expert Joanne Miller of the University of Minnesota. I planned a telephone survey that included approximately 150 questions, many of them asked contingent on responses to preceding questions. The questions were entirely closed-ended, though in a few instances an open-ended response was sought if the respondent answered "other." The policy usage questions were phrased in an iterative fashion and required only "yes" or "no" responses, easing the task for respondents; those who answered affirmatively to specific policies were asked several follow-up questions about their experiences. The format of the survey began with questions about current political attitudes and views about government, phrased in the typical manner. Next it proceeded to ask about political participation, asking first whether individuals had ever participated in particular activities and, if they replied affirmatively, asking follow-up questions. Questions about policy usage followed only after these sections, in order to avoid influencing responses to the attitudinal and participation questions.

A unique aspect of the SGIP is that it inquired about lifetime policy usage rather than only present usage, and it also asked whether individuals had ever participated in various political activities. Accordingly, I aimed to design the survey to facilitate recall and to minimize the potential source of bias that could be introduced by memory concerns. I did not ask about obscure details but rather framed questions and response options to solicit general indicators of program participation and civic engagement in general periods of respondents' lives. I also conducted several qualitative, open-ended, in-person interviews on the same topics before writing the survey instrument, and this provided me with a sense of which kinds of questions respondents answered with confidence and which they did not. I decided, for example, that I could not ask about *attitudes* from the past because it would be difficult for individuals to remember and to distinguish past and present attitudes. I focused instead on *activities*—that is, on what respondents had *done* rather than on what they had *thought*—and I asked about the social benefits they claimed and their forms of political participation. Following literature about survey research, I structured the survey questionnaire in a manner designed to stimulate memory.[1]

I took care in crafting the questions about policy usage, including various names by which such programs are known and qualifiers aimed at helping respondents recall and correctly identify which programs they had utilized. The earlier pilot survey and the in-person interviews enabled me to refine the instrument. Careful studies about recall of program usage that link survey responses with administrative data do not find large or consistent evidence of underreporting or overreporting.[2] Some might worry that such data are subject to underreporting, given the stigma attached to some kinds of policy receipt. Scholars find, however, that any such underreporting tends to be quite minimal.[3] Although even such minimal discrepancies can lead to large errors if the effort is to estimate rates of policy usage, the aim here is not to offer a precise estimate of such usage (I use the administrative data in chapter 2 for that purpose) but rather to investigate broadly the relationship between policy usage and political attitudes and participation.

The survey was conducted by telephone, administered by the Survey Research Institute at Cornell University, and sought participation by a national random sample of American adults.

There were three sampling approaches to this study, with an identical survey instrument for all three groups:

1. National random digit dial (RDD)
2. Oversample of "young" individuals, using a listed household sample targeting individuals between eighteen and thirty-four years of age
3. Oversample of "low-income" households, using a national RDD sample targeting households with annual incomes under $35,000

All samples were drawn from the forty-eight contiguous United States. Data collection began on August 23, 2008, and was completed by November 1, 2008.

All adults in the national sample were eligible to participate, and none were offered any financial incentive. The majority of these data were collected by Cornell's Survey Research Institute, but a portion was collected by the Indiana University Center for Survey Research. A total of one thousand surveys were completed as a part of this national sample.

Potential respondents in the young oversample were immediately screened for eligibility—only individuals in the target age range (eighteen to thirty-four) were allowed to complete a survey. These respondents were offered a $10 incentive for their participation. A total of two hundred surveys were completed as a part of this young oversample.

All adults in the low-income oversample were eligible to participate and were also offered a $10 incentive. Since there was no screening based on income, some respondents completed the survey but reported a household income of $35,000 or more. In these cases, the respondent's data were combined with the data collected using the national sample. This ensured that all data collected as a part of the low-income oversample was in fact for low-income households. A total of two hundred surveys were completed as a part of this low-income oversample.

Weighting for the survey consisted of two adjustments: a weight for nonresponse and a weight for calibrating the sample to population totals. Differences in nonresponse across U.S. Census regions and Metropolitan Statistical Areas are accounted for in the weight adjustment for nonresponse. Differences between sample and population characteristics are accounted for with a poststratification weight adjustment. The poststratification balances the sample according to person-level population data obtained from the 2007 Current Population Survey (CPS). The poststratification variables are gender, age, education, and ethnicity (Hispanic).

QUESTIONNAIRE FOR THE SOCIAL AND GOVERNMENTAL ISSUES AND PARTICIPATION STUDY

This is a condensed version of the survey instrument. Question wording is reported "as is," but with some omissions, including: instructions to interviewers (for example, to randomize responses, or to skip questions depending on specific answers); the list of possible responses to each question; and a few follow-up questions about the timing of participation or benefit usage, which are not utilized in the analysis in this book.

Hello! I am calling from Cornell University. One of our faculty, Professor Suzanne Mettler, would like to request your participation in an academic research study she is conducting. The goal of this project is to better understand Americans' views about social and governmental issues and their participation in public life.

Before we begin, there are a few points I need to cover: I want to assure you that all the information you give will be kept completely confidential and that none of it will be released in any way that would permit identification of you. Your participation in this study is, of course, voluntary. If there is any question you would prefer not to answer, just tell me and we will go on to the next question.

Section 1: Introduction

1. Some people, when they think through their life experiences, report that they have at some point used a government social program. Others report that they have never used a government social program. What about you: have you ever used a government social program, or not?

2. What is the year of your birth? 19_____ (*range: 1916 to 1991*)

3. On the whole, are you very satisfied, somewhat satisfied, somewhat dissatisfied, or very dissatisfied with the way democracy works in the United States?

Section 2: Attitudes About Public Policies

1. I am going to read you a list of federal government programs. For each one please tell me if you have a favorable or an unfavorable opinion of that program. How about . . . [ask each item from list below, randomize please]. Do you have a favorable or an unfavorable opinion? (If favorable/unfavorable, ask:) Is that a very favorable or somewhat favorable/very unfavorable or somewhat unfavorable opinion?

  a. Head Start—a preschool and nutritional program for children from low-income families
  b. Social Security
  c. Medicare—that's health care coverage for those who are eligible for Social Security
  d. Medicaid—that's health care coverage for low-income elderly, disabled, and children (same as Medi-Cal in California)
  e. Welfare or public assistance
  f. The Earned Income Tax Credit (EITC)—that's a tax benefit for people who work but don't make much money
  g. Student loans—that's money students can borrow to help pay for college; they must repay it later on, with interest
  h. Pell Grants—that's money to help low-income students pay for college; they do not need to repay it
  i. Unemployment Insurance—that's the same as unemployment compensation
  j. Food stamps
  k. Government-subsidized housing for low-income people—such as Section 8 and public housing
  l. The GI Bill, which pays for veterans' education and training
  m. The home mortgage interest deduction—that's a tax benefit for people who have mortgages on their homes

2. There is much concern about the rapid rise in medical and hospital costs. Some people feel there should be a government insurance plan which would cover all medical and hospital expenses for everyone. Others feel that

all medical expenses should be paid by individuals through private insurance plans like Blue Cross or other company-paid plans. Which is closer to the way you feel?

3. There's also concern about Social Security. Some people feel that workers should be allowed to invest part of their Social Security taxes in the stock market or in bonds because it would give them more control over their money. Other people feel that workers should *not* be allowed to invest part of their Social Security taxes in the stock market or in bonds because it would reduce guaranteed retirement benefits from government. Which is closer to the way you feel?

4. All in all, do you favor or oppose the United States government guaranteeing health insurance for all citizens, even if it means raising taxes? Do you [favor it/oppose it] strongly or somewhat?

5. We are faced with many problems in this country, none of which can be solved easily or inexpensively. I'm going to name some of these problems, and for each one I'd like you to tell me whether you think we're spending too much money on it, too little money, or about the right amount. Are we spending too much, too little, or about the right amount on . . .

    a. Housing for the poor
    b. Social Security
    c. Welfare
    d. Military or defense spending
    e. Aid for poor people
    f. Aid for college students
    g. Health care
    h. Assistance for child care
    i. Aid for the unemployed
    j. Economic aid to other nations

6. When it comes to paying federal income taxes, do you feel you are asked to pay your fair share, more than your fair share, or less than your fair share?

Section 3: Political Efficacy and Other Attitudes

Now I'd like to read you a few statements about public life.

    1. I'll read them one at a time and please tell me whether you agree or

disagree with each of them. [*Read.*] Do you agree or disagree? Is that agree/disagree strongly or agree/disagree somewhat?

a. "Public officials don't care much what people like me think."
b. "People like me don't have any say about what the government does."
c. "I feel that I have a pretty good understanding of the important political issues facing this country."
d. "I consider myself well qualified to participate in politics."
e. "Generally, I feel like a full and equal citizen in this country with all the rights and protections that other people have."
f. "Government social programs have helped me in times of need."
g. "Government has imposed costly burdens on me."
h. "Government has given me opportunities to improve my standard of living."
i. "Government has greatly limited my freedom."
j. "Generally, I feel proud to be an American."
k. "I feel I owe a great deal back to this country."
l. "I want to help make our society more fair and equitable."

2. Do you feel that the distribution of money and wealth in this country today is fair, or do you feel that the money and wealth in this country should be more evenly distributed among a larger percentage of the people?

Section 4: Voting

Now I'd like to ask you some questions about voting.

1. Which of the following applies to you: you are currently registered to vote, you are not sure if you are registered to vote, you could register but have not, or you are not eligible to vote for some reason?

2. Thinking back to the national election in November 2004, when the presidential candidates were John Kerry, the Democrat, and George W. Bush, the Republican, did you happen to vote in that election?

3. In talking to people about elections, we find that they are sometimes not able to vote because they're not registered, they don't have time, or they have difficulty getting to the polls. Think about the *presidential elections*

since you were old enough to vote. Have you voted in all of them, voted in most of them, voted in some of them, rarely voted in them, or have you never voted in a presidential election?

4. Now, think about the *nonpresidential elections*—meaning elections for state, local, or congressional leaders when no presidential candidates are on the ballot—that have been held since you were old enough to vote. Have you voted in all of them, voted in most of them, voted in some of them, rarely voted in them, or have you never voted in a nonpresidential election?

Section 5: Other Political Activities

Now I am going to ask you about your political involvement.

1. Have you *ever in your life* done any volunteer work for a political candidate who is running for national, state, or local office? For instance, you might have made calls, distributed literature, prepared mailings, or gathered signatures.

2. Have you *ever* contributed money to an individual candidate, a party group, a political action committee, or any other organization that supported candidates?

3. Have you *ever* served in a voluntary capacity on any local governmental board, council, committee, or group that deals with community problems and issues?

4. Have you *ever* contacted a government official or someone on the staff of such an official—either in person, by phone, or by email—about problems or issues with which you were concerned?

5. Have you *ever* taken part in a protest, march, or demonstration on some national or local issue?

Section 6: Social Program Experiences

Now I'd like to ask you about your experience with several government policies over the course of your life.

1. Could you tell me if you personally have ever at any time received benefits or payments from any of the following social programs?

  a. Social Security
  1. Was that either the retirement and survivors' type of Social

Security benefits, or was it Social Security disability benefits, or was it both types?

b. Supplemental Security Income (SSI, also referred to as "disability" benefits)

c. Medicare (that's health care coverage for those who are eligible for Social Security)

d. Medicaid (that's health care coverage for low-income elderly, disabled, and children; same as Medi-Cal in California)

e. Unemployment Insurance or unemployment compensation

f. Pell Grants or their precursors from 1965 to 1972 (that's money to help low-income students pay for college; they do not repay it; precursors were called Educational Opportunity Grants)

g. Student loans (for example, Stafford or Perkins loans; money students borrow to go to college; they must repay it later on with interest)

h. Welfare or public assistance (Temporary Assistance to Needy Families, TANF)

i. Food stamps

j. Government-subsidized housing (including public housing and Section 8 housing)

k. Head Start

Now I need to ask you, have you ever served or are you currently serving in the U.S. military, the National Guard, or military reserves?

l. GI Bill for education or training

m. Other veterans' benefits (such as disability or VA hospital benefits)

Now I want to ask you about your experiences with [*program*].

2. What is the total amount of time in your life during which you received benefits from [*program*]: was it two years or less, or was it more than two years? [*If more than two years, ask:*] Was it from two to five years, from five to ten years, or more than ten years? [*If two years or less, ask:*] Was it less than six months, from six to twelve months, or from one to two years? [*If respondents are unsure, prompt with "Do you have a best guess?"*]

3. To what extent did [*program*] help you: a great deal, to some extent, a little, or not at all?

4. When people apply for government benefits, sometimes they find that the process is easy, while on other occasions it is complicated. In your own experience with [*program*], would you say that qualifying for benefits was easy or complicated, or don't you remember? Was it very easy/complicated or somewhat easy/complicated?

5. When people are beneficiaries of a government program, sometimes they feel that the program is well run and sometimes they feel that it is poorly run. In your own experience with [*program*], would you say that it is well run or poorly run, or don't you remember? Is that very well run/poorly run or somewhat well run/poorly run?

6. Have you ever taken into account the position of a candidate on [*program*] in deciding either how to vote or whether to vote?

7. When you contributed money to an individual candidate, a party group, a political action committee, or any other organization that supports candidates, have you ever done so, at least in part, because of your concern about [*program*]?

8. Have you ever contacted an elected official or someone on the staff of such an official regarding [*program*]?

Section 7: Tax Benefits

Now I'd like to ask you about your experience with several federal income tax benefits.

1. Could you tell me if you (or whoever files taxes on your behalf) have ever claimed any of the following benefits?

   a. Home mortgage interest deduction—a tax benefit for people who have mortgages on their homes
   b. Earned Income Tax Credit (EITC)—a tax benefit for people who work but don't make much money
   c. Child and Dependent Care Tax Credit—a tax benefit for people who pay someone else to care for their child or other family member so they can work or look for work
   d. Hope Credit or Lifetime Learning Credit—tax benefits for people paying college tuition
   e. Either a qualified tuition program ("529 plan") or a Coverdell Education Savings Account (education IRA)

Now I want to ask you about your experiences with the [*tax benefit*].

2. What is the total number of years in your life during which you claimed benefits from the [*tax benefit*]: one year only, from two to five years, from six to ten years, or more than ten years? [*If respondents are unsure, prompt with "Do you have a best guess?"*]

3. To what extent did [*tax benefit*] help you: a great deal, to some extent, a little, or not at all?

4. When people try to claim tax benefits, sometimes they find that the process is easy, while on other occasions it is complicated. In your own experience with the [*tax benefit*], would you say that qualifying for it was easy or complicated, or don't you remember? Is that very easy/complicated or somewhat easy/complicated?

5. Have you ever taken into account the position of a candidate on the [*tax benefit*] in deciding either how to vote or whether to vote?

6. When you contributed money to an individual candidate, a party group, a political action committee, or any other organization that supports candidates, have you ever done so, at least in part, because of your concern about the [*tax benefit*]?

7. Have you ever contacted an elected official or someone on the staff of such an official regarding the [*tax benefit*]?

Section 8: Educational Benefits

[*For recipients of Pell Grants, guaranteed student loans, GI Bill, and/or Hope/ Lifetime Learning Tax Credit, ask questions in this section; for others, skip to section 9*]

1. Did you complete the educational degree or certificate for which you used [*Read names of all that apply: Pell Grants or their precursor, student loans, the GI Bill, the Hope and Lifetime Learning Tax Credits*]?

2. Please indicate whether you agree or disagree with each of the following statements about your use of the following educational benefits: [*Read names of all that apply: Pell Grants or their precursor, student loans, the GI Bill, the Hope and Lifetime Learning Tax Credits*]:

a. If these/this educational benefit(s) had not existed, I would *not have considered* acquiring additional educational or training.

b. If these/this educational benefit(s) had not existed, I could *not have afforded* acquiring additional educational or training.

c. I would still have acquired further education or training even without these/this educational benefit(s) but *in a program of lesser cost, quality, or reputation.*

d. I would still have acquired further education or training even without these/this educational benefit(s) but *it would have taken me longer.*

e. I am satisfied that the education or training that I paid for with my student loan(s) was worth it.

3. Do you think of student loans *primarily* as a *public* program—that is, belonging to government—or as a *private* program—that is, belonging to lenders, banks, or academic institutions?

4. In your own personal experience, to what extent did student loans expand your opportunity to acquire more education or training: a great deal, quite a bit, some, very little, or not at all?

5. In your own personal experience, to what extent did student loans burden you with debts that are or were difficult to repay: a great deal, quite a bit, some, very little, or not at all?

6. What is the total amount, approximately, that you ever borrowed in student loans?

[*Prompt, if respondent has trouble remembering: "What is your best guess? For example, was it less than $2,000, $2,000 to less than $5,000, $5,000 to less than $10,000; $10,000 to less than $15,000; $15,000 to less than $20,000; $20,000 to under $25,000; $25,000 to under $35,000; $35,000 to under $50,000; $50,000 to under $75,000; or more than $75,000?"*]

Section 9: Political Interest

Now I'd like to ask you about your interest in politics.

1. Some people don't pay much attention to political campaigns. How about you? Thinking about the *presidential political campaign this year,* have you been extremely interested, very interested, somewhat interested, slightly interested, or not at all interested?

2. Some people seem to follow what's going on in government and public affairs most of the time, *whether there's an election or not.* Others aren't that interested. Would you say you follow what's going on in government and public affairs most of the time, some of the time, only now and then, or hardly at all?

Section 10: Political Knowledge

Now here are a few questions about the government in Washington.

1. Do you happen to know what job or political office is now held by Dick Cheney?

2. Whose responsibility is it to determine if a law is constitutional or not?

    a. The president
    b. Congress
    c. The Supreme Court
    d. Don't know

3. How much of a majority is required for the U.S. Senate and House to override a presidential veto?

4. Do you happen to know which major political party currently has the most members in the House of Representatives?

Section 11: Mobilization

1. As you know, the political candidates and parties try to talk to as many people as they can to get them to vote or to engage in other political activities. In the past five years, did any candidate for political office or anyone from one of the political parties call you up or come around and talk to you about voting or engaging in other political activities?

2. In the past five years, did anyone from a group *other than a political party,* not counting members of your own family, ever communicate with you about voting or engaging in other political activities?

Section 12: Political Views

Next, here are a few questions about your own political opinions.

1. When it comes to politics, do you usually think of yourself as extremely liberal, liberal, slightly liberal, moderate or middle-of-the-road, slightly conservative, conservative, or extremely conservative?

2. Generally speaking, do you think of yourself as a Republican, a Democrat, an independent, or what?

[If answer Republican/Democrat]:

Generally speaking, do you think of yourself as a strong Republican (Democrat) or not a very strong Republican (Democrat), or haven't you thought much about this?

[If answer independent]:

Would you say that you lean toward one of the two major parties—either Republican or Democratic—or haven't you thought much about this? If so, which party do you lean toward?

a. Republican
b. Democratic
c. Neither
d. Haven't thought much about this

Section 13: Demographics

1. What is the last grade or class that you completed in school or college?

a. Less than high school degree
b. High school degree (grade 12 or GED certificate)
c. Technical, trade, or vocational school *after* high school
d. Some college, no degree
e. Two-year college degree (associate's)
f. Four-year college degree (BA, BS, bachelor's)
g. Some postgraduate training or professional school *after* college, no degree
h. Master's degree
i. Doctoral degree (PhD) or professional degree (JD, DDS, MD, etc.)
j. Don't know
k. Refused

2. As an undergraduate student, did you attend a public college or university or a private college or university?

3. Are you currently single, married, separated, divorced, or widowed?

4. How many children do you yourself have?

5. Are you currently a citizen of the United States, or not?

6. What is the last grade or class that your mother completed in school or college?

7. What is the last grade or class that your father completed in school or college?

8. Thinking about the time when you were sixteen years old, compared with American families in general then, would you say your family income was far below average, below average, average, above average, or far above average?

9. We'd like to know your current employment status: are you employed now in a full-time, permanent or long-term position? Employed now in a part-time or temporary position? Are you temporarily laid off, unemployed, retired, permanently disabled, a homemaker, a student, or what?

10. Which describes your current primary health insurance coverage: do you have a plan offered through your employer (or your spouse/partner's employer), such as Blue Cross? Are you covered by a government plan such as Medicare or Medicaid? Do you have a plan that is not through an employer and for which you or your family pays? Or don't you currently have health insurance?

11. Do you have a retirement plan through an employer—either (a) an employer-provided traditional *pension* that pays you a set amount each month for life in retirement (a "defined benefit" plan—promises a specific monthly benefit at retirement; typically one must work a number of years in a job to be "vested" with pension benefits) or (b) an employer-sponsored *savings plan* such as a 401(k), 403(b), etc. (a "defined contribution" plan—requires employee to make investment decisions; no promises of a set monthly benefit at retirement; contributions are set aside "pretax" and are "tax-deferred"). Or do you have neither of these?

12. Are you of Hispanic origin or descent, such as Mexican, Puerto Rican, Cuban, or some other Spanish background?

13. What racial or ethnic group best describes you?

a. White or Caucasian
b. Black or African American
c. American Indian, Aleut, Eskimo
d. Asian or Pacific Islander
e. Something else (please specify)

14. Do you own your home or do you pay rent?

15. Have you ever belonged to a labor union?

16. What is your religious affiliation? Is it Protestant, Catholic, Christian Orthodox, Jewish, Muslim, some other religion, or no religion?

17. Last year, in 2007, what was your total household income from all sources, before taxes: was it under $50,000 or was it $50,000 or over? [*If under $50,000, read:*] Was it less than $10,000, $10,000 to under $20,000, $20,000 to under $30,000, $30,000 to under $40,000, or $40,000 to under $50,000? [*If $50,000 or over, read:*] Was it $50,000 to under $75,000, $75,000 to under $100,000, $100,000 to under $150,000, or $150,000 or more?

18. Have you ever been convicted of a felony?

19. We are looking for survey respondents who are willing to have an additional follow-up interview at some point in the next year, so that we can ask you more about the topics covered in today's interview. This may be another telephone interview, or it may be in-person, in which case the researcher would arrange to meet you at a location convenient to you. Might you be willing to be interviewed in this way, and if so, could we contact you about it?

SURVEY RESPONSE RATE AND COMPARISON TO EXISTING STUDIES

The overall response rate for the Social and Governmental Issues and Participation survey (SGIP), meaning the percentage of households *sampled* that yielded an interview, was 21 percent according to the guidelines for AAPOR response rate number 1, and 34 percent according to response rate number 3. The cooperation rate, meaning the percentage of households *contacted* that yielded an interview, was 56 percent, and the contact rate, meaning the percentage of households in which an adult was reached, was 65 percent. The refusal rate was 16 percent (AAPOR response rate number 1). These rates compare favorably to those of other surveys conducted in the same period.[1]

As noted in appendix A, the survey was data weighted. Table C.1 shows how survey demographics, weighted and unweighted, compared to those in the American National Election Study and General Social Survey conducted in the same year.

The SGIP is unique in that it asks a national random sample of Americans whether they have *ever* used any of several social policies. One other survey, conducted four years later, asked a similar question: the Gender and Generations Survey, conducted by the Pew Research Center in November 2012. It asked about only eight policies, in contrast to the twenty-one investigated in the SGIP. It also used different question wording, asking respondents to distinguish whether "you or anyone in your household" had ever received each policy, whereas the SGIP study said, "Now I'd like to ask you about your experiences with several government policies over the course of your life. Could you tell me if you personally have at any time received benefits or payments from any of the following social programs?"[2] The participation rates reported in each study are shown in table C.2.

Table C.1 Demographics of Sample in Social and Governmental Issues and Participation Study (SGIP) Compared to Demographics in American National Election Studies (ANES) and General Social Survey (GSS)

	ANES 2008		GSS 2008		SGIP 2008	
	UNWEIGHTED	**WEIGHTED**	**UNWEIGHTED**	**WEIGHTED**	**UNWEIGHTED**	**WEIGHTED**
Gender						
Male	43%	44.9%	45.97%	47.44%	45.6%	48.8%
Female	57.0	55.1	54.03	52.56	54.3	51.1
Age						
Eighteen to thirty-four	27.4	30.0	26.20	28.70	27.5	28.2
Thirty-five to forty-four	17.7	15.8	18.83	19.46	16.4	17.2
Forty-five to fifty-four	21.6	21.6	20.57	21.48	21.8	23.9
Fifty-five to sixty-four	15.9	15.1	15.60	15.01	17.3	14.7
Sixty-five and older	16.5	1.07	18.63	15.37	17.0	16.1
Education						
High school graduate or less	46.8	43.2	45.50	44.40	27.2	37.2
Some college/associate's degree	31.2	28.8	25.27	27.43	33.1	37.1
College graduate or higher	21.6	28.0	29.09	28.13	39.7	25.7

(continued)

Table C.1 (*continued*)

	ANES 2008		GSS 2008		SGIP 2008	
	UNWEIGHTED	WEIGHTED	UNWEIGHTED	WEIGHTED	UNWEIGHTED	WEIGHTED
Race-ethnicity						
White (may include Hispanic)	62.5	79.5	77.06	77.08	74.7	71.1
African American	25.0	12.0	13.89	13.31	14.9	16.6
Some other race	11.0	7.4	9.05	9.62	10.3	12.3
More than one race	1.1.0	1.0	–	–	–	–
Latino (yes/no)						
Latino	21.3	9.0	11.74	13.75	8.7	12.1
Region						
Northeast	10.7	14.1	17.55	17.17	16.7	17.5
North Central	17.0	21.0	23.18	22.08	22.8	20.3
South	47.6	43.5	37.07	37.88	41.9	42.2
West	24.7	21.4	22.19	22.88	18.7	19.9

Source: 2008 ANES; 2008 GSS; 2008 SGIP.

Table C.2 Participation Rates for Social and Governmental Issues and Participation Study and Gender and Generation Survey

	SGIP 2008	PEW 2012: RESPONDENT	PEW 2012: NET (RESPONDENT OR SOMEONE IN HOUSEHOLD)
Federal grants or loans for college	32.0% (student loans and/or Pell Grants)	26%	38%
Food stamps	25.4	18	26
Medicaid	17.5	11	20
Medicare	22.2	22	31
Social Security benefits	15.8 (retirement and survivors') + 9.7 (disability) = 25.5	26	36
Unemployment benefits	38.5	27	38
Veterans' benefits	4.6 (other than GI Bill) + 5.9 (GI Bill) = 10.5	8	14
Welfare benefits	13.9	8	11

Source: 2008 SGIP; 2012 Gender and Generations Survey.

Comparing the first two columns in table C.2, the SGIP yielded identical response rates for the two programs that were entitlements and not countercyclical, Social Security and Medicare.[3] Respondents reported higher lifetime usage rates of the countercyclical programs in the SGIP study than in the Pew study. Several factors may account for this: for example, the 2008 study was conducted near the beginning of the financial downturn, when usage of the countercyclical programs spiked, making usage of them more common and probably more salient in respondents' memories. In the case of some policies such as food stamps and Unemployment Insurance, the SGIP individual usage rates more closely reflect the net household usage rates reported by Pew (right-hand column), possibly suggesting that it effectively generated answers indicating general household use.[4] Also, the SGIP study was explicitly designed to prompt memory of past experiences, through a long battery of questions about political participation at specific junctures in individuals' lives that preceded the policy questions, the inclusion of careful descriptors to help respondents identify programs, and several follow-up questions about program delivery and policy experiences for any policy to which a respondent indicated prior usage, a process that probably predisposed respondents to more careful memory retrieval and reporting.[5] Unlike the Pew study, the SGIP followed several procedures to avoid undersampling those with lower socioeconomic status: (a) because low-income and young people are typically underrepresented in surveys, the SGIP study included an oversample of two hundred of each (see appendix A), whereas Pew used only a national random sample; (b) the SGIP was in the field for seventy-one days compared to only eight days by Pew; and (c) respondents for the SGIP were called as many as thirty times compared to only seven times in the case of the Pew study. Finally, the Pew study was conducted shortly after the 2012 presidential campaign, during which political discourse had criticized beneficiaries of social programs, possibly making individuals less willing to report prior usage.

The policy usage estimates reached through these cross-sectional approaches are likely to be conservative compared to what would be gained by panel data. This is evidenced in the use by researchers Mark Rank and Thomas Hirschl of the Panel Study of Income Dynamics, which permits overall lifetime assessments of usage of a small number of programs from 1968 to 1997. They arrive at higher rates than those in the SGIP: by age fifty, they estimate, 30 percent of Americans will have used a cash welfare program and 50 percent will have used in-kind assistance.[6] For food stamps in particular, they estimate that over half of Americans (50.8 percent) will use them at some point between ages twenty and sixty-five.[7]

INTERVIEW SCHEDULE FOR OPEN-ENDED PHONE INTERVIEWS

Hello, my name is _____, and I'm calling from Cornell University. I'd like to speak with _____.

Hello, my name is _____, and I'm calling from Cornell University. I'm calling in reference to the follow-up interview for the study of Americans' experiences of public policy; you recently sent a form back to us indicating that you are willing to be interviewed once again. Is now a good time for that interview? [*If not, ask: "When shall I call back?"*]

1. Several years have passed since we spoke with you last. Many Americans have faced economic challenges at some point in recent years. How about you? How have you and your family gotten by over these years? Have you had any major changes in your circumstances in terms of (a) jobs or employment; (b) health (c) going to school, or (d) any other developments that affect your economic security?

2. To what extent does or has government helped you and your family in terms of economic security, health coverage, or educational opportunity? Would you say it has helped you or not helped you? [*Distinguish between whether government is helping "presently," "in recent years," and/or "ever in your life."*] [*If "helped" at any of these times, ask:*]: Would you say it has helped you some or a great deal? [*If "not helped," ask:*]: Would you say it has not helped you much, or not helped you at all? Explain. [*If respondent feels that government has helped, probe how, through which policies, how did it make a difference, etc. If respondent feels that government has not helped, ask him or her to explain: is it a matter of not having qualified for any policies, or using policies that were not helpful, etc.*]

3. I'm going to use a term that means different things to different people:

"government social programs." What do you think of when you hear that phrase? Is there a particular policy or policies that come to mind? Do you think of "government social programs" in a mostly positive or mostly negative way? Why? Explain.

4. Some people tell us that they claim various tax preferences or tax breaks—for example, the home mortgage interest deduction, a lower rate for capital gains, and so forth.

    a. Do you consider these policies to be a form of government social benefits, like Unemployment Insurance or grants to go to college, for example, in which government is helping to provide people with economic security and opportunity, or do you think of them differently? Why do you think of them the way you do?

    b. These policies mean that some people pay less in taxes than others who have the same income. For example, someone who owns a house and has a mortgage pays less in taxes than someone with the same income who rents an apartment. Do you think that's fair and appropriate? Why/why not?

    c. Let's imagine that these policies operated differently: instead of people who qualify for them getting a tax break, government could send them a check for the same amount. Would you be in favor of that, or do you think it's better that they operate as they do, with people claiming them just by paying less in taxes? Why?

5. Have you ever used or received any of these policies: The home mortgage interest deduction? The Earned Income Tax Credit? Employer-provided retirement benefits? Employer-provided health coverage? If so, which one(s)? [*If yes to EITC, ask question 6; if others, continue here, then go to question 7.*] What was that experience like? Did it make much of a difference in your life? If so, how? Do you think of the reduction in your taxes that comes with this policy as a government benefit, something owed to you because of your employment, or what?

6. Tell me about receiving EITC. How did you learn about it? How did you claim it? Did you fill out the forms yourself, or did someone or an organization help you? Who/where? What was that experience like? How do you feel you were treated? What difference did EITC make in your life? Explain. Do you think of EITC as a government benefit, or as something owed to you because of your employment, or what? Why?

7.

   a. Have you ever been unemployed? [*If no, go to question 8. If yes, continue.*] Roughly how long ago was that? What state were you living in at the time?

   b. Did you receive unemployment insurance/compensation? [*If no, go to question 7(d).*]

   c. Tell me about that experience. Was it hard/easy to apply for unemployment insurance/compensation and to claim it, and why? What was the process like? For how long did you use it? Were the funds sufficient? Explain. How helpful were the benefits? If you could change some aspect of how the program is run, what would it be?

   d. Why not? Did you try to claim unemployment insurance/compensation and were denied, and if so, why? Did you not try to claim it, and if not, why not? What state were you living in? If you could change some aspect of how the program is run, what would it be?

8. Have you ever used food stamps, or SNAP? When was that? What was/is the experience like? How did/do you feel you were/are treated in the process? Was it hard/easy to apply for it and to claim it, and why? For how long did you use it? Was the amount of the benefits sufficient? Explain. What difference did/does it make in your life? How helpful were the benefits? If you could change some aspect of how the program is run, what would it be?

9. Have you ever used Medicaid [*or same program with state-level name*]? When was that? What was/is the experience like? How did/do you feel you were/are treated in the process? Was it hard/easy to apply for it and to claim it, and why? For how long did you use it? Was the amount of the benefits sufficient? Explain. What difference did/does it make in your life? How helpful were the benefits? If you could change some aspect of how the program is run, what would it be?

10. Has the new health care law enacted in 2010 made any difference in your life? For example, have you gained coverage under the state exchanges, or through expanded Medicaid benefits, or for an adult child under age twenty-six? [*If yes, ask:*] What was/is the experience like? How did/do you feel you were/are treated in the process? Was it hard/easy to apply for it and

to claim it, and why? Explain. What difference did/does it make in your life? How helpful were the benefits? If you could change some aspect of how the program is run, what would it be?

11. Do you think government should do *more* or *less* than it does in: (a) helping people to get jobs? (b) helping to raise how much people get paid? (c) other ways providing for the economic security of individuals and families? Why? What do you think it could/should do differently? Explain. [*If less, probe rationale: Is it because respondent thinks people are deserving/undeserving? Or is it because respondent has not experienced government to be valuable/effective?*]

12. Is there anything else you'd like to say about the topics we've covered?

That's all. Thank you so much for your time! We very much appreciate your participation in this study.

ADDITIONAL CHAPTER 4 AND 5 TABLES

Chapter 4 Analyses

Table E.1 Determinants of Favorable Attitude Toward Welfare

	FAVORS WELFARE		FAVORS WELFARE
High school graduate	−0.49	Male	−0.197
	(0.361)		(0.130)
Some college or associate's degree	−0.603	Black or African American	0.482*
	(0.356)		(0.192)
Bachelor's degree	−0.493	American Indian, Aleut, Eskimo	0.772
	(0.372)		(0.482)
Graduate degree	−0.431	Asian or Pacific Islander	1.685**
	(0.392)		(0.632)
$20,000 to $34,999	−0.0000334	Other race	−0.0902
	(0.238)		(0.291)
$35,000 to $49,999	−0.848***	Hispanic	0.118
	(0.219)		(0.264)
$50,000 to $74,999	−0.497*	Constant	1.199***
	(0.230)		(0.349)
$75,000 to $99,999	−0.990***	N	1238
	(0.257)		
$100,000 or more	−0.39		
	(0.249)		

Source: 2008 SGIP.
Note: Weighted binary logistic regression. Standard errors in parentheses.
***$p < .001$; **$p < .01$; *$p < .05$

Table E.2 Determinants of Attitudes About Government: Considering Lifetime Policy Usage

	GOVERNMENT HAS HELPED ME IN TIMES OF NEED		GOVERNMENT HAS GIVEN ME OPPORTUNITIES		PUBLIC OFFICIALS DON'T CARE MUCH WHAT PEOPLE LIKE ME THINK	
	CO-EFFICIENT	MARGINAL EFFECTS	CO-EFFICIENT	MARGINAL EFFECTS	CO-EFFICIENT	MARGINAL EFFECTS
Age	0.003	0.001	0.006	0.001	0.004	0.001
	(0.006)	(0.001)	(0.005)	(0.001)	(0.006)	(0.001)
Nonwhite	−0.608**	−0.121**	0.129	0.029	−0.093	−0.019
	(0.202)	(0.038)	(0.174)	(0.039)	(0.197)	(0.041)
Hispanic	0.435	0.088	0.119	0.027	−0.319	−0.068
	(0.297)	(0.059)	(0.268)	(0.059)	(0.281)	(0.062)
Male	0.169	0.034	0.252	0.057	0.223	0.045
	(0.158)	(0.032)	(0.143)	(0.032)	(0.149)	(0.030)
Some college	−0.026	−0.005	0.037	0.008	−0.100	−0.020
	(0.201)	(0.041)	(0.180)	(0.041)	(0.199)	(0.039)
College graduate	0.171	0.035	0.404*	0.0893*	−0.514*	−0.108*
	(0.210)	(0.042)	(0.202)	(0.044)	(0.210)	(0.044)
Income	−0.060	−0.012	0.005	0.001	−0.097	−0.020
	(0.059)	(0.012)	(0.056)	(0.013)	(0.059)	(0.012)
Partisanship (Republican = 1)	0.069	0.014	−0.140**	−0.0315**	0.118*	0.0240*
	(0.046)	(0.009)	(0.044)	(0.010)	(0.047)	(0.010)
Attitude toward welfare	0.451***	0.0920***	0.519***	0.117***	−0.343***	−0.0699***
	(0.084)	(0.016)	(0.077)	(0.016)	(0.084)	(0.017)
Number of visible and means-tested policies used	0.596***	0.122***	0.067	0.015	0.008	0.002
	(0.084)	(0.015)	(0.057)	(0.013)	(0.061)	(0.012)
Number of submerged and means-tested policies used	0.178	0.036	−0.282*	−0.0632*	0.339*	0.0692*
	(0.141)	(0.029)	(0.133)	(0.030)	(0.138)	(0.028)
Number of visible and non-means-tested policies used	0.141	0.029	0.101	0.023	−0.061	−0.013
	(0.089)	(0.018)	(0.078)	(0.017)	(0.084)	(0.017)
Number of submerged and non-means-tested policies used	−0.020	−0.004	−0.013	−0.003	−0.069	−0.014
	(0.068)	(0.014)	(0.063)	(0.014)	(0.066)	(0.014)
Constant	−1.919***		−1.074**		1.522***	
	(0.461)		(0.398)		(0.427)	
N	1,036	1,036	1,115	1,115	1,120	1,120

Source: 2008 SGIP.

Note: First six models are weighted binary logistic regressions. Standard errors are in parentheses. Final model is a weighted generalized ordinal logit model.

†indicates coefficient does not meet parallel lines assumption. Coefficient = −.023*, OR = .977*

***p < .01; **p < .05; *p < .10

PEOPLE LIKE ME DON'T HAVE ANY SAY		I FEEL LIKE A FULL CITIZEN		SATISFIED WITH THE WAY DEMOCRACY WORKS IN THE UNITED STATES		I PAY MY FAIR SHARE IN TAXES	
CO-EFFICIENT	MARGINAL EFFECTS	CO-EFFICIENT	MARGINAL EFFECTS	CO-EFFICIENT	MARGINAL EFFECTS	CO-EFFICIENT	ODDS RATIOS
0.000	0.000	0.0155*	0.00252*	0.001	0.000	0.00511†	1.005
(0.005)	(0.001)	(0.006)	(0.001)	(0.005)	(0.001)	(0.005)	[0.995, 1.016]
-0.183	-0.042	-0.782***	-0.139***	0.068	0.016	-0.770***	0.463***
(0.178)	(0.041)	(0.201)	(0.038)	(0.174)	(0.041)	(0.181)	[0.324, 0.661]
-0.140	-0.032	0.728*	0.104**	0.686*	0.154**	0.204	1.227
(0.262)	(0.061)	(0.324)	(0.040)	(0.275)	(0.057)	(0.271)	[0.721, 2.087]
0.177	0.041	0.298	0.049	-0.013	-0.003	0.622***	1.862***
(0.140)	(0.032)	(0.176)	(0.029)	(0.140)	(0.033)	(0.137)	[1.423, 2.436]
-0.639***	-0.152***	0.048	0.008	0.076	0.018	0.173	1.189
(0.179)	(0.042)	(0.205)	(0.035)	(0.176)	(0.042)	(0.175)	[0.844, 1.675]
-0.939***	-0.223***	0.374	0.059	0.256	0.060	0.542**	1.719**
(0.196)	(0.046)	(0.239)	(0.038)	(0.193)	(0.046)	(0.197)	[1.167, 2.531]
-0.142**	-0.0330**	0.042	0.007	0.101	0.024	-0.107*	0.899*
(0.054)	(0.012)	(0.066)	(0.011)	(0.054)	(0.013)	(0.050)	[0.814, 0.992]
0.115**	0.0267**	-0.187***	-0.0304***	-0.200***	-0.0468***	-0.030	0.970
(0.043)	(0.010)	(0.054)	(0.009)	(0.043)	(0.010)	(0.044)	[0.891, 1.057]
-0.245**	-0.0568***	0.294***	0.0478***	0.298***	0.0697***	0.229**	1.257**
(0.076)	(0.017)	(0.088)	(0.014)	(0.075)	(0.017)	(0.075)	[1.086, 1.456]
-0.032	-0.007	-0.094	-0.015	-0.014	-0.003	0.0523	1.054
(0.056)	(0.013)	(0.062)	(0.010)	(0.055)	(0.013)	(0.055)	[0.947, 1.173]
0.259*	0.0601*	-0.305*	-0.0497*	-0.097	-0.023	0.307*	1.360*
(0.127)	(0.029)	(0.152)	(0.025)	(0.126)	(0.030)	(0.121)	[1.073, 1.724]
-0.018	-0.004	-0.027	-0.004	-0.031	-0.007	0.0643	1.066
(0.077)	(0.018)	(0.093)	(0.015)	(0.080)	(0.019)	(0.077)	[0.917, 1.240]
-0.001	0.000	0.138	0.022	0.012	0.003	-0.0322	0.968
(0.060)	(0.014)	(0.073)	(0.012)	(0.060)	(0.014)	(0.058)	[0.863, 1.086]
0.976*		0.188		-0.272		-0.550	
(0.398)		(0.457)		(0.392)		(0.395)	
1,134	1,134	1,131	1,131	1,137	1,137	1,135	1,135

Table E.3 Relationship Between EITC and AFDC/TANF Receipt and Attitudes About Government

	GOVERNMENT HAS HELPED ME IN TIMES OF NEED	GOVERNMENT HAS GIVEN ME OPPORTUNITIES	PUBLIC OFFICIALS DON'T CARE MUCH WHAT PEOPLE LIKE ME THINK	PEOPLE LIKE ME DON'T HAVE ANY SAY	I PAY MY FAIR SHARE IN TAXES
Used EITC only	0.0531	-0.0799*	0.0693*	0.0855*	1.5220**
	(0.040)	(0.0390)	(0.0340)	(0.0380)	[1.1084, 2.0894]
Used AFDC/TANF only	0.228**	0.064	-0.0751	-0.0158	1.5650
	(0.080)	(0.076)	(0.0780)	(0.0800)	[0.8297, 2.9533]
Used both EITC and AFDC/TANF	0.382**	-0.00635	-0.0602	0.0291	1.6690
	(0.048)	(0.06300)	(0.0690)	(0.0650)	[0.9878, 2.8188]
Income (five categories)	-0.0470**	-0.00616	-0.0355**	-0.0348*	0.8660*
	(0.015)	(0.014)	(0.014)	(0.014)	[0.7691, 0.9745]
Partisanship (5-point scale, 1 = Republican)	0.0340***	-0.0200*	0.0214*	0.0233*	0.9930
	(0.0100)	(0.0100)	(0.0090)	(0.0100)	[0.9138, 1.0782]
Current age	0.00076	0.000548	0.0015	0.000882	0.9450*
	(0.00100)	(0.001000)	(0.0010)	(0.00100)	[0.8997, 0.9928]
Age-squared	(0.00100)	(0.001000)	(0.0010)	(0.00100)	1.0010*

	Model 1	Model 2	Model 3	Model 4	Model 5
					[1.0001, 1.0011]
Nonwhite	-0.073	0.0357	-0.0388	-0.0733	0.4860***
	(0.040)	(0.0400)	(0.0410)	(0.0400)	[0.3428, 0.6886]
Hispanic	0.0262	0.00112	-0.036	-0.0133	1.2060
	(0.0600)	(0.06100)	(0.060)	(0.0610)	[0.7034 - 2.0670]
Male	0.0376	0.0409	0.0419	0.0402	1.7950***
	(0.0330)	(0.0320)	(0.0300)	(0.0320)	[1.3756, 2.3411]
Some college	0.00329	-0.0198	0.0166	-0.132**	1.2090
	(0.04300)	(0.0420)	(0.0390)	(0.042)	[0.8607, 1.6975]
Bachelor's degree or higher	0.0438	0.0744	-0.108*	-0.211***	1.8730***
	(0.0440)	(0.0430)	(0.042)	(0.044)	[1.2964, 2.7056]
Has felony record	0.135	0.124	0.132	0.187*	1.0210
	(0.077)	(0.072)	(0.073)	(0.085)	[0.4734, 2.2015]
Observations	1,033	1,110	1,116	1,132	1,135
F	5.345	2.992	3.742	5.104	5.059

Source: 2008 SGIP.

Note: Models 1 to 4 are weighted logistic regressions; average marginal effects are presented, and standard errors are in parentheses. Model 5 is a weighted ordinal logit model; odds ratios are presented, and confidence intervals are in brackets.

***$p < .01$; **$p < .05$; *$p < .10$

Table E.4 Higher Education Policy Receipt and Determinants of View That Government Provided Opportunities to Improve Standard of Living

	GI BILL		PELL GRANTS		STUDENT LOANS	
	CO-EFFICIENT	MARGINAL EFFECTS	CO-EFFICIENT	MARGINAL EFFECTS	CO-EFFICIENT	MARGINAL EFFECTS
Education policy	0.998**	0.229**	0.419*	0.0968*	0.271	0.063
	(0.344)	(0.077)	(0.203)	(0.046)	(0.180)	(0.041)
Age	0.001	0.000	0.007	0.002	0.007	0.002
	(0.005)	(0.001)	(0.005)	(0.001)	(0.006)	(0.001)
Nonwhite	−0.073	−0.017	−0.105	−0.024	−0.065	−0.015
	(0.210)	(0.049)	(0.212)	(0.049)	(0.212)	(0.049)
Hispanic	−0.283	−0.066	−0.311	−0.073	−0.365	−0.087
	(0.351)	(0.083)	(0.348)	(0.083)	(0.349)	(0.084)
Male	0.065	0.015	0.219	0.051	0.198	0.046
	(0.173)	(0.040)	(0.167)	(0.038)	(0.166)	(0.039)
College graduate	0.190	0.044	0.171	0.039	0.141	0.033
	(0.170)	(0.039)	(0.171)	(0.039)	(0.174)	(0.041)
Income	0.034	0.008	0.026	0.006	0.013	0.003
	(0.056)	(0.013)	(0.055)	(0.013)	(0.054)	(0.013)
Partisanship	−0.037	−0.008	−0.037	−0.008	−0.037	−0.009
(Republican = 1)	(0.050)	(0.012)	(0.051)	(0.012)	(0.051)	(0.012)
Attitude toward welfare	0.425***	0.098***	0.392***	0.090***	0.392***	0.091***
	(0.094)	(0.020)	(0.094)	(0.021)	(0.094)	(0.021)
Constant	−0.846*		−1.090**		−1.030*	
	(0.394)		(0.407)		(0.414)	
N	797	797	797	797	798	798

Source: 2008 SGIP.

Note: All models are binary logistic regressions. Second column presents average marginal effects. Standard errors are in parentheses.

***p < .01; **p < .05; *p < .10

HOPE CREDIT		529 PLANS		PELL GRANTS AND STUDENT LOANS	
CO-EFFICIENT	MARGINAL EFFECTS	CO-EFFICIENT	MARGINAL EFFECTS	CO-EFFICIENT	MARGINAL EFFECTS
−0.099	−0.023	−0.171	−0.040	0.353	0.081
(0.217)	(0.051)	(0.320)	(0.074)	(0.218)	(0.050)
				0.179	0.041
				(0.192)	(0.044)
0.004	0.001	0.004	0.001	0.008	0.002
(0.005)	(0.001)	(0.005)	(0.001)	(0.006)	(0.001)
−0.046	−0.011	−0.046	−0.011	−0.106	−0.025
(0.210)	(0.049)	(0.211)	(0.049)	(0.213)	(0.050)
−0.365	−0.087	−0.306	−0.072	−0.321	−0.076
(0.348)	(0.084)	(0.352)	(0.084)	(0.348)	(0.083)
0.192	0.045	0.214	0.050	0.226	0.052
(0.166)	(0.039)	(0.167)	(0.039)	(0.167)	(0.038)
0.199	0.046	0.184	0.043	0.145	0.033
(0.171)	(0.040)	(0.171)	(0.040)	(0.175)	(0.040)
0.015	0.004	0.024	0.006	0.024	0.005
(0.054)	(0.013)	(0.054)	(0.013)	(0.055)	(0.013)
−0.028	−0.007	−0.026	−0.006	−0.038	−0.009
(0.051)	(0.012)	(0.051)	(0.012)	(0.051)	(0.012)
0.384***	0.090***	0.404***	0.094***	0.390***	0.090***
(0.094)	(0.021)	(0.095)	(0.021)	(0.094)	(0.021)
−0.814*		−0.907*		−1.173**	
(0.397)		(0.390)		(0.420)	
792	792	788	788	797	797

Chapter 5 Analyses

Table E.5 Determinants of Support for Social Provision: Considering Lifetime Policy Usage

	SPENDING IDEOLOGY		FAVORS HEALTH INSURANCE FOR ALL	
	COEFFICIENT[a]	ODDS RATIOS[b]	COEFFICIENT[a]	MARGINAL EFFECTS[a]
Age	-0.0228***	0.977***	-0.0174*	-0.00307**
	(0.0060)	[0.967, 0.988]	(0.0070)	(0.00100)
Nonwhite	0.512*	1.668*	-0.331	-0.0579
	(0.219)	[1.085, 2.565]	(0.215)	(0.0370)
Hispanic	-0.0709	0.932	0.417	0.0718
	(0.3230)	[0.494, 1.755]	(0.351)	(0.058)
Male	-0.278	0.757	0.00791	0.00139
	(0.147)	[0.567, 1.010]	(0.15900)	(0.02800)
Some college	-0.425*	0.654*	-0.111	-0.0196
	(0.190)	[0.450, 0.949]	(0.214)	(0.0380)
College graduate	-0.263	0.768	0.0784	0.0137
	(0.206)	[0.513, 1.151]	(0.2250)	(0.0390)
Income	-0.0481	0.953	0.0905	0.016
	(0.0550)	[0.856, 1.061]	(0.0650)	(0.011)
Partisanship (Republican = 1)	0.464***	1.591***	0.498***	0.0878***
	(0.045)	[1.456, 1.739]	(0.050)	(0.0070)
Attitude toward welfare	0.910***c	2.484***	0.579***	0.102***
	(0.116)	[1.980, 3.118]	(0.089)	(0.015)
Number of visible and means-tested policies used	0.217***	1.243***	0.191**	0.0336**
	(0.066)	[1.093, 1.414]	(0.068)	(0.0120)
Number of submerged and means-tested policies used	0.250	1.284	0.119	0.0209
	(0.138)	[0.979, 1.685]	(0.150)	(0.0270)
Number of visible and non-means-tested policies used	0.231**	1.259**	0.103	0.0181
	(0.082)	[1.071, 1.480]	(0.095)	(0.0170)
Number of submerged and non-means-tested policies used	0.0764	1.079	0.00821	0.00145
	(0.0670)	[0.947, 1.231]	(0.07000)	(0.01200)
Constant	-0.696		-2.106***	
	(0.430)		(0.480)	
N	1,143	1,143	1,126	1,126

Source: 2008 SGIP.

Note: First model is a weighted generalized ordinal logit model. Second model is a weighted binary logistic regression.

[a] Standard errors are in parentheses.

[b] Exponentiated coefficients; 95 percent confidence intervals are in brackets.

[c] Coefficient does not meet parallel assumptions. Second coefficient = 0.0534*** (0.0830); marginal effect = 1.706*** [1.450, 2.007].

***$p < .001$; **$p < .01$; *$p < .05$

Table E.6 Relationship Between EITC or AFDC/TANF Receipt and Political Behavior

	REGISTERED TO VOTE	VOTED IN PRESIDENTIAL ELECTIONS	VOTED IN NON-PRESIDENTIAL ELECTIONS	PARTICI-PATION INDEX
Used EITC only	0.0886***	0.1120	0.2120*	1.1760**
	(0.0223)	(0.0873)	(0.0875)	[1.0463, 1.3223]
Used AFDC/TANF only	0.0346	−0.240	−0.238	0.8000
	(0.0502)	(0.218)	(0.229)	[0.5624, 1.1369]
Used both EITC and AFDC/TANF	−0.00476	−0.0802	0.0448	1.1700
	(0.04300)	(0.1670)	(0.1670)	[0.9621, 1.4219]
Income (five categories)	0.0474***	0.1260***	0.1110**	1.0820**
	(0.0092)	(0.0362)	(0.0373)	[1.0307, 1.1364]
Partisanship (5-point scale, 1 = Republican)	0.0112	−0.00175	0.00659	1.0300
	(0.0063)	(0.02040)	(0.02220)	[0.9997, 1.0607]
Current age	0.00357***	0.0177	0.0251**	1.0350**
	(0.00080)	(0.0030)	(0.0028)	[1.0134, 1.0569]
Age-squared				1.0000*
				[0.9996, 1.0000]
Nonwhite	0.0292	0.170	−0.0860	0.9620
	(0.0267)	(0.104)	(0.1010)	[0.8439, 1.0959]
Hispanic	−0.1390**	−0.494**	−0.346*	0.8410
	(0.0470)	(0.189)	(0.165)	[0.6569, 1.0757]
Male	−0.0437*	−0.1670*	0.00523	1.2010***
	(0.0216)	(0.0763)	(0.07910)	[1.0881, 1.3260]
Some college	0.0355	0.241*	0.196	1.5060***
	(0.0260)	(0.102)	(0.103)	[1.2748, 1.7796]
Bachelor's degree or higher	0.0992***	0.5190***	0.4910***	2.1670***
	(0.0244)	(0.0945)	(0.1000)	[1.8268, 2.5710]
Has felony record	−0.0969	−0.528*	−0.419*	0.8150
	(0.0533)	(0.227)	(0.209)	[0.6246, 1.0624]
Constant		1.730***	0.386	
		(0.445)	(0.404)	
Observations	1,140	1,074	1,110	1,136
F	7.665			21.97
R-squared	.	0.168	0.164	

Source: 2008 SGIP.
Note: Model 1 is weighted logistic regressions; average marginal effects are presented, and standard errors are in parentheses. Models 2 and 3 are weighted OLS; average marginal effects are presented, and standard errors are in parentheses. Model 4 is weighted poisson regression; incidence rate ratios are presented, and confidence intervals are in brackets.
***$p < .01$; **$p < .05$; *$p < .10$

APPENDIX F

T-TESTS OF KENTUCKY VOTER TURNOUT

Table F.1 *T*-Tests of Kentucky Voter Turnout by County, Overall and Among Registered Voters by Party, 2012 and 2014

	REPUBLICAN		DEMOCRAT		TOTAL	
	MEAN	**MEDIAN**	**MEAN**	**MEDIAN**	**MEAN**	**MEDIAN**
2012						
High transfer	0.5708	0.5763	0.4938	0.5043	0.5291	0.5360
Low transfer	0.6172	0.6188	0.5991	0.6046	0.5985	0.6022
Difference	−0.0463***	−0.0425***	−0.1053***	−0.1002***	−0.0693***	−0.0662***
2014						
High transfer	0.4917	0.4926	0.4451	0.4500	0.4740	0.4756
Low transfer	0.4650	0.4619	0.4982	0.4977	0.4771	0.4757
Difference	0.02670**	0.03070**	−0.0530***	−0.0477***	−0.0030	−0.0001

Source: 2008 SGIP.

Note: Tables show *t*-tests of registered voter turnout for Kentucky counties, comparing means in counties with high levels of federal government social transfers and low levels of transfers. Differences are the mean voter turnout in high-transfer counties minus the mean in low-transfer counties, and hypothesis tests were conducted relative to zero. Counties are coded as high or low counties in two ways. The "mean" columns show the averages based on whether counties are above or below the mean level of government transfers as a percentage of personal income for the state of Kentucky. The "median" columns show the averages based on whether counties are above or below the median level of transfers for Kentucky. In Kentucky, the mean level of transfer is 0.31, and the median is 0.29. Medians here might be preferred, since they are less susceptible to outlier biases. Nonetheless, these findings are robust to either coding decision.

***p < .01; **p < .05; *p < .10

NOTES

CHAPTER 1: A TIME OF CONTRADICTION

1. Apologies to Charles Dickens, *A Tale of Two Cities* (1859).
2. Pew Research Center 2015.
3. Author's analysis, American National Election Studies (ANES), Cumulative Data, 1948–2012.
4. Gallup 2017a; Fournier and Quinton 2012; Associated Press/NORC 2015.
5. Riffkin 2015.
6. In fact, the "entitlement" benefits comprised 58 percent of all benefits in 2014—almost identical to the 57 percent in 1969. This figure crested at a high point of 64 percent in the late 1980s.
7. Organization for Economic Cooperation and Development 2016, figs. 1 and 4.
8. These policies include: Head Start; Social Security Disability Insurance (SSDI), Social Security retirement, and Supplemental Security Income (SSI); Medicaid and Medicare; Temporary Assistance for Needy Families (TANF, or welfare); the GI Bill and other veterans' benefits; Unemployment Insurance (UI); the Supplemental Nutrition Assistance Program (SNAP, or food stamps); government-subsidized housing and the home mortgage interest deduction; the Hope Credit, the Lifetime Learning Credit, the Child and Dependent Care Tax Credit, and the Earned Income Tax Credit (EITC); Pell Grants, federal student loans, 529 plans (qualified tuition programs), and Coverdell Education Savings Accounts (education IRAs); and employer-subsidized health insurance and retirement benefits.
9. Author's analysis of the Social and Governmental Issues and Participation Study (SGIP), conducted in 2008.
10. Morone 1990.
11. On the end of the draft, see Borstelmann 2011, 153–54.
12. Mettler 2011.
13. I am grateful to Steven Maynard-Moody, at the University of Kansas, who made me aware of the data utilized here, which are from the U.S. Bureau of Economic Analysis. These data have also been showcased in White et al. (2012) and Eberstadt (2012).

14. The exceptions—those tax expenditures included among "federal transfers"—are the EITC, the child tax credits, and a few other smaller tax expenditures.

15. Howard 1997; Hacker 2002; Mettler 2011.

16. The Tax Cuts and Jobs Act of 2017 scaled back the value of the home mortgage interest deduction in a couple of major ways, and these categories are expected to reduce the percentage of homeowners who claim it from 44 to 14 percent. First, it reduced the amount of interest that can be deducted, from that incurred on mortgages of up to $750,000, not 1.1 million as was the case previously, though this change will expire in 2026. Second, the standard deduction was increased, such that many fewer homeowners will find it worthwhile to itemize deductions, and therefore will not claim it. Engquist 2018.

17. Pew Charitable Trusts 2013.

18. Reagan 1981.

19. Brewer and Stonecash 2015; Mounk 2017.

20. The social science literature illuminating this approach is voluminous. For examples, see Wilson (1996) and Hochschild (1996).

21. The Personal Responsibility and Work Opportunity Reconciliation Act (PRWORA) of 1996 was signed into law by Democratic president Bill Clinton, but it represents only a partial exception to the rule, as it was designed by the Republican-dominated Congress. Still, by vowing to "end welfare as we know it," Clinton was responding to a strongly held view among the white working class (Williams 2017, 23).

22. Murray 2012; Harsanyi 2007.

23. Sykes 1993, 2011; Eberstadt 2012.

24. Pew Research Center 2012a; Brewer and Stonecash 2015.

25. Brewer and Stonecash 2015, chap. 9 (esp. 122–25), appendix.

26. Other scholars have also observed this paradox; see Krimmel and Rader (2017), Francia and Levine (2006), and Lacy (2014).

27. O'Keefe 2014.

28. Moorhead 2012.

29. These six states were Alabama, Arkansas, Kentucky, Mississippi, South Carolina, and West Virginia.

30. Among this group of states, Obama gained fifty-seven electoral votes from Colorado, Connecticut, Maryland, New Jersey, New Hampshire, and Virginia, and Romney gained fifty-five electoral votes from Nebraska, North Dakota, Texas, Utah, and Wyoming.

31. In the other two states, Iowa and Wisconsin, with sixteen electoral votes, transfers account for 15 to 17 percent of average income. One more electoral vote for Trump came from Maine, where social transfers surpass 22 percent of average income. Maine splits its four votes between the candidates if its two congressional districts diverge in their preferences.

32. Rudowitz, Artiga, and Young 2016.

33. Cheves 2016.

34. Shesgreen 2014.

35. U.S. House of Representatives 2013.

36. Lubell 1952, 60–61, 196.

37. Roosevelt 1944.
38. Marshall 1992, 6, also 33.
39. Dahl 2003, 153; see also Dahl 1989, 114–15.
40. Some might wonder whether causality runs in the other direction—whether political attitudes or partisanship affect later willingness to utilize policies (or not). The data used here do not permit us to explore this possibility, because they are drawn from a survey that asked for a *life history* of policy usage but probed only *current* attitudes about policies and current partisanship. Research on what survey respondents can remember and reliably report suggests that only present attitudes can be explored, but that previous events, such as policy usage, can be investigated (Mettler 2005, appendix B). For an exploration of how political attitudes or partisanship affect policy utilization, see Lerman, Sadin, and Trachtman (2017).
41. Pierson 1994.
42. Campbell 2003.
43. Verba, Schlozman, and Brady 1995, 394–97; Wolfinger and Rosenstone 1980, 32.
44. Schneider and Ingram 1993, 340.
45. Soss 1999.
46. Mettler 2005.
47. Mettler and Soss 2004.
48. Patashnik and Zelizer 2013; Galvin and Thurston 2017.
49. Hochschild 1981, chap. 8, 34.
50. Free and Cantril 1968, 5–6.
51. Free and Cantril 1968, chap. 3.
52. Free and Cantril 1968, chap. 2.
53. McCall 2013, 33–34.
54. Page and Shapiro 1992, chap. 4; Jacobs and Page 2009; Gilens 1999, 27–29; Cook and Barrett 1992; Ellis and Stimson 2012.
55. Hibbing and Theiss-Morse 2002, 151.
56. For example, Bailey and Danziger 2013; Beland, Howard, and Morgan 2015; Cancian and Danziger 2009; Currie 2006; Howard 2007.
57. For example, Morgan and Campbell 2011; Erkulwater 2006; Grogan and Patashnik 2003; Jacobs and Skocpol 2010; Hacker 2004.
58. For example, Ben-Shalom, Moffit, and Scholz 2011; U.S. Congressional Budget Office 2011, 2013; Edin and Shaefer 2015.
59. Recent books that delve deeply into how these policy attributes influence individuals' experiences of public policy include Andrea Campbell's *Trapped in America's Safety Net* (2014), which explores rules in a variety of means-tested policies; *Disciplining the Poor,* an examination of post-AFDC (Aid to Families with Dependent Children) welfare implementation by Joe Soss, Richard Fording, and Sanford Schram (2011); and a study of the experience of using the Earned Income Tax Credit by Sarah Halpern-Meekin, Kathryn Edin, Laura Tach, and Jennifer Sykes called *It's Not Like I'm Poor* (2015). See also Edin and Lein 1997.
60. At the same time, resources were redistributed away from some households and toward others: away from working-age and nondisabled people and toward the elderly and disabled; away from families of single parents and toward those of married parents,

and within the latter, away from those with lower incomes and toward those with somewhat higher incomes (Moffitt 2015).

61. Schneider and Ingram 1993; Pierson 1993; Soss 1999; Campbell 2003; Mettler 2005.

62. Skocpol 1991; Mettler and Stonecash 2008; Gordon 1994; Mink 1996. For an argument to the contrary, see Soss 1999.

63. Mettler 2011; see also Arnold 1992; Pierson 1993; Howard 1997; Hacker 2004.

64. Studies have tended to focus on the impact of one or a few specific policies, making it difficult to generalize. This is compounded by the fact that most means-tested policies feature a visible role for government, and most social benefits in the tax code are not means-tested, such that it is not clear which of these design features makes more of a difference. Scholars have only begun, furthermore, to consider how policy effects on political behavior compare to those emanating from other attributes, such as partisanship. On the latter, see Lerman and McCabe 2017; Jacobs and Mettler 2018.

65. The literature is vast: see, for example, Gilens 1999; Lieberman 1998; Mettler 1998; Katznelson 2005; Soss, Fording, and Schram 2011.

66. Hochschild 2016, 35.

67. Some other scholars have probed this paradox by using national data to explore aggregate trends. See Krimmel and Rader (2017) and Lacy (2014).

68. I assumed at the outset that this would involve the simple task of downloading data from a single government agency. That turned out not to be the case. Rather, data on different programs had to be collected from the myriad agencies that oversee different components of the complex U.S. welfare state, and sometimes historical data had to be gathered from different sources entirely. I included the same policies that are investigated in the Social and Governmental Issues and Participation Study (SGIP). This is not a comprehensive list.

69. Examples of policy feedback analyses using panel data include Bruch, Ferree, and Soss (2010), Morgan and Campbell (2011), and Jacobs and Mettler (2018), and a notable field experiment is featured in Lerman, Sadin, and Trachtman (2017).

70. This component of the project was used for illustrative purposes only, not analytical ones, and as such I did not aim to contact a representative sample.

71. Out of a possible 727 who fit the criteria, I sent letters to 500. I soon heard back from 53 who were willing to be reinterviewed. I succeeded in interviewing 21 of these individuals during the summer of 2015. I sent them $20 each in appreciation of their sharing of their time, perspectives, and experiences.

72. Lane and Oreskes 2007, 199–221.

CHAPTER 2: THE MARKET RECEDES, GOVERNMENT RESPONDS

1. Lou Clark, interview with the author, Syracuse, N.Y., January 28, 2016.

2. New York Department of Labor 2015.

3. Data for 2000 and 2014 from U.S. Census Bureau, *American Fact Finder* (for 2000, Summary File 3, https://www.census.gov/census2000/sumfile3.html, accessed February 15, 2018; for 2014, American Community Survey Five-Year Estimates, https://www.census.gov/programs-surveys/acs/news/data-releases/2014/release.html, accessed

February 15, 2018). Data for 1979 from U.S. Census Bureau, Decennial Census 1980, "T100: Poverty Status in 1979" (short version), *Social Explorer* (https://www.social explorer.com/data/C1980/metadata/?ds=SE&table=T100, accessed February 15, 2018).

4. U.S. Census Bureau, *American Fact Finder,* 2010–2014 American Community Survey Five-Year Estimates, "S1701: Poverty Status in the Past 12 Months," https://factfinder .census.gov/faces/tableservices/jsf/pages/productview.xhtml?src=bkmk (accessed February 15, 2018).

5. U.S. Census Bureau, *American Fact Finder,* 2010–2014 American Community Survey Five-Year Estimates, "S1701: Poverty Status in the Past 12 Months"; U.S. Census Bureau, Decennial Census 1980, "T100: Poverty Status in 1979" ("T102: White Alone," "T103: Black Alone," and "T107: Population of Spanish Origin"), *Social Explorer.*

6. U.S. Census Bureau, 1979 data from *Social Explorer,* "T71: Households with Public Assistance Income" (which includes supplemental security income [SSI], aid to families with dependent children, and general assistance), https://www.socialexplorer.com /tables/C1980, accessed February 15, 2018; 2014 data from U.S. Census Bureau, *American Fact Finder,* 2010–2014 American Community Survey Five-Year Estimates, "Selected Economic Characteristics," https://factfinder.census.gov/faces/tableservices/jsf /pages/productview.xhtml?src=bkmk, accessed February 15, 2018 (SSI and cash public assistance reported separately, with usage rates at 11.1 percent and 8.8 percent, respectively, in 2014). The rate of Social Security usage remained quite stable, at 27 percent in 2014.

7. Data for 2014 from U.S. Census Bureau, *American Fact Finder,* 2010–2014 American Community Survey Five-Year Estimates, "Selected Economic Characteristics."

8. See figures 3.6 and 3.7. On rising poverty in Upstate New York generally, see Pendall and Christopherson (2004). On changes in rural areas of the United States, see Johnson (2006).

9. Kennedy 1963. Apparently the phrase was used by others prior to Kennedy.

10. Economic Policy Institute 2014.

11. Saez 2016.

12. Economic Policy Institute 2016.

13. For example, Goldin and Margo 1992; Piketty and Saez 2003.

14. Mettler 2005; Featherman and Hauser 1978.

15. Donahue and Heckman 1991; Heckman and Payner 1989.

16. Mettler 1998.

17. Freeman and Medoff 1984.

18. Hacker 2002, 203, 239–42.

19. Borstelmann 2011, 53–63.

20. U.S. Department of Labor 2012.

21. Borstelmann 2011, 133–34.

22. Lee and Mather 2008, fig. 5, "Share of Nonfarm Employment by Major Industrial Sector, 1950 to 2007" (chart), accessed March 29, 2016; Economic Policy Institute 2012; National Employment Law Project 2014.

23. Mishel et al. 2012, 188.

24. Gould, Schieder, and Geier 2016.

25. Rodgers 2011, chap. 2; Borstelmann 2011, chap. 3.

26. Rodgers 2011, 44.

27. Borstelmann 2011, 132.

28. Cowie 2010, 262, 291.

29. Cowie 2010, 362.

30. Rosenfeld 2014, 29; Freeman 2007, 80–82; see also chapter 7.

31. Walker 2014.

32. Freeman 2007, 50–51.

33. Rosenfeld 2014, chap. 3.

34. Radcliff and Davis 2000; Leighley and Nagler 2007; Kerrissey and Schofer 2013.

35. Gitterman 2010, 60, quote on 77.

36. Freeman 2007, 50–51; Mishel et al. 2012, 279–86.

37. Mishel et al. 2012, 282–83.

38. Meyerson 2013.

39. Meyerson 2013; Mishel et al. 2012, 198–204.

40. Mishel et al. 2012, 182, 201.

41. White House 2016.

42. Pierson 1994, 65; Campbell 2003, 90.

43. Campbell 2003, 93.

44. Campbell 2003, 104.

45. In 1982, Social Security was stripped of its minimum benefit, which was intended for workers who had contributed to the system for forty quarters despite some periods of zero or no contributions. The omission of this minimum benefit hurt women in particular and exacerbated a racial bias in program benefits (Harrington-Meyer 1996, 457–58). The Medicare changes occurred in 2004, when "Medicare Advantage" plans were created as part of the Medicare Modernization Act (Morgan and Campbell 2011).

46. Medicare distinguishes between those who are "enrolled" and those who are "served." Those served among the aged grew from 7.1 percent of all Americans in 1980 to 8.7 percent in 2013; for the disabled, the percentage rose from 0.8 percent to 2.0 percent over the same period.

47. Amounts are in 2015 dollars. Also, for disabled recipients, average benefits increased from $7,312 in 1980 to $11,107 in 2013 (also in 2015 dollars).

48. Pierson 1994; Campbell 2003.

49. Moffitt 2013, 24; Bitler and Hoynes 2014, 40.

50. Edin and Shaefer 2016, 15.

51. Edin and Shaefer 2016, 16.

52. Gilens 1999, chap. 6; Quadagno 1996; Soss, Fording, and Schram 2011.

53. Gilens 1999, 37–38.

54. Weaver 2015, 360–61.

55. Hays 2003, 16, 60. In fact, program benefits failed to provide enough to permit mothers to stay out of the workforce. For historical treatments, see Mettler (1998), chap. 6, and Mink (1996); on the 1990s, see Edin and Lein (1997).

56. Halpern-Meekin et al. 2015.

57. Edin and Shaefer 2016.
58. Moffitt 2014, 62–63.
59. Center on Budget and Policy Priorities 2017.
60. Gruber 2003, 16.
61. Howard 2007, 96–98; Grogan and Patashnik 2003, 829–33.
62. Kaiser Family Foundation, "Current Status of State Medicaid Expansion Decision," as of February 8, 2008, https://www.kff.org/health-reform/slide/current-status-of-the-medicaid-expansion-decision/ (accessed February 15, 2018).
63. Center on Budget and Policy Priorities 2016a. Although seniors make up such a small percentage of beneficiaries, they utilize a larger share of program spending, as do others in need of long-term care. Forty-two percent of program spending is used for long-term care for patients in nursing homes, though they account for only 6 percent of all beneficiaries (Rau 2017).
64. Gundersen 2015, 399.
65. Bitler and Hoynes 2014, 8.
66. Hoynes 2016, 3. Although seniors make up such a small percentage of beneficiaries, they utilize a large share of program spending.
67. College Board 2015, 3.
68. Mettler 2014.
69. For example, Autor 2011; Ledbetter 2010; Burkhauser 2012; Orlet 2011; Eberstadt 2012, 51–58; quote in Citizens Against Government Waste 2013. For a succinct reply, see Pollack 2013.
70. Erkulwater 2015, 435.
71. Quoted in Erkulwater 2015, 441.
72. For SSDI, 53 percent of applicants from 2001 to 2010 had their claims denied. See Social Security Administration (2012).
73. Autor and Duggan 2006, 75.
74. Outlays for the program amount to $51.6 billion for SSI in 2018 and $143 billion for SSDI in 2016 (Social Security Administration 2017; U.S. Congressional Budget Office 2016).
75. Krawak 2015.
76. Ben-Shalom, Moffitt, and Scholz 2011; Ziliak 2006, 37; Ziliak 2008.
77. Rogers and Toder 2011, 3. On the development of these policies, see Howard (1997), Hacker (2002), and Faricy (2015).
78. Mettler 2011, 20–21.
79. Mettler 2011, chap. 4.
80. Data provided by the Urban-Brookings Tax Policy Center, table T16-0164, "Tax Benefit of the Deduction for Home Mortgage Interest by Expanded Cash Income Percentile, 2016."
81. Howard 1997, 2007.
82. Center on Budget and Policy Priorities 2015.
83. U.S. Congressional Budget Office 2013, 15.
84. U.S. Congressional Budget Office 2013, 15.
85. Burman and Slemrod 2013, 41–42.

86. White House 2013.
87. Organization for Economic Cooperation and Development 2014, figure 7.
88. Mettler 2011; Hacker 2002; Howard 2007.
89. Eberstadt 2012.
90. Vroman 2009, 8.
91. Wenger and Wilkins 2008.
92. See the list of states permitting this at Food and Nutrition Service, U.S. Department of Agriculture (USDA), "Supplemental Nutrition Assistance Program (SNAP)," https://www.fns.usda.gov/snap/apply (accessed February 15, 2018).
93. For example, Levedahl 1998; Malonebeach, Frank, and Heuberger 2012.
94. Wenger 2014, 248.
95. Mettler 1998, 143–58.
96. Wenger 2014, 259; Woodbury 2015, 477–48.
97. Shaefer 2010, 450.
98. Shaefer 2010, 457.
99. Zedlewski and Rader 2005, 538–42.
100. Bitler and Hoynes 2014, 6; Waldfogel 2013, 156.
101. Gundersen 2015, 401.
102. Waldfogel 2013, 2–13, 158.
103. Center on Budget and Policy Priorities 2016b.
104. Campbell 2014, 85.
105. Gundersen 2015, 398, 403.
106. Halpern-Meekin et al. 2015, 21, 198–99.
107. Edin and Shaefer 2015, "Introduction."
108. Campbell 2014.
109. This theme is well developed in Michener (2018).
110. Hacker 2004.
111. Mettler 2014, 2016.
112. Kohler-Hausmann 2017.
113. Bonczar 2003, 1.
114. Soss and Weaver 2017, 565.
115. Soss and Weaver 2017, 584.
116. Eisenstadt 2013.
117. Quoted in Campbell 2014, 39.
118. For example, Gallup 2017b.

CHAPTER 3: WE ARE ALL BENEFICIARIES NOW

1. For example, Cramer 2016; Mink 1996; Gordon 1994; Mettler 1998; Lieberman 1998; Gilens 1999; Fox 2012.
2. Quoted in Edin and Shaefer 2015, 15–16.
3. For example, see Eberstadt 2012, 41–58.
4. Corn 2012, 2016.

5. Brewer and Stonecash 2015; Hochschild 2016; Mounk 2017.

6. SIPP collects data on general assistance, SSI, TANF, SNAP, Social Security, UI, disability, and veterans' benefits, as well as a few others.

7. Hirschl and Rank 2002.

8. If respondents hesitated, interviewers provided descriptions of each policy in order to improve their recall and the accuracy of their responses; respondents were also given a "don't know" option.

9. The SGIP includes a random national sample (N = 1,000). In addition, because young people and low-income people are particularly important to a study of social policy but tend to be underrepresented in surveys because they are harder to reach, we included an oversample of 200 eighteen- to thirty-four-years-olds and an oversample of 200 individuals from households with annual incomes below $35,000. The data were weighted through two adjustments: first, a weighting for nonresponse, relative to U.S. census regions and metropolitan statistical areas; and second, because of the oversamples, a weighting to calibrate the sample to population totals, using the following poststratification variables: age, gender, education, and ethnicity (Hispanic).

10. Bureau of Economic Analysis 2016.

11. Counts of each policy indicate whether the respondent "ever" used the policy, with two exceptions. Because we asked only about current benefits when we asked about employer-provided health and retirement benefits, these numbers understate actual usage of these policies across respondents' lifetimes.

12. Among nonbeneficiaries, 45 percent were born between 1980 and 1990, and 48 percent between 1955 and 1979.

13. These data are confirmed by a more recent survey that asked the same questions about program usage, but only for eight policies, making it less useful for analysis. The Pew Survey found that 55 percent of Americans had used at least one of the following six: Social Security, Medicare, Unemployment Insurance, Medicaid, food stamps, and welfare benefits (Pew Research Center 2012c, 1).

14. Rank, Hirschl, and Foster 2014, 35–37.

15. 2008 SGIP.

16. 2008 SGIP.

17. Hirschl and Rank 2002; Rank, Hirschl, and Foster 2014.

18. Hacker 2002; Howard 1997; Mettler 2011.

19. Seven of the twenty-one policies fit this criterion. In the interest of avoiding overcrowding, figure 3.3 shows all of them except employer-provided retirement benefits because usage patterns for this type of benefit largely duplicate those of employer-provided health benefits.

20. Pew Research Center, 2012a, 20, 56; see also Brewer and Stonecash 2015.

21. Skocpol and Williamson 2012, 64–68, 72–74.

22. For calculations of usage by age, unlike those related to income or party, employer-provided benefits are not included given that "current use" is highly correlated to age.

23. Those ages seventy and older were significantly more likely to be veterans—28.2 percent compared to 10.8 percent among those under age seventy. As a result, GI Bill

usage was more common among the seventy-and-older group (12.2 percent had used it versus 4.8 percent) as were other veterans' benefits (used by 6.8 percent compared to 4.1 percent).

24. Mettler 2014, chap. 2.

25. For example, see Lieberman 1998; Katznelson 2005; Fox 2012.

26. Gilens 1999; Soss et al. 2001.

27. "Nonwhite non-Hispanics" are treated as a single group here because the limited number of cases prevents greater disaggregation.

28. Pallarito 2011.

29. Frankel 2015.

30. The correlation coefficient between the percentage of county income from government transfers and the percentage of the population composed of white residents is −0.18, significant at the $p < 0.001$ level.

31. The Middle Atlantic states include New York, Pennsylvania, New Jersey, Maryland, Delaware, and the District of Columbia. See U.S. Bureau of Economic Analysis, "Measuring the Nation's Economy: A Guide to the Bureau of Economic Analysis," http://www.bea.gov/agency/pdf/BEA_Customer_Guide.pdf (accessed February 15, 2018), 18.

32. Corn 2012.

33. Craw and Carter 2012.

34. Piketty 2014, 349.

35. U.S. Congressional Budget Office 2014, 13, 25–27.

36. U.S. Congressional Budget Office 2014, 22.

37. Williams 2016.

38. Robertson C. Williams (2016) of the Tax Policy Center estimates that of those Americans who do not owe income taxes, 60 percent are employed and owe payroll taxes and most of the others are retired and have incomes too low to owe taxes.

39. U.S. Congress, Joint Committee on Taxation 2015, 23.

40. U.S. Congress, Joint Committee on Taxation 2015, 29.

41. Schlesinger 1958, 308–9.

42. DeSilver 2015; Jacobs and Page 2009, 68–70.

43. Fitzgerald 1995.

44. Hemingway 1961.

CHAPTER 4: DIFFERENT LENSES

1. For example, Hetherington 2005; Hetherington and Rudolph 2015; Hibbing and Theiss-Morse 2001. In addition, to the extent that views about policies are affected by diminished trust in government, as Marc Hetherington (2005) has suggested, one result might be less support for social provision.

2. For example, Gilens 1999.

3. For example, Hetherington 2005; Hetherington and Rudolph 2015; Hibbing and Theiss-Morse 2002.

4. Levi and Stoker 2000, 491, 495–97; see also Cook, Jacobs, and Kim 2010.

5. Some other scholars have explored the geographic paradox. See Krimmel and Rader 2017; Lacy 2014.

6. Campbell 2014; Soss, Fording, and Schram 2011; Michener 2018; Vargas 2016; Hays 2003.

7. The means are 3.08 and 3.82, respectively, and the confidence intervals do not overlap. Data are weighted.

8. Strach 2007, 102, 124–25.

9. Schneider and Ingram 1993, 340–41; Pierson 1993.

10. Arnold 1992; Pierson 1993.

11. Campbell 2003.

12. Howard 1997.

13. Hacker 2002; Morgan and Campbell 2011.

14. Skocpol 1991; Wilson 1987, chap. 7; Greenstein 1991.

15. Esping-Andersen 1990; Gordon 1994; Mink 1996; Skocpol 1992; Mettler 1998.

16. Skocpol 1991.

17. Soss 1999.

18. Halpern-Meekin et al. 2015.

19. Cramer 2016; Dawson 2003.

20. Achen and Bartels 2016, especially chaps. 8 and 9.

21. Lee 2009, 2016; McCarty, Poole, and Rosenthal 2006.

22. Layman et al. 2010; Layman and Carsey 2002a, 2002b; Achen and Bartels 2016, 264.

23. Brewer and Stonecash 2015.

24. Teles 1996; Gilens 1999.

25. Halpern-Meekin et al. 2015.

26. Gilens 1999, 8.

27. Cramer 2016, 166.

28. Among respondents, views of welfare were as follows: 19.4 percent, very unfavorable; 24.5 percent, somewhat unfavorable; 42 percent, somewhat favorable; and 14.1 percent, very favorable.

29. Income was included as five bins with the lowest income category missing, as the reference category (under $20,000).

30. For this analysis, we collapsed the welfare favorability scale into a dichotomous scale in which 1=favorable and 0=unfavorable.

31. Results persist when we control for partisanship, ideology, and other factors.

32. The differences between blacks and whites disappear once we control for partisanship and ideology. Not surprisingly, ideology emerges as a highly significant determinant of welfare attitudes, with conservatives more likely to disapprove of it, but interestingly the results for partisanship, which show that Democrats are more supportive, disappear once we accounted for region and religion. None of the other factors reached the level of significance.

33. For example, Lieberman 1998; Katznelson 2005; Gilens 1999.

34. The inclusion of an interaction term between race and income revealed that the results remain broadly consistent, with the exception of the $75,000 to $99,000 income bin, in which black's views of welfare diminished below that of whites.

35. Gilens 1999, 8. Hetherington (2005) explores a similar relationship, but in reverse, showing that declining trust in government undermines support for spending on various priorities, such as welfare.

36. Hochschild 2016, 114–15, and chap. 9.

37. Achen and Bartels 2016.

38. For example, Crenshaw 1991; Cortez 2017.

39. The limited size of the data set used here does not permit rigorous intersectional analysis.

40. Skocpol 1992.

41. Mettler 1998.

42. Mettler 2005; on limits by race, see Katznelson 2005.

43. Mettler 2005, 144.

44. Mettler 1998; Mettler 2005, chap. 9; Burns, Schlozman, and Verba 2001, 340.

45. Burns, Schlozman, and Verba 2001; Delli Carpini and Keeter 1996, chap. 4.

46. Lawless and Fox 2013; Center for American Women and Politics 2017; Thomsen 2017.

47. McDonagh 2009.

48. Valelly 2004, chaps. 1, 3, 4.

49. Smith 1999.

50. Weaver 2007.

51. Krogstad and Lopez 2016.

52. Soss and Weaver 2016.

53. Mettler 2005.

54. Mettler 2014.

55. For example, Verba, Schlozman, and Brady 1995.

56. Nie, Junn, and Stehlik-Barry 1996.

57. Gilens 2012; Bartels 2008; Gilens and Page 2014.

58. In the survey, those who volunteered the answer "neutral" were assigned a 3 on a 5-point scale. Since fewer than 2 percent of respondents offered this voluntary answer, however, we omitted those in this analysis and used a 4-point scale to reflect the options actually given to respondents.

59. As factor analysis makes evident, the measures associated with the "social contract" dimension of attitudes about government are predicted by a common set of variables. Similarly, the four attitudes discussed in the next paragraph also share common determinants.

60. Scholars familiar with the literature on trust may be curious about the omission of trust here as a dependent variable and the inclusion of these other measures. Unfortunately, the standard trust question was not included in the 2008 SGIP. Using the 2008 and 2016 American National Election Studies, however, I have analyzed determinants of trust using the same models used here, with the exception of the policy usage variables, which ANES does not include, and I have done the same for the two political efficacy dependent variables. I found that the political efficacy models performed simi-

larly using the ANES data as they did with the SGIP data. The results for the trust model resembled the political efficacy models, but the latter were generally more robust, containing more significant variables.

61. Soss 1999; Mettler 2005.

62. The scale is "Republican" (1), "leaning Republican" (2), "independent" (3), "leaning Democrat" (4), and "Democrat" (5).

63. I have also examined all models with age considered in a nonlinear manner, with six age bins (for example, "twenty-eight- to thirty-seven-years-old," "thirty-eight- to forty-seven-years old," and so forth, with those age eighteen to twenty-seven as the missing reference group). This made a difference only in a couple of models, as noted later.

64. I have also examined all models with income considered in a nonlinear manner, with five income bins (for example, "$20,000 to $34,999," "$35,000 to $49,999," and so forth, with income below $20,000 as the missing reference group). As with age, this made a difference only in a couple of models, as noted later.

65. Figure 4.3 indicates adjusted predictions for relationships involving variables that emerged as significant in the logistic regressions, except those involving dummy variables, which are described in the text only. The same approach is used for similar figures later in this chapter.

66. I briefly examine some of these relationships in *The Submerged State* (Mettler 2011, 40–44), using simpler models that compare only visible versus submerged policy experiences and exclude partisanship and welfare attitudes. With those variations, individuals who had used more visible policies were also more likely to think that government had provided them with opportunities and that taxes were fair. The reason for the different models is that, in *The Submerged State,* I was aiming to describe attitudes while controlling only for socioeconomic characteristics, whereas here—given the findings in chapter 3 about widespread policy usage across parties, and because partisanship is widely understood to be related to views about government—I have added the additional controls.

67. Some might wonder whether welfare attitudes are themselves influenced by policy usage, creating post-treatment bias. An examination of correlations between welfare attitudes and policy receipt of the four sum variables revealed no significant relationships, however, nor did the same evaluation of welfare attitudes and use of EITC or AFDC/TANF. In addition, each of the models examined in table 4.1 was also run with welfare attitudes and partisanship excluded, as well as with only one or the other included; in each case, the results for the policy variables remained consistent throughout every model, and all of the group and demographic variables remained consistent as well, with only one exception. The exception emerged in the "full citizen" model, in which the exclusion of partisanship revealed that men were significantly more likely than women to agree. Aside from this, the tests provided assurance that post-treatment bias does not affect the results.

68. Hochschild 2016, chap. 9.

69. Curious about this result, I examined the determinants of political efficacy measures in the 2008 and 2016 ANES, using the same model used here but without the policy variables (which ANES lacks). I found consistent results, with Democrats significantly

more likely to have low efficacy on the "no say" measure in 2016; for both models in 2008 and the "government doesn't care" model in 2016, the signs also indicated the same relationship, but it lacked significance.

70. Hetherington and Rudolph 2015, 29.

71. Lieberman 1998; Katznelson 2005; Mettler 1998, 2005.

72. The likelihood that nonwhites would feel that government had helped them was 45 percent, compared to whites at 57 percent.

73. I also considered income nonlinearly (not shown) and found that, in the political efficacy models, those in the highest income group ($100,000 and more) were the only ones to differ significantly from the reference group, the lowest income group: they were significantly more likely to disagree with the negative statements that "public officials don't care" and "people like me don't have any say," indicating higher political efficacy.

74. Gilens 2012; Bartels 2008; Gilens and Page 2014.

75. I also analyzed age nonlinearly and found that, in the political efficacy models, those in each of the four age groups—covering those ages twenty-eight to sixty-seven—were significantly more likely than the youngest group to agree with one or both statements, indicating lower political efficacy. The two oldest age groups, those above age sixty-seven, did not differ significantly from the young.

76. The only significant results that contradict the general theoretical expectations offered earlier were that higher-income people perceived taxes to be unfair compared to lower-income people, which makes sense given the progressive nature of the income tax, and that Hispanics perceived democracy to be functioning well compared to non-Hispanics, which may be an anomaly resulting from the relatively small number of cases; table 4.1 includes eighty-nine Hispanics in the analysis. An equivalent proportion of Hispanics and non-Hispanics reported being "somewhat satisfied" or "very satisfied" with the way democracy works in the United States.

77. This is not to suggest that most such individuals voted for Trump, only that enough of them did so to have an impact on the election (Carnes and Lupu 2017).

78. Halpern-Meekin et al. 2015, 20.

79. Soss 1999; Soss, Fording, and Schram 2011; Campbell 2003, chap 7.

80. Soss 1999.

81. Soss, Fording, and Schram 2011, 288.

82. Halpern-Meekin et al. 2015, 10.

83. Halpern-Meekin et al. 2015, 118.

84. Halpern-Meekin et al. 2015, 8.

85. Halpern-Meekin et al. 2015, 8, 107, 121.

86. Halpern-Meekin et al. 2015, 83.

87. Halpern-Meekin et al. 2015, 125.

88. Halpern-Meekin et al. 2015, 114.

89. Halpern-Meekin et al. 2015, 20.

90. Jones 2014, 13–14. These figures represent the low and high take-up rates between 2005 and 2009.

91. To avoid concerns about post-treatment bias, we did not control for attitudes about welfare in these models. We conducted the analyses in both ways, however, and the

results were essentially the same. Also, we did not include the models examining satisfaction with democracy or feeling like a full and equal citizen, as the policy variables were not significant in those models and added nothing to the understanding we had already gained from the general analysis earlier in this chapter.

92. Lerman and Weaver 2014.

93. I am indebted to Kathryn Edin for pointing this out.

94. In figures 4.5, 4.5, 5.7, and 5.8, the lines indicating usage of "welfare" and "both" (meaning both EITC and welfare) are shorter than other lines due to the small number of cases in the upper income levels.

95. Gilens 2012.

96. Results are presented as odds ratios.

97. Mettler 2014.

98. Mettler 2005, chap. 5.

99. A further distinction between these policies is that those in the tax code are likely to be claimed by parents rather than by students themselves, further obscuring their value in students' own minds.

100. In a separate model, we examined the combined usage of Pell Grants and student loans. It failed to reach the level of significance.

CHAPTER 5: UNEQUAL VOICE

1. Skocpol and Hertel-Fernandez 2016; Skocpol and Williamson 2012.

2. For example, Frank 2005.

3. For example, see Achen and Bartels 2016; Stonecash and Brewer 2007; Schaffner, MacWilliams, and Nteta 2017; Bartels 2008.

4. Cramer 2016, 166, 17, 89.

5. Results are presented as odds ratios.

6. Sides and Vavreck 2013.

7. For an excellent study, see Leighley and Nagler 2014.

8. DeSilver 2016.

9. In 2008, 38.4 percent of Americans failed to participate in the presidential election, and in 2012 the figure was 41.4 percent (McDonald 2014).

10. Author's calculations from data on voting-eligible population from McDonald (2016).

11. Cohn 2017.

12. DeSilver 2016.

13. For example, Leighley and Nagler 2014, chap. 4; Powell 1986; Rigby and Springer 2011; Rosenstone and Hansen 1993.

14. Verba, Schlozman, and Brady 1995, 51.

15. For example, Leighley and Nagler 2014.

16. File 2015.

17. Skocpol and Williamson 2012.

18. Skocpol and Williamson 2012.

19. Bump 2016.

20. Gould and Harrington 2016. Support for Trump ran highest among middle-income voters ($50,000 to $99,900). It is the case that compared to 2012, lower-income voters

were somewhat more likely to vote for the Republican candidate than they had been previously, and the reverse was the case among upper-income voters (Huang et al. 2016). Also, educational level proved to be more influential in voting patterns than income levels (Silver 2016).

21. For example, Leighley and Nagler 2014.
22. Verba, Schlozman, and Brady 1995; Schlozman, Verba, and Brady 2012.
23. Verba, Schlozman, and Brady 1995, 365.
24. Verba, Schlozman, and Brady 1995, 51.
25. Campbell 2003; Mettler 2005.
26. Rosenstone and Hansen 1993, chaps. 6 and 7.
27. For example, Verba, Schlozman, and Brady 1995; Lerman and Weaver 2014.
28. Burns, Schlozman, and Verba 2001.
29. Rosenbaum, Schmucker, and Rothenberg 2016; Gourevitch and Sommers 2016.
30. U.S. Bureau of Economic Analysis 2016.
31. Kentucky Energy and Environment Cabinet 2014; Cohen 2016.
32. Konty and Bailey 2009, 3–4.
33. Thompson et al. 2001; Konty and Bailey 2009, 3–4.
34. Brammer and Musgrave 2013.
35. Gerth 2016; *New York Times* 1995.
36. *Fresh Air* 2014.
37. Fineman 2015.
38. Brammer 2013.
39. Vance 2016, 57.
40. Commonwealth of Kentucky 2015.
41. Commonwealth of Kentucky 2016.
42. Kanik 2016.
43. Commonwealth of Kentucky 2017.

CHAPTER 6: RECONNECTING CITIZENS AND GOVERNMENT

1. *Fox News* 2016.
2. For example, Brettschneider 2016; Colvin 2016.
3. Authors' analysis of 2016 ANES. These results come from two separate models, each with the dependent variable indicating a vote for Trump, but one with the level of agreement with "trust the government in Washington to do what is right" as an independent variable and one with the level of agreement with "politicians don't care about people like me." Additional significant variables included college degree (the more educated were less likely to support Trump), race (white people were more likely to support Trump), party identification (Republicans and Republican leaners were more likely to support Trump), and income (those with above median income were less likely to support Trump).
4. Pew Research Center 2016.
5. Cohen 2016.
6. Kliff 2016.

7. Altman 2017.
8. The 2017 tax bill has scaled back the scope of a few of the policies embedded in the tax code, most notably the home mortgage interest deduction and the state and local tax deduction.
9. For example, Schneider and Ingram 1993.
10. Mettler 2005.
11. Lee 2016.
12. Weaver 2007; Kohler-Hausmann 2017; Sears and Citrin 1982; Kruse 2005.
13. Sinclair 2005, chap. 2; Hayes and McKee 2008; Shafer and Johnston 2006.
14. Stonecash 2000.
15. Achen and Bartels 2016.
16. Skocpol and Williamson 2012.
17. Prior 2007; Mutz 2015; Baum 2011; Berry and Sobieraj 2016.
18. Rose and Baumgartner 2013, 22–23.
19. Skocpol 2004.
20. Skocpol and Williamson 2012; Parker and Barreto 2013; Skocpol and Hertel-Fernandez 2016.
21. Drutman 2015.
22. For example, Ansolabehere, de Figueiredo, and Snyder 2003; Hall and Wayman 1990.
23. Gilens 2012; Carnes 2013.
24. Valelly 2004.
25. Dahl 2003, 43–45, 187.
26. Aidt and Trannatos 2002.
27. Mettler 2014, 22.
28. Gilens 2012; Gilens and Page 2014; Bartels 2008.
29. Mettler 2011.
30. Frank 2016.
31. Mettler 2005, 105.
32. Han 2009, 2014.
33. Mettler 2014.

APPENDIX A: DESIGN AND PROCEDURES FOR THE SOCIAL AND GOVERNMENTAL ISSUES AND PARTICIPATION STUDY

1. Tourangeau, Rips, and Rasinski 2000; Fowler 1984.
2. See Mathiowetz, Brown, and Bound 2001; Marquis and Moore 2013. The sociologist Jane L. Collins at the University of Wisconsin recently used a survey design similar to the SGIP in a study of over fifty women on welfare in Wisconsin. She had access to public records about each woman's receipt of several different programs over time, and this permitted her to verify the accuracy of respondents' answers. In personal communication with me, she reported that women's responses to interview questions were consistent with the official data in all instances.
3. See Marquis and Moore 2013, 8–13.

APPENDIX C: SURVEY RESPONSE RATE AND COMPARISON TO EXISTING STUDIES

1. Pew Research Center 2012b.
2. The Pew Research Center kindly shared with me the study questionnaire, methodology report, and topline results, which are used throughout this appendix.
3. From the SGIP, 27 percent had used either student loans only (16 percent) or student loans plus Pell Grants (11 percent), for a total amount nearly identical to the Pew figure. Another 5 percent had used Pell Grants only.
4. The Pew study asked respondents to specify whether they themselves or another household member had received benefits, whereas the SGIP did not.
5. For example, for Medicaid, the interviewer added the descriptor, "That's health care coverage for low-income elderly, disabled, and children"; for welfare, the interviewer actually said, "Welfare or public assistance (Temporary Assistance to Needy Families, TANF)." See survey questionnaire for more details.
6. Rank and Hirschl 2002.
7. Rank and Hirschl 2005.

REFERENCES

Achen, Christopher H., and Larry M. Bartels. 2016. *Democracy for Realists: Why Elections Do Not Produce Responsive Government.* Princeton, N.J.: Princeton University Press.

Aidt, Toke, and Zafiris Tzannatos. 2002. *Unions and Collective Bargaining: Economic Effects in a Global Environment.* Washington, D.C.: World Bank.

Altman, Drew. 2017. "The Health Care Plan Trump Voters Really Want." *New York Times,* January 5.

Ansolabehere, Stephen, John M. de Figueiredo, and James M. Snyder Jr. 2003. "Why Is There So Little Money in U.S. Politics?" *Journal of Economic Perspectives* 17: 105–30.

Arnold, J. Douglas. 1992. *The Logic of Congressional Action.* New Haven, Conn.: Yale University Press.

Associated Press. NORC Center for Public Affairs Research. 2015. "Confidence in Institutions: Trends in American Attitudes toward Government, Media, and Business." Issue brief. http://www.apnorc.org/projects/Pages/HTML%20Reports/confidence-in-insti tutions-trends-in-americans-attitudes-toward-government-media-and-busi ness0310-2333.aspx (accessed February 15, 2018).

Autor, David H. 2011. "The Unsustainable Rise of the Disability Rolls in the United States: Causes, Consequences, and Policy Options." Working Paper 17697. National Bureau of Economic Research, Cambridge, Mass. http://www.nber.org/papers/w17697.pdf (accessed February 15, 2018).

Autor, David H., and Mark G. Duggan. 2006. "The Growth in the Social Security Disability Rolls: A Fiscal Crisis Unfolding." *Journal of Economic Perspectives* 20(3): 71–60.

Bailey, Martha J., and Sheldon Danziger, eds. 2013. *Legacies of the War on Poverty.* New York: Russell Sage Foundation.

Bartels, Larry M. 2008. *Unequal Democracy: The Political Economy of the Gilded Age.* New York: Russell Sage Foundation.

Baum, Matthew A. 2011. "Red State, Blue State, Flu State: Media Self-Selection and Partisan Gaps in Swine Flu Vaccinations." *Journal of Health, Policy, Politics, and Law* 36(December): 1021–60.

Beland, Daniel, Christopher Howard, and Kimberly J. Morgan, eds. 2015. *The Oxford Handbook of U.S. Social Policy.* New York: Oxford University Press.

Ben-Shalom, Yonatan, Robert A. Moffit, and John Karl Scholz. 2011. "An Assessment of the Effectiveness of Anti-poverty Programs in the United States." Working Paper 17042. National Bureau of Economic Research, Cambridge, Mass. http://www.nber.org/papers /w17042.pdf (accessed February 15, 2018).

Berry, Jeffrey M., and Sarah Sobieraj. 2016. *The Outrage Industry: Political Opinion Media and the New Incivility.* New York: Oxford University Press.

Bitler, Marianne, and Hilary Hoynes. 2013. "The More Things Change, the More They Stay the Same? The Safety Net and Poverty in the Great Recession." Working Paper 19449. National Bureau of Economic Research, Cambridge, Mass. (September). http://www .nber.org/papers/w19449.pdf (accessed February 15, 2018).

Bonczar, Thomas P. 2003. "Prevalence of Imprisonment in the U.S. Population, 1974– 2001." Washington: U.S. Department of Justice, Office of Justice Programs.

Borstelmann, Thomas. 2011. *The 1970s: A New Global History from Civil Rights to Economic Inequality.* Princeton, N.J.: Princeton University Press.

Brammer, Jack. 2013. "Several Kentucky Tea Party Groups Seek to Defeat McConnell in 2014." *Lexington Herald Leader,* January 22. http://www.mcclatchydc.com/news /politics-government/article24743575.html (accessed February 15, 2018).

Brammer, Jack, and Beth Musgrave. 2013. "Kentucky's Religious Freedom Bill Divided Politicians, Public, Ministers." *Lexington Herald Leader,* March 30. http://www.ken-tucky.com/news/politics-government/article44415102.html (accessed February 15, 2018).

Brettschneider, Corey. 2016. "Trump vs. the Constitution: A Guide." *Politico,* August 4. http://www.politico.com/magazine/story/2016/08/2016-donald-trump-constitution-guide-unconstitutional-freedom-liberty-khan-214139 (accessed February 15, 2018).

Brewer, Mark D., and Jeffrey M. Stonecash. 2015. *Polarization and the Politics of Personal Responsibility.* New York: Oxford University Press.

Bruch, Sarah K., Myra Marx Ferree, and Joe Soss. 2010. "From Policy to Polity: Democracy, Paternalism, and the Incorporation of Disadvantaged Citizens." *American Sociological Review* 75(2): 205–26.

Bump, Phillip. 2016. "Donald Trump Will Be President Thanks to 80,000 People in Three States." *Washington Post,* December 1. https://www.washingtonpost.com/news/the-fix /wp/2016/12/01/donald-trump-will-be-president-thanks-to-80000-people-in -three-states/ (accessed February 15, 2018).

Bureau of National Affairs. (BNA). 1997. *Union Membership and Earnings Data Book: Compilations from the Current Population Survey.* Washington, D.C.: BNA Plus.

Burkhauser, Richard V. 2012. "A Proposal for Fundamental Change in Social Security Disability Insurance." Statement before the House Committee on Ways and Means, Subcommittee on Social Security, September 14. http://waysandmeans.house.gov/Uploaded Files/Burkhauser_Testimony_SS914.pdf (accessed February 15, 2018).

Burman, Leonard E., and Joel Slemrod. 2013. *Taxes in America: What Everyone Needs to Know.* New York: Oxford University Press.

Burns, Nancy, Kay Lehman Schlozman, and Sidney Verba. 2001. *The Private Roots of Public*

Action: Gender, Equality, and Political Participation. Cambridge, Mass.: Harvard University Press.

Campbell, Andrea Louise. 2003. *How Policies Make Citizens: Senior Political Activism and the American Welfare State.* Princeton, N.J.: Princeton University Press.

———. 2014. *Trapped in America's Safety Net: One Family's Struggle.* Chicago: University of Chicago Press.

Cancian, Maria, and Sheldon Danziger, eds. 2009. *Changing Poverty, Changing Policies.* New York: Russell Sage Foundation.

Carnes, Nicholas. 2013. *White-Collar Government: The Hidden Role of Class in Economic Policy Making.* Chicago: University of Chicago Press.

Carnes, Nicholas, and Noam Lupu. 2017. "It's Time to Bust the Myth: Most Trump Voters Were Not Working Class." *Monkey Cage* (blog), *Washington Post,* June 5. https://www.washingtonpost.com/news/monkey-cage/wp/2017/06/05/its-time-to-bust-the-myth-most-trump-voters-were-not-working-class/?utm_term=.aff414b6c0e3 (accessed February 15, 2018).

Center for American Women and Politics. 2017. "Facts—Current Numbers." Eagleton Institute of Politics, Rutgers University, New Brunswick, N.J. http://www.cawp.rutgers.edu/current-numbers (accessed February 15, 2018).

Center on Budget and Policy Priorities. 2015. "Policy Basics: The Earned Income Tax Credit." Center on Budget and Policy Priorities, Washington, D.C., October 21. http://www.cbpp.org/cms/?fa=view&id=2505 (accessed February 15, 2018).

———. 2016a. "Policy Basics: Introduction to Medicaid." Center on Budget and Policy Priorities, Washington, D.C., updated August 16. http://www.cbpp.org/research/health/policy-basics-introduction-to-medicaid (accessed February 15, 2018).

———. 2016b. "The Future of SNAP: Testimony of Stacy Dean, Vice President for Food Assistance Policy, Center on Budget and Policy Priorities, Before the House Agriculture Committee's Nutrition Subcommittee." March 28. http://agriculture.house.gov/uploaded files/dean_testimony.pdf (accessed February 15, 2018).

———. 2017. "Chart Book: TANF at 20." Center on Budget and Policy Priorities, Washington, D.C., (updated) August 16. http://www.cbpp.org/research/family-income-support/chart-book-tanf-at-20 (accessed February 15, 2018).

Cheves, John. 2016. "War on Poverty Failed Because It Trapped People with Handouts, Andy Barr Says." *Lexington Herald Leader,* August 12. http://www.kentucky.com/news/politics-government/article95320067.html (accessed February 15, 2018).

Citizens Against Government Waste (CAGW) Staff. 2013. "Disability Is the New Welfare." CAGW, Washington, D.C., April 3. http://www.cagw.org/media/wastewatcher/disability-new-welfare (accessed February 15, 2018).

Cohen, Roger. 2016. "We Need 'Somebody Spectacular': Views from Trump Country." *New York Times,* September 9. https://www.nytimes.com/2016/09/11/opinion/sunday/we-need-somebody-spectacular-views-from-trump-country.html (accessed February 15, 2018).

Cohn, Nate. 2017. "Turnout Wasn't the Driver of Clinton's Defeat." *New York Times,* March 28. https://www.nytimes.com/2017/03/28/upshot/a-2016-review-turnout-wasnt-the-driver-of-clintons-defeat.html?mcubz=1 (accessed February 15, 2018).

College Board. 2015. "Trends in Student Aid 2015." College Board, New York. http://trends.collegeboard.org/sites/default/files/trends-student-aid-web-final-508-2.pdf (accessed February 15, 2018).

———. 2016. "Trends in College Pricing." College Board, New York. https://trends.collegeboard.org/sites/default/files/2016-trends-college-pricing-web_0.pdf (accessed February 15, 2018).

Colvin, Jill (Associated Press). 2016. "Trump Challenges Legitimacy of Election." *PBS News-Hour,* October 15. http://www.pbs.org/newshour/rundown/trump-challenges-legitimacy-election/ (accessed February 15, 2018).

Commonwealth of Kentucky. 2015. "Voter Turnout Report for the 2014 General Election (11/4/2014)." Kentucky State Board of Elections, February 5. http://elect.ky.gov/SiteCollectionDocuments/Election%20Statistics/turnout/2011-2019/2014/trnout2014.pdf (accessed February 15, 2018).

———. 2016. "Voter Turnout by Age and Sex." Kentucky State Board of Elections, January 26. http://elect.ky.gov/statistics/Documents/voterturnoutagesex-2015G-20160126-033122.pdf (accessed February 15, 2018).

———. 2017. "Voter Turnout by Age and Sex." Kentucky State Board of Elections, February 7. https://elect.ky.gov/statistics/Documents/voterturnoutagesex-2016G-20170207-045855.pdf (accessed February 15, 2018).

Cook, Fay Lomax, and Edith J. Barrett. 1992. *Support for the American Welfare State: The Views of Congress and the Public.* New York: Columbia University Press.

Cook, Fay Lomax, Lawrence R. Jacobs, and Dukhong Kim. 2010. "Trusting What You Know: Information, Knowledge, and Confidence in Social Security." *Journal of Politics* 72: 397–412.

Corn, David. 2012. "Secret Video: Romney Tells Millionaire Donors What He Really Thinks of Obama Voters." *Mother Jones,* September 17. http://www.motherjones.com/politics/2012/09/secret-video-romney-private-fundraiser (accessed February 15, 2018).

———. 2016. "Donald Trump's 47 Percent Moment." *Mother Jones,* March 7. http://www.motherjones.com/politics/2016/03/donald-trump-mitt-romney-47-percent (accessed February 15, 2018).

Cortez, David. 2017. "Broken Mirrors: Identity, Duty, and Belonging in the Age of the New *La(tinx) Migra.*" PhD diss., Department of Government, Cornell University, Ithaca, N.Y.

Cowie, Jefferson. 2010. *Stayin' Alive: The 1970s and the Last Days of the Working Class.* New York: New Press.

Cramer, Katherine J. 2016. *The Politics of Resentment: Rural Consciousness in Wisconsin and the Rise of Scott Walker.* Chicago: University of Chicago Press.

Craw, Ben, and Zach Carter. 2012. "Paul Ryan: 60 Percent of Americans Are Takers, Not Makers." *Huffington Post,* October 5. https://www.huffingtonpost.com/2012/10/05/paul-ryan-60-percent-of-a_n_1943073.html (accessed February 15, 2018).

Crenshaw, Kimberle. 1991. "Mapping the Margins: Intersectionality, Identity Politics, and Violence against Women of Color." *Stanford Law Review* 43: 1241–99.

Currie, Janet M. 2006. *The Invisible Safety Net: Protecting the Nation's Poor Children and Families.* Princeton, N.J.: Princeton University Press.

Dahl, Robert A. 1989. *Democracy and Its Critics.* New Haven, Conn.: Yale University Press.

———. 2003. *How Democratic Is the American Constitution?* 2nd ed. New Haven, Conn.: Yale University Press.

Dawson, Michael. 2003. *Black Visions: The Roots of African American Political Ideologies.* Chicago: University of Chicago Press.

Delli Carpini, Michael X., and Scott Keeter. 1996. *What Americans Know about Politics and Why It Matters.* New Haven, Conn.: Yale University Press.

DeSilver, Drew. 2015. "5 Facts about Social Security." Pew Research Center, Washington, D.C., August 18. www.pewresearch.org/fact-tank/2015/08/18/5-facts-about-social -security/ (accessed February 15, 2018).

———. 2016. "U.S. Voter Turnout Trails Most Developed Countries." Pew Research Center, Washington, D.C., May 15. http://www.pewresearch.org/fact-tank/2016/08/02 /u-s-voter-turnout-trails-most-developed-countries/ (accessed February 15, 2018).

Donahue, John J., and James Heckman. 1991. "Continuous versus Episodic Change: The Impact of Civil Rights Policy on the Economic Status of Blacks." *Journal of Economic Literature* 29: 1603–43.

Drutman, Lee. 2015. *The Business of America Is Lobbying.* New York: Oxford University Press.

Eberstadt, Nicholas. 2012. *A Nation of Takers: America's Entitlement Epidemic.* West Conshohocken, Penn.: Templeton Press.

Economic Policy Institute (EPI). 2012. "Distribution of Employment, by Industry, Selected Years, 1979–2011 (and 2020 Projections)" (chart). *The State of Working America,* Economic Policy Institute, Washington, D.C., March 28. http://stateofworkingamerica .org/chart/swa-jobs-figure-5b-distribution-employment/.

———. 2014. "Average Family Income Growth, by Income Group, 1947–2013." *The State of Working America,* EPI, Washington, D.C., updated September 25. http://www.stateof workingamerica.org/charts/real-annual-family-income-growth-by-quintile-1947 -79-and-1979-2010/ (accessed February 15, 2018).

———. 2016. "Wages." *The State of Working America,* EPI, Washington, D.C. http://www .stateofworkingamerica.org/fact-sheets/wages/ (accessed February 15, 2018).

Edin, Kathryn J., and Laura Lein. 1997. *Making Ends Meet: How Single Mothers Survive Welfare and Low-Wage Work.* New York: Russell Sage Foundation.

Edin, Kathryn J., and H. Luke Shaefer. 2016. *$2.00 a Day: Living on Almost Nothing in America.* New York: Houghton Mifflin Harcourt.

Eisenstadt, Marnie. 2013. "Syracuse Working Mom Defends Food Stamps as Congress Debates Cuts." (Syracuse) *Post Standard,* October 3. http://www.syracuse.com/news/index .ssf/2013/10/syracuse_working_mom_defends_food_stamps_as_congress_debates_cuts .html (accessed February 15, 2018).

Ellis, Christopher, and James A. Stimson. 1992. *Ideology in America.* New York: Cambridge University Press.

Engquist, Erik. 2018. "Mortgage Interest Deduction Down But Not Out." *Crain's,* January 11. http://www.crainsnewyork.com/article/20180111/REAL_ESTATE/180109947 /mortgage-interest-deduction-down-but-not-out (accessed February 15, 2018).

Erkulwater, Jennifer L. 2006. *Disability Rights and the American Social Safety Net.* Ithaca, N.Y.: Cornell University Press.

———. 2015. "Social Security Disability Insurance and Supplemental Security Income." In *The Oxford Handbook of U.S. Social Policy,* edited by Daniel Beland, Christopher Howard, and Kimberly J. Morgan. New York: Oxford University Press.

Esping-Andersen, Gøsta. 1990. *The Three Worlds of Welfare Capitalism.* Princeton, N.J.: Princeton University Press.

Faricy, Christopher G. 2015. *Welfare for the Wealthy: Parties, Social Spending, and Inequality in the United States.* New York: Cambridge University Press.

Featherman, David L., and Robert M. Hauser. 1978. *Opportunity and Change.* New York: Academic Press.

Federal Election Commission (FEC). 2012. "Federal Elections 2012." FEC, Washington. http://www.fec.gov/pubrec/fe2012/2012presmaps.pdf (accessed February 15, 2018).

File, Thom. 2015. "Who Votes? Congressional Elections and the American Electorate, 1978–2014." P20-577. U.S. Census Bureau, Washington, July. https://www.census .gov/content/dam/Census/library/publications/2015/demo/p20-577.pdf (accessed February 15, 2018).

Fineman, Howard. 2015. "GOP's Kentucky Wins a Good Sigh for the Tea Party." *Huffington Post,* November 3. http://www.huffingtonpost.com/entry/gop-wins-kentucky-tea -party_us_56392f27e4b0b24aee47f61f (accessed February 15, 2018).

Fitzgerald, F. Scott. 1995. "The Rich Boy." In *The Short Stories of F. Scott Fitzgerald: A New Collection,* edited by Matthew J. Bruccoli. New York: Simon & Schuster.

Floyd, Ife. 2016. "TANF Cash Benefits Have Fallen by More than 20 Percent in Most States and Continue to Erode." Center on Budget and Policy Priorities, Washington, D.C., October 13. https://www.cbpp.org/sites/default/files/atoms/files/10-30-14tanf.pdf (accessed February 15, 2018).

Fournier, Ron, and Sophie Quinton. 2012. "How Americans Lost Trust in Our Greatest Institutions." *Atlantic,* April 20.

Fowler, Floyd, Jr. 1984. *Survey Research Methods.* Beverly Hills, Calif.: Sage Publications.

Fox, Cybelle. 2012. *Three Worlds of Relief: Race, Immigration, and the American Welfare State from the Progressive Era to the New Deal.* Princeton, N.J.: Princeton University Press.

Fox News. 2016. "Sarah Palin, 'Donald J. Trump Is That Revolutionary!'" March 14. https:// www.youtube.com/watch?v=F9-S-oTY5oY (accessed February 15, 2018).

Francia, Peter L., and Renan Levine. 2006. "Feast or Famine at the Federal Luau? Understanding Net Federal Spending Under Bush." *The Forum* 4(2). DOI:10.2202/1540 -8884.1114.

Frank, Robert. 2016. *Success and Luck: Good Fortune and the Myth of Meritocracy.* Princeton, N.J.: Princeton University Press.

Frank, Thomas. 2005. *What's the Matter with Kansas? How Conservatives Won the Heart of America.* New York: Henry Holt & Co.

Frankel, Matthew. 2015. "The Ten Richest Counties in the United States." *Motley Fool,* September 20. http://www.fool.com/investing/general/2015/09/20/the-top-10-richest -counties-in-the-united-states.aspx (accessed February 15, 2018).

Free, Lloyd A., and Hadley Cantril. 1968. *The Political Beliefs of Americans: A Study of Public Opinion*. New York: Simon & Schuster/Clarion.

Freeman, Richard B. 2007. *America Works: Critical Thoughts on the Exceptional U.S. Labor Market*. New York: Russell Sage Foundation.

Freeman, Richard B., and James Medoff. 1984. *What Do Unions Do?* New York: Basic Books.

Fresh Air. 2014. "Senator Mitch McConnell's Political Life, Examined, in 'The Cynic.'" *NPR, Fresh Air*, November 20. http://www.npr.org/2014/11/20/365484670/sen-mitch-mcconnells-political-life-examined-in-the-cynic (accessed February 15, 2018).

Gallup. 2017a. "Confidence in Institutions." *Gallup News*. http://www.gallup.com/poll/1597/confidence-institutions.aspx (accessed February 15, 2018).

———. 2017b. "Satisfaction with the United States." *Gallup News*. http://www.gallup.com/poll/1669/general-mood-country.aspx (accessed February 15, 2018).

Galvin, Daniel J., and Chloe N. Thurston. 2017. "The Democrats' Misplaced Faith in Policy Feedback." *The Forum*. 15(2): 333–43.

Gerth, Joseph. 2016. "Bevin: Beshear Officials Shook Down Workers." *Courier Journal*, April 19. www.courier-journal.com/story/news/politics/ky-governor/2016/04/19/bevin-alleges-ethical-lapses-beshear-administration/83227646/ (accessed February 15, 2018).

Gilens, Martin. 1999. *Why Americans Hate Welfare: Race, Media, and the Politics of Antipoverty Policy*. Chicago: University of Chicago Press.

———. 2012. *Affluence and Influence: Economic Inequality and Political Power in America*. New York: Russell Sage Foundation.

Gilens, Martin, and Benjamin I. Page. 2014. "Testing Theories of American Politics: Elites, Interest Groups, and Average Citizens." *Perspectives on Politics* 12(3): 564–81.

Gitterman, Daniel P. 2010. *Boosting Paychecks: The Politics of Supporting America's Working Poor*. Washington, D.C.: Brookings Institution Press.

Goldin, Claudia, and Robert A. Margo. 1992. "The Great Compression: The Wage Structure in the United States at Mid-century." *Quarterly Journal of Economics* 107(1, February): 1–34.

Gordon, Linda. 1994. *Pitied but Not Entitled: Poor Women and the History of Welfare*. New York: Free Press.

Gould, Elise, Jessica Schieder, and Kathleen Geier. 2016. "What is the Gender Pay Gap and Is It Real?" Economic Policy Institute. Report. www.epi.org/publication/what-is-the-gender-pay-gap-and-is-it-real/ (accessed April 2, 2018).

Gould, Skye, and Rebecca Harrington. 2016. "7 Charts Show Who Propelled Trump to Victory." *Business Insider*, November 10. http://www.businessinsider.com/exit-polls-who-voted-for-trump-clinton-2016-11/#more-women-voted-for-clinton-as-expected-but-trump-still-got-42-of-female-votes-1 (accessed February 15, 2018).

Gourevitch, Rebecca, and Benjamin D. Sommers. 2016. "Medicaid Expansion in Kentucky: Early Successes, Future Uncertainty." Commonwealth Fund, July 8. http://www.commonwealthfund.org/publications/blog/2016/jul/medicaid-expansion-in-kentucky (accessed February 15, 2018).

Greenstein, Robert. 1991. "Universal and Targeted Approaches to Relieving Poverty: An Alternative View." In *The Urban Underclass*, edited by Paul E. Peterson and Christopher Jencks. Washington, D.C.: Brookings Institution.

Grogan, Colleen, and Eric Patashnik. 2003. "Between Welfare Medicine and Mainstream Entitlement: Medicaid at the Crossroads." *Journal of Health Policy, Politics, and Law* 28(5): 821–58.

Gruber, Jonathan. 2003. "Medicaid." In *Means-Tested Transfer Programs in the United States,* edited by Robert A. Moffitt. Chicago: National Bureau of Economic Research.

Gundersen, Craig. 2015. "Food-Assistance Programs and Food Security." In *The Oxford Handbook of U.S. Social Policy,* edited by Daniel Beland, Christopher Howard, and Kimberly J. Morgan. New York: Oxford University Press.

Hacker, Jacob S. 2002. *The Divided Welfare State: The Battle over Public and Private Social Benefits in the United States.* New York: Cambridge University Press.

———. 2004. "Privatizing Risk without Privatizing the Welfare State: The Hidden Politics of Social Policy Retrenchment in the United States." *American Political Science Review* 98(2): 243–60.

Hall, Richard L., and Frank W. Wayman. 1990. "Buying Time: Moneyed Interests and the Mobilization of Bias in Congressional Committees." *American Political Science Review* 84: 797–820.

Halpern-Meekin, Sarah, Kathryn Edin, Laura Tach, and Jennifer Sykes. 2015. *It's Not Like I'm Poor: How Working Families Make Ends Meet in a Post-Welfare World.* Oakland: University of California Press.

Han, Hahrie. 2009. *Moved to Action: Motivation, Participation, and Inequality in American Politics.* Stanford, Calif.: Stanford University Press.

———. 2014. *How Organizations Develop Activists: Civic Associations and Leadership in the Twenty-First Century.* New York: Oxford University Press.

Harrington-Meyer, Madonna. 1996. "Making Claims as Workers or Wives: The Distribution of Social Security Benefits." *American Sociological Review* 61(3): 449–65.

Harsanyi, David. 2007. *The Nanny State: How Food Fascists, Teetotaling Do-Gooders, Priggish Moralists, and Other Bone-Headed Bureaucrats Are Turning America into a Nation of Children.* New York: Broadway Books.

Hayes, Danny, and Seth C. McKee. 2008. "Toward a One-Party South?" *American Politics Research* 36: 3–32.

Hays, Sharon. 2003. *Flat Broke with Children: Women in the Age of Welfare Reform.* New York: Oxford University Press.

Heckman, James, and Brook S. Payner. 1989. "Determining the Impact of Federal Antidiscrimination Policy on the Economic Status of Blacks: A Study of South Carolina." *American Economic Review* 79(1): 138–77.

Hemingway, Ernest. 1961. *The Snows of Kilimanjaro.* New York: Charles Scribner and Sons.

Hetherington, Marc J. 2005. *Why Trust Matters: Declining Political Trust and the Demise of American Liberalism.* Princeton, N.J.: Princeton University Press.

Hetherington, Marc J., and Thomas J. Rudolph. 2015. *Why Washington Won't Work.* Chicago: University of Chicago Press.

Hibbing, John R., and Elizabeth Theiss-Morse, eds. 2001. *What Is It About Government That Americans Dislike?* New York: Cambridge University Press.

———. 2002. *Stealth Democracy: Americans' Beliefs about How Government Should Work.* New York: Cambridge University Press.

Hirschl, Thomas A., and Mark R. Rank. 2002. "Welfare Use as a Life Course Event: Toward a New Understanding of the U.S. Safety Net." *Social Work* 47(July): 237–48.

Hochschild, Arlie Russell. 2016. *Strangers in Their Own Land: Anger and Mourning on the American Right.* New York: New Press.

Hochschild, Jennifer. 1981. *What's Fair? American Beliefs about Distributive Justice.* Cambridge, Mass.: Harvard University Press.

———. 1996. *Facing Up to the American Dream: Race, Class, and the Soul of the Nation.* Princeton, N.J.: Princeton University Press.

Howard, Christopher. 1997. *The Hidden Welfare State: Tax Expenditures and Social Policy in the United States.* Princeton, N.J.: Princeton University Press.

———. 2007. *The Welfare State Nobody Knows.* Princeton, N.J.: Princeton University Press.

Hoynes, Hilary. 2016. "Why SNAP Matters." GSPP Working Paper. https://gspp.berkeley .edu/assets/uploads/research/pdf/Hoynes_Why_SNAP_Matters_1-25-16.pdf (accessed February 15, 2018).

Huang, Jon, Samuel Jacoby, Michael Strickland, and K. K. Rebecca Lai. 2016. "Election 2016: Exit Polls." *New York Times,* November 8. https://www.nytimes.com/interactive /2016/11/08/us/politics/election-exit-polls.html (accessed February 15, 2018).

Jacobs, Eva E., and Mary Meghan Ryan. 2003. *Handbook of U.S. Labor Statistics: Employment, Earnings, Prices, Productivity, and Other Labor Data.* 6th ed. Lanham, Md.: Bernan Press.

Jacobs, Lawrence R., and Suzanne Mettler. 2018. "When and How New Policy Creates New Politics: Examining the Feedback Effects of the Affordable Care Act on Public Opinion." *Perspectives on Politics* 16(2).

Jacobs, Lawrence R., and Benjamin Page. 2009. *Class War? What Americans Really Think about Economic Inequality.* Chicago: University of Chicago Press.

Jacobs, Lawrence R., and Theda Skocpol. 2010. *Health Care Reform and American Politics: What Everyone Needs to Know.* New York: Oxford University Press.

Johnson, Kenneth. 2006. "Demographic Trends in Rural and Small Town America." Carsey Institute, University of New Hampshire, Durham.

Johnson, Paul D., Trudi Renwick, and Kathleen Short. 2010. "Estimating the Value of Federal Housing Assistance for the Supplemental Poverty Measure." SEHSD Working Paper 2010-13. Washington: U.S. Census Bureau (December). https://cps.ipums.org /cps/resources/spm/SPM_HousingAssistance.pdf (accessed February 15, 2018).

Jones, Maggie R. 2014. "Changes in EITC Eligibility and Participation, 2005–2009." CARRA Working Paper Series, Working Paper 2014-04. Center for Administrative Records, Research, and Applications, U.S. Census Bureau, Washington, July 11. https:// www.census.gov/content/dam/Census/library/working-papers/2014/adrm/carra -wp-2014-04.pdf (accessed February 15, 2018).

Kanik, Alexandra. 2016. "Kentucky Turned a Deeper Shade of Red on Election Day." Kentucky Center for Investigative Reporting, November 9. http://kycir.org/2016/11/09 /kentucky-turned-a-deeper-shade-of-red-on-election-day-see-just-how-much/ (accessed February 15, 2018).

Katznelson, Ira. 2005. *When Affirmative Action Was White.* New York: W. W. Norton.

Kennedy, John F. 1963. "400—Remarks at Heber Springs, Arkansas, at the Dedication of

Greers Ferry Dam, October 3." American Presidency Project. http://www.presidency
.ucsb.edu/ws/index.php?pid=9455 (accessed February 15, 2018).

Kentucky Energy and Environment Cabinet, Department for Energy Development and Independence. 2014. "Kentucky Coal Facts." http://energy.ky.gov/Coal%20Facts%20 Library/Kentucky%20Coal%20Facts%20-%2014th%20Edition%20(2014).pdf (accessed February 15, 2018).

Kerrissey, Jasmine, and Evan Schofer. 2013. "Union Membership and Political Participation in the United States." *Social Forces* 91(3): 895–928.

Kliff, Sarah. 2016. "Why Obamacare Enrollees Voted for Trump." *Vox,* December 13. http:// www.vox.com/science-and-health/2016/12/13/13848794/kentucky-obamacare-trump (accessed February 15, 2018).

Kohler-Hausmann, Julilly. 2017. *Getting Tough: Welfare and Imprisonment in 1970s America.* Princeton, N.J.: Princeton University Press.

Konty, Melissa Fry, and Jason Bailey. 2009. "The Impact of Coal on the Kentucky State Budget." Mountain Association of Community Economic Development. http://maced .org/coal/documents/Impact_of_Coal.pdf (accessed February 15, 2018).

Krawak, Paul M. 2015. "Warnings Sounded for Disability Fund." *Congressional Quarterly Weekly,* April 27, 22.

Krimmel, Katherine, and Kelly Rader. 2017. "The Federal Spending Paradox: Economic Self-Interest and Symbolic Racism in Contemporary Fiscal Politics." *American Politics Research* 45(5): 727–54.

Krogstad, Jens Manuel, and Gustavo Lopez. 2016. "Roughly Half of Hispanics Have Experienced Discrimination." Pew Research Center, Washington, D.C., June 29. http:// www.pewresearch.org/fact-tank/2016/06/29/roughly-half-of-hispanics-have-experi enced-discrimination/ (accessed February 15, 2018).

Kruse, Kevin M. 2005. *White Flight: Atlanta and the Making of Modern Conservatism.* Princeton, N.J.: Princeton University Press.

Lacy, Dean. 2014. "Moochers and Makers in the Voting Booth: Who Benefits from Federal Spending and How Did They Vote in the 2012 Presidential Election?" *Public Opinion Quarterly* 78: 255–75.

Lane, Eric, and Michael Oreskes. 2007. *The Genius of America: How the Constitution Saved Our Country and Why It Can Again.* New York: Bloomsbury.

Layman, Geoffrey C., and Thomas M. Carsey. 2002a. "Party Polarization and 'Conflict Extension' in the American Electorate." *American Journal of Political Science* 46(4): 786.

———. 2002b. "Party Polarization and Party Structuring of Policy Attitudes: A Comparison of Three NES Panel Studies." *Political Behavior* 24(3): 199–236.

Layman, Geoffrey C., Thomas M. Carsey, John C. Green, Richard Herrera, and Rosalyn Cooperman. 2010. "Activists and Conflict Extension in American Party Politics." *American Political Science Review* 104(02), 324–46.

Lawless, Jennifer L., and Richard L. Fox. 2013. "Girls Just Wanna Not Run: The Gender Gap in Young Americans' Political Ambition." Women and Politics Institute, American University, Washington, D.C., March. https://www.american.edu/spa/wpi/upload /Girls-Just-Wanna-Not-Run_Policy-Report.pdf (accessed February 15, 2018).

Ledbetter, James. 2010. "America's Hidden Welfare Program." *Slate,* September 13. http://

www.slate.com/articles/business/moneybox/2010/09/americas_hidden_welfare
_program.html (accessed February 15, 2018).

Lee, Frances E. 2009. *Beyond Ideology: Politics, Principles, and Partisanship in the U.S. Senate.* Chicago: University of Chicago Press.

———. 2016. *Insecure Majorities: Congress and the Perpetual Campaign.* Chicago: University of Chicago Press.

Lee, Marlene A., and Mark Mather. 2008. "U.S. Labor Force Trends." *Population Bulletin* (publication of the Population Reference Bureau) 63(2, June): 1–16. http://www.prb.org/pdf08/63.2uslabor.pdf (accessed February 15, 2018).

Leighley, Jan E., and Jonathan Nagler. 2007. "Unions, Voter Turnout, and Class Bias in the U.S. Electorate, 1964–2004." *Journal of Politics* 69(2).

———. 2014. *Who Votes Now? Demographics, Issues, Inequality, and Turnout in the United States.* Princeton, N.J.: Princeton University Press.

Lerman, Amy E., and Katherine T. McCabe. 2017. "Personal Experiences and Public Opinion: A Theory and Test of Conditional Policy Feedback." *Journal of Politics* 79(2): 624–41.

Lerman, Amy E., Meredith L. Sadin, and Samuel Trachtman. 2017. "Policy Uptake as Political Behavior: Evidence from the Affordable Care Act." *American Political Science Review* 111(4): 755–70.

Lerman, Amy E., and Vesla Mae Weaver. 2014. *Arresting Citizenship: The Democratic Consequences of American Crime Control.* Chicago: University of Chicago Press.

Levedahl, J. William. 1998. "The Effect of an Electronic Benefit Transfer (EBT) System on Food Expenditure of Food Stamp Recipients: Evidence from the Maryland Statewide Implementation." Paper presented to the annual meeting of the American Agricultural Economics Association, Salt Lake City, Utah, August 2–5. http://ageconsearch.umn.edu/bitstream/20905/1/spleve01.pdf (accessed February 15, 2018).

Levi, Margaret, and Laura Stoker. 2000. "Political Trust and Trustworthiness." *Annual Review of Political Science* 3: 475–507.

Lewis, Jeffrey B., Keith Poole, Howard Rosenthal, Adam Boche, Aaron Rudkin, and Luke Sonnet. 2017. *Voteview: Congressional Roll-Call Votes Database.* https://voteview.com/ (accessed February 15, 2018).

Lieberman, Robert C. 1998. *Shifting the Color Line: Race and the American Welfare State.* Cambridge, Mass.: Harvard University Press.

Lubell, Samuel. 1952. *The Future of American Politics.* New York: Harper & Brothers.

Malonebeach, Eileen E., Cindy S. Frank, and Roschelle A. Heuberger. 2012. "Electronic Access to Food and Cash Benefits." *Social Work in Public Health* 27: 424–40.

Marquis, K. H., and J. C. Moore. 2013. "The Survey of Income and Program Participation: SIPP Record Check Results: Implications for Measurement Principles and Practice." Working Paper 126. Washington: U.S. Department of Commerce, Census Bureau.

Marshall, T. H. 1992. "Citizenship and the Social Class" (1950). Reprinted in *Citizenship and Social Class* by T. H. Marshall and Tom Bottomore. London: Pluto Press.

Mathiowetz, Nancy A., Charlie Brown, and John Bound. 2001. "Measurement Error in Surveys of the Low-Income Population." In *Studies of Welfare Population: Data Collection and Research Issues,* edited by Michele Ver Ploeg, Robert A. Moffitt, and Constance

F. Citro. Washington, D.C.: Committee of National Statistics, National Research Council.

McCall, Leslie. 2013. *The Undeserving Rich: American Beliefs about Inequality, Opportunity, and Redistribution.* New York: Cambridge University Press.

McCarty, Nolan, Keith T. Poole, and Howard Rosenthal. 2006. *Polarized America: The Dance of Ideology and Unequal Riches.* Cambridge, Mass.: MIT Press.

McDonagh, Eileen. 2009. *The Motherless State: Women's Political Leadership and American Democracy.* Chicago: University of Chicago Press.

McDonald, Michael P. 2014. "National General Election VEP Turnout Rates, 1789–Present." United States Election Project, Gainesville, Fla., June 11. http://www.electproject.org/national-1789-present (accessed February 15, 2018).

———. 2016. "2016 November General Election Turnout Rates." United States Election Project, Gainesville, Fla., http://www.electproject.org/2016g (accessed February 15, 2018).

Mettler, Suzanne. 1998. *Dividing Citizens: Gender and Federalism in New Deal Public Policy.* Ithaca, N.Y.: Cornell University Press.

———. 2005. *Soldiers to Citizens: The GI Bill and the Making of the Greatest Generation.* New York: Oxford University Press.

———. 2011. *The Submerged State: How Invisible Government Policies Undermine American Democracy.* Chicago: University of Chicago Press.

———. 2014. *Degrees of Inequality: How the Politics of Higher Education Policy Sabotaged the American Dream.* New York: Basic Books.

———. 2016. "The Policyscape and the Challenges of Contemporary Politics to Policy Maintenance." *Perspectives on Politics* 14(2, June): 369–90.

Mettler, Suzanne, and Andrew Milstein. 2007. "American Political Development from Citizens' Perspective: Tracking Federal Government's Presence in Individual Lives over Time." *Studies in American Political Development* (Spring): 110–30.

Mettler, Suzanne, and Joe Soss. 2004. "The Consequences of Public Policy for Democratic Citizenship: Bridging Policy Studies and Mass Politics." *Perspectives on Politics* 2(1): 55–73.

Mettler, Suzanne, and Jeff Stonecash. 2008. "Government Program Usage and Political Voice." *Social Science Quarterly* 89(2): 273–93.

Meyerson, Harold. 2013. "The Forty-Year Slump." *American Prospect,* November 12. http://prospect.org/article/40-year-slump (accessed February 15, 2018).

Michener, Jamila. 2018. *Fragmented Democracy: Medicaid, Federalism, and Unequal Politics.* New York Cambridge University Press.

Mink, Gwendolyn. 1996. *The Wages of Motherhood: Inequality in the Welfare State, 1917–1942.* Ithaca, N.Y.: Cornell University Press.

Mishel, Lawrence, Josh Bivens, Elise Gould, and Heidi Shierholz. 2012. *The State of Working America.* 12th ed. Washington, D.C., and Ithaca, N.Y.: Economic Policy Institute and Cornell University Press.

Moffitt, Robert A. 2013. "The Great Recession and the Social Safety Net." *Annals of the American Academy of Political and Social Science* 650(1).

———. 2014. "The Social Safety Net in the Great Recession: Success, Failure, or a Little of Each?" *Milken Institute Review* (fourth quarter). http://assets1b.milkeninstitute.org/assets/Publication/MIReview/PDF/55-65-MR64.pdf (accessed February 15, 2018).

———. 2015. "The Deserving Poor, the Family, and the U.S. Welfare System." *Demography* 52: 729–49.

Moorhead, Molly. 2012. "Romney Says 47 Percent of Americans Pay No Income Tax." *PolitiFact,* September 18. http://www.politifact.com/truth-o-meter/statements/2012/sep/18/mitt-romney/romney-says-47-percent-americans-pay-no-income-tax/ (accessed February 15, 2018).

Morgan, Kimberly J., and Andrea Louise Campbell. 2011. *The Delegated Welfare State: Medicare, Markets, and the Governance of Social Policy.* New York: Oxford University Press.

Morone, James A. 1990. *The Democratic Wish: Popular Participation and the Limits of American Government.* New York: Basic Books.

Mounk, Yascha. 2017. *The Age of Responsibility: Luck, Choice, and the Welfare State.* Cambridge, Mass.: Harvard University Press.

Murray, Charles A. 2012. *Coming Apart: The State of White America, 1960–2010.* New York: Crown Forum.

Mutz, Diana C. 2015. *In Your Face Politics: The Consequences of Incivility.* Princeton, N.J.: Princeton University Press.

National Employment Law Project (NELP). 2014. "The Low-Wage Recovery: Industry Employment and Wages Four Years into the Recovery." NELP data brief. National Employment Law Project, New York, April. http://www.nelp.org/content/uploads/2015/03/Low-Wage-Recovery-Industry-Employment-Wages-2014 Report.pdf (accessed February 15, 2018).

New York Department of Labor. 2015. "Central New York Projections, 2012–2022: Top 15 Fastest Growing Job Titles." Occupational Projections and Occupational Employment Statistics programs, New York Department of Labor, Albany. https://labor.ny.gov/stats/cen/CentralNY-Fastest-Growing-2012-2022.xls (accessed February 15, 2018).

New York Times. 1995. "Prison for Ex-Congressman." *New York Times,* March 14. http://www.nytimes.com/1995/03/14/us/prison-for-ex-congressman.html (accessed February 15, 2018).

Nie, Norman H., Jane Junn, and Kenneth Stehlik-Barry. 1996. *Education and Democratic Citizenship in America.* Chicago: University of Chicago Press.

O'Keefe, Ed. 2014. "The House Has Voted 54 Times in 4 Years on Obamacare. Here's the Full List." *Washington Post,* March 21. https://www.washingtonpost.com/news/the-fix/wp/2014/03/21/the-house-has-voted-54-times-in-four-years-on-obamacare-heres-the-full-list/ (accessed February 15, 2018).

Organization for Economic Cooperation and Development (OECD). 2014. "Social Expenditure Update." OECD, Paris, November. http://www.oecd.org/els/soc/OECD2014-Social-Expenditure-Update-Nov2014-8pages.pdf (accessed February 15, 2018).

———. 2016. "OECD. Stat: Social Expenditure: Aggregated Data." OECD, Paris. http://stats.oecd.org/Index.aspx?datasetcode=SOCX_AGG (accessed February 15, 2018).

Orlet, Christopher. 2011. "The New Welfare Swindle." *American Spectator,* November 17. https://spectator.org/36566_new-welfare-swindle/ (accessed February 15, 2018).

Page, Benjamin I., and Robert Y. Shapiro. 1992. *The Rational Public: Fifty Years of Americans' Policy Preferences*. Chicago: Chicago University Press.

Pallarito, Karen. 2011. "Life Expectancy in U.S. Trails Top Nations." CNN, June 16. http://www.cnn.com/2011/HEALTH/06/15/life.expectancy.united.states/index.html?hpt=hp_c2 (accessed February 15, 2018).

Parker, Christopher, and Matt Barreto. 2013. *Change They Can't Believe In: The Tea Party and Reactionary Politics in America*. Princeton, N.J.: Princeton University Press.

Patashnick, Eric M., and Julian E. Zelizer. 2013. "The Struggle to Remake Politics: Liberal Reform and the Limits of Policy Feedback in the Contemporary American State." *Perspectives on Politics* 11(4): 1071–87.

Pendall, Rolf, and Susan Christopherson. 2004. "Losing Ground: Income and Poverty in Upstate New York, 1980–2000." Metropolitan Policy Program, Brookings Institution, Washington, D.C.

Pew Charitable Trusts. 2013. "The Geographic Distribution of the Mortgage Interest Deduction." Pew Charitable Trusts, Philadelphia. http://www.pewtrusts.org/~/media/legacy/uploadedfiles/pcs_assets/2013/midreport2.pdf (accessed February 15, 2018).

Pew Research Center. 2012a. "Partisan Polarization Surges in Bush, Obama Years: Trends in American Values, 1987–2012." U.S. Politics & Policy. Pew Research Center, Washington, D.C., June 4. http://www.people-press.org/2012/06/04/partisan-polarization-surges-in-bush-obama-years/.

———. 2012b. "Assessing the Representativeness of Public Opinion Surveys." U.S. Politics & Policy. Pew Research Center, Washington, D.C., May 15. http://www.people-press.org/2012/05/15/assessing-the-representativeness-of-public-opinion-surveys/ (accessed February 15, 2018).

———. 2012c. "A Bipartisan Nation of Beneficiaries." Pew Social & Demographic Trends. Pew Research Center, Washington, D.C., December 18. http://www.pewsocialtrends.org/files/2012/12/Benefits_FINAL_12-20.pdf (accessed February 15, 2018).

———. 2015. "Beyond Distrust: How Americans View Their Government: 1. Trust in Government, 1958–2015." U.S. Politics & Policy. Pew Research Center, Washington, D.C., November 23. http://www.people-press.org/2015/11/23/1-trust-in-government-1958-2015/ (accessed February 15, 2018).

———. 2016. "A Divided and Pessimistic Electorate." Pew Research Center, Washington, D.C., November 10. http://assets.pewresearch.org/wp-content/uploads/sites/5/2016/11/10151213/11-10-16-election-release.pdf (accessed February 15, 2018).

Pierson, Paul. 1993. "When Effect Becomes Cause: Policy Feedback and Political Change." *World Politics* 45(4): 595–628.

———. 1994. *Dismantling the Welfare State? Reagan, Thatcher, and the Politics of Retrenchment*. New York: Cambridge University Press.

Piketty, Thomas. 2014. *Capital in the Twenty-First Century*. Cambridge, Mass.: Harvard University Press.

Piketty, Thomas, and Emmanuel Saez. 2003. "Income Inequality in the United States, 1913–1998." *Quarterly Journal of Economics* 117(1): 1–39.

Pollack, Harold. 2013. "Misleading 'Trends with Benefits.'" Century Foundation, March

28. https://tcf.org/content/commentary/misleading-trends-with-benefits/ (accessed February 15, 2018).

Powell, G. Bingham. 1986. "American Voter Turnout in Comparative Perspective." *American Political Science Review* 80(1): 17–43.

Prior, Markus. 2007. *Post-Broadcast Democracy: How Media Choice Increases Inequality in Political Involvement and Polarizes Elections.* New York: Cambridge University Press.

Quadagno, Jill. 1996. *The Color of Welfare: How Racism Undermined the War on Poverty.* New York: Oxford University Press.

Radcliff, Benjamin, and Patricia A. Davis. 2000. "Labor Organization and Electoral Participation in Industrial Democracies." *American Journal of Political Science* 44(1): 132.

Rank, Mark R., and Thomas A. Hirschl. 2002. "Welfare Use as a Life Course Event: Toward a New Understanding of the U.S. Safety Net." *Social Work* 47: 237–48.

———. 2005. "Likelihood of Using Food Stamps during the Adulthood Years." *Journal of Nutrition Education and Behavior* 37: 137–46.

Rank, Mark Robert, Thomas A. Hirschl, and Kirk A. Foster. 2014. *Chasing the American Dream: Understanding What Shapes Our Fortunes.* New York: Oxford University Press.

Rau, Jordan. 2017. "Medicaid Cuts May Force Retirees Out of Nursing Homes." *New York Times,* June 24. https://www.nytimes.com/2017/06/24/science/medicaid-cutbacks -elderly-nursing-homes.html (accessed February 15, 2018).

Reagan, Ronald. 1981. "Inaugural Address, January 20, 1981." American Presidency Project. http://www.presidency.ucsb.edu/ws/?pid=43130 (accessed February 15, 2018).

Riffkin, Rebecca. 2015. "Big Government Still Named as Biggest Threat to U.S." *Gallup News,* December 22. http://www.gallup.com/poll/187919/big-government-named -biggest-threat.aspx (accessed February 15, 2018).

Rigby, Elizabeth, and Melanie J. Springer. 2011. "Does Electoral Reform Increase (or Decrease) Electoral Inequality?" *Political Research Quarterly* 64(2): 420–34.

Rodgers, Daniel T. 2011. *Age of Fracture.* Cambridge, Mass.: Harvard University Press.

Rogers, Allison, and Eric Toder. 2011. "Trends in Tax Expenditures, 1985–2016." Tax Policy Center, Urban Institute and Brookings Institution, Washington, D.C., September 16. http://www.taxpolicycenter.org/UploadedPDF/412404-Tax-Expenditure-Trends.pdf (accessed February 15, 2018).

Roosevelt, Franklin D. 1944. "State of the Union Message to Congress, January 11, 1944." Franklin D. Roosevelt Presidential Library and Museum. http://www.fdrlibrary.marist .edu/archives/address_text.html (accessed February 15, 2018).

Rose, Max, and Frank R. Baumgartner. 2013. "Framing the Poor: Media Coverage and U.S. Poverty Policy, 1960–2008." *Policy Studies Journal* 41: 22–53.

Rosenbaum, Sara, Sara Schmucker, and Sara Rothenberg. 2016. "Will Kentucky Roll Back Its Medicaid Expansion?" Commonwealth Fund, July 8. http://www.commonwealth fund.org/publications/blog/2016/jul/will-kentucky-roll-back-its-medicaid-expansion (accessed February 15, 2018).

Rosenfeld, Jake. 2014. *What Unions No Longer Do.* Cambridge, Mass.: Harvard University Press.

Rosenstone, Steven J., and John Mark Hansen. 1993. *Mobilization, Participation, and Democracy in America.* New York: Macmillan.

Rudowitz, Robin, Samantha Artiga, and Katherine Young. 2016. "What Coverage and Financing Is at Risk under a Repeal of the ACA Medicaid Expansion?" Kaiser Family Foundation, Menlo Park, Calif., December 6. http://kff.org/medicaid/issue-brief/what-coverage-and-financing-at-risk-under-repeal-of-aca-medicaid-expansion/ (accessed February 15, 2018).

Saez, Emmanuel. 2016. "U.S. Top One Percent of Income Earners Hit New High in 2015 amid Strong Economic Growth." Washington Center for Equitable Growth, Washington, D.C., July 1. http://equitablegrowth.org/research-analysis/u-s-top-one-percent-of-income-earners-hit-new-high-in-2015-amid-strong-economic-growth/ (accessed February 15, 2018).

Schaffner, Brian, Matthew MacWilliams, and Tatishe Nteta. 2017. "Explaining White Polarization in the 2016 Vote for President: The Sobering Role of Racism and Sexism." University of Massachusetts, Amherst. Paper prepared for presentation at the conference on "The U.S. Elections of 2016: Domestic and International Aspects," IDC Herzliya, Herzliya, Israel, January 8–9. http://people.umass.edu/schaffne/schaffner_et_al_IDC_conference.pdf (accessed February 15, 2018).

Schlesinger, Arthur. 1958. *The Coming of the New Deal, 1933–1935.* Boston: Houghton Mifflin.

Schlozman, Kay Lehman, Sidney Verba, and Henry E. Brady. 2012. *The Unheavenly Chorus: Unequal Political Voice and the Broken Promise of American Democracy.* Princeton, N.J.: Princeton University Press.

Schneider, Anne, and Helen Ingram. 1993. "Social Constructions of Target Populations: Implications for Politics and Policy." *American Political Science Review* 87: 334–47.

Sears, David O., and Jack Citrin. 1982. *Tax Revolt: Something for Nothing in California.* Cambridge, Mass.: Harvard University Press.

Shaefer, H. Luke. 2010. "Identifying Key Barriers to Unemployment Insurance for Disadvantaged Workers in the United States." *Journal of Social Policy* 39(3, May): 439–60.

Shafer, Byron E., and Richard Johnston. 2006. *The End of Southern Exceptionalism.* Cambridge, Mass.: Harvard University Press.

Shesgreen, Deidre. 2014. "A Congressman Thinks 'No' Is the Answer," *USA Today,* June 15. http://www.cincinnati.com/story/news/politics/2014/06/15/congressman-thinks-answer/10565771/ (accessed February 15, 2018).

Sides, John, and Lynn Vavreck. 2013. *The Gamble: Choice and Chance in the 2012 Presidential Election.* Princeton, N.J.: Princeton University Press.

Silver, Nate. 2016. "Education, Not Income, Predicted Who Would Vote for Trump." *FiveThirtyEight,* November 22. http://fivethirtyeight.com/features/education-not-income-predicted-who-would-vote-for-trump/ (accessed February 15, 2018).

Sinclair, Barbara. 2005. *Party Wars: Polarization and the Politics of National Policy Making.* Norman: University of Oklahoma Press.

Skocpol, Theda. 1991. "Targeting within Universalism: Politically Viable Policies to Combat Poverty in the United States." In *The Urban Underclass,* edited by Christopher Jencks and Paul E. Peterson. Washington, D.C.: Brookings Institution.

———. 1992. *Protecting Soldiers and Mothers: The Political Origins of Social Policy in the United States.* Cambridge, Mass.: Harvard University Press.

————. 2004. *Diminished Democracy: From Membership to Management in American Civic Life.* Norman, Okla.: University of Oklahoma Press.

Skocpol, Theda, and Alexander Hertel-Fernandez. 2016. "The Koch Network and the Rightward Shift in U.S. Politics." Paper presented at the Annual Meeting of the American Political Science Association. Chicago, April 8. https://www.scholarsstrategynetwork.org/sites/default/files/mpsa_koch_network.pdf (accessed February 15, 2018).

Skocpol, Theda, and Vanessa Williamson. 2012. *The Tea Party and the Remaking of Republican Conservatism.* New York: Oxford University Press.

Smith, Rogers M. 1999. *Civic Ideals: Conflicting Visions of Citizenship in U.S. History.* New Haven, Conn.: Yale University Press.

Social Security Administration (SSA). 2006. *Annual Statistical Supplement to the Social Security Bulletin, 2005.* SSA Publication 13-11700. Washington, D.C.: SSA (February). http://www.ssa.gov/policy/docs/statcomps/supplement/2005/supplement05.pdf (accessed February 15, 2018).

————. 2012. *Annual Statistical Report on the Social Security Disability Insurance Program, 2011.* SSA Publication 13-11826. Washington, D.C.: SSA (July). https://www.ssa.gov/policy/docs/statcomps/di_asr/2011/di_asr11.pdf (accessed February 15, 2018).

————. 2015. *Annual Statistical Supplement,* table 8.E. Washington, D.C.: SSA (February). https://www.ssa.gov/policy/docs/statcomps/supplement/2015/8e.pdf (accessed February 15, 2018).

————. 2017. "Supplemental Security Income Program: FY 2018 Congressional Justification—Budget Estimates." SSA, Washington, D.C. https://www.ssa.gov/budget/FY18Files/2018SSI.pdf (accessed February 15, 2018).

Soss, Joe. 1999. "Lessons of Welfare: Policy Design, Political Learning, and Political Action." *American Political Science Review* 93(2): 363–80.

Soss, Joe, Richard C. Fording, and Sanford Schram. 2011. *Disciplining the Poor: Neoliberal Paternalism and the Persistent Power of Race.* Chicago: University of Chicago Press.

Soss, Joe, Sanford F. Schram, Thomas P. Vartanian, and Erin O'Brien. 2001. "Setting the Terms of Relief: Explaining State Policy Choices in the Devolution Revolution." *American Journal of Political Science* 45(2, April): 378–95.

Soss, Joe, and Vesla Weaver. 2016. "Learning from Ferguson: Welfare, Criminal Justice, and the Political Science of Race and Class." In *The Double Bind: The Politics of Racial and Class Inequalities in the Americas: A Report of the Task Force on Racial and Social Class,* edited by Juliet Hooker and Alvin B. Tillery Jr. Washington, D.C.: American Political Science Association.

————. 2017. "Police Are Our Government: Politics, Political Science, and the Policing of Race-Class Subjugated Communities." *Annual Review of Political Science* 20: 565–91.

Stonecash, Jeffrey M. 2000. *Class and Party in American Politics.* Boulder, Colo.: Westview Press.

Stonecash, Jeffrey M., and Mark Brewer. 2007. *Split: Class and Cultural Divides in American Politics.* Washington, D.C.: CQ Press.

Strach, Patricia. 2007. *All in the Family: The Private Roots of American Public Policy.* Stanford, Calif.: Stanford University Press.

Sykes, Charles J. 1993. *A Nation of Victims: The Decay of American Character.* New York: St. Martin's Press.

———. 2011. *A Nation of Moochers: America's Addiction to Getting Something for Nothing.* New York: St. Martin's Press.

Teles, Steven M. 1996. *Whose Welfare? AFDC and Elite Politics.* Lawrence: University Press of Kansas.

Thompson, Eric C., Mark C. Berger, Steven N. Allen, and Jonathan Roenker. 2001. "A Study of the Current Economic Impacts of the Appalachian Coal Industry and Its Future in the Region: Final Report." Center for Business and Economic Research, University of Kentucky, March 27. https://www.arc.gov/assets/research_reports/Current EconomicImpactsofAppalachianCoalIndustry.pdf (accessed February 15, 2018).

Thomsen, Danielle M. 2017. *Opting Out of Congress: Partisan Polarization and the Decline of Moderate Candidates.* New York: Cambridge University Press.

Tourangeau, Roger, Lance J. Rips, and Kenneth Rasinski. 2000. *The Psychology of Survey Response*, 1st edition. New York: Cambridge University Press.

U.S. Bureau of Economic Analysis (BEA). 2016. "Interactive Data: GDP and Personal Income: Regional Data: Local Area Personal Income and Employment: Personal Current Transfer Receipts (CA35). U.S. Department of Commerce, Washington. https://www. bea.gov/itable/iTable.cfm?ReqID=70&step=1#reqid=70&step=1&isuri=1 (accessed February 15, 2018).

U.S. Congress. Joint Committee on Taxation (JCT). 2015. "Overview of the Federal Tax System as in Effect for 2015." JCX-70-15. JCT, Washington, March 30. https://www. jct.gov/publications.html?func=startdown&id=4763 (accessed February 15, 2018).

U.S. Congressional Budget Office (CBO). 2011. "Trends in the Distribution of Household Income Between 1979 and 2007." CBO, Washington, October 25. http://www .cbo.gov/sites/default/files/10-25-HouseholdIncome_0.pdf (accessed February 15, 2018).

———. 2013. "The Distribution of Major Tax Expenditures in the Individual Income Tax System." CBO, Washington, May 29. http://www.cbo.gov/publication/43768 (accessed February 15, 2018).

———. 2014. "The Distribution of Household Income and Federal Taxes, 2011." CBO, Washington, November 12. https://www.cbo.gov/publication/49440 (accessed February 15, 2018).

———. 2016. "Social Security Disability Insurance: Participation and Spending." CBO, Washington, June. https://www.cbo.gov/sites/default/files/114th-congress-2015-2016 /reports/51443-ssdiparticipationspending.pdf (accessed February 15, 2018).

U.S. Department of Labor. Bureau of Labor Statistics (BLS). 1975. *Handbook of Labor Statistics 1975.* Reference ed. Washington: U.S. Government Printing Office.

———. 2012. "The Recession of 2007–2009." Washington, February 12. http://www.bls .gov/spotlight/2012/recession/ (accessed February 15, 2018).

———. 2015. "Employee Benefits in the United States: March 2015." Bulletin 2782. U.S. Department of Labor, BLS, Washington, September. https://www.bls.gov/ncs/ebs /benefits/2015/ebbl0057.pdf (accessed February 15, 2018).

U.S. House of Representatives. Office of Congressman Thomas Massie. 2013. "U.S. Representative Massie Votes in Favor of Agriculture Reform." Press release, July 12. https://massie.house.gov/press-release/press-release-us-representative-massie-votes-favor-agriculture-reform (accessed February 15, 2018).

Valelly, Richard M. 2004. *The Two Reconstructions: The Struggle for Black Enfranchisement.* Chicago: University of Chicago Press.

Vance, J. D. 2016. *Hillbilly Elegy: A Memoir of a Family and a Culture in Crisis.* New York: HarperCollins.

Vargas, Robert. 2016. "How Health Navigators Legitimize the Affordable Care Act to the Uninsured Poor." *Social Science and Medicine* 165: 263–70.

Verba, Sidney, Kay Lehman Schlozman, and Henry E. Brady. 1995. *Voice and Equality: Civic Voluntarism in American Politics.* Cambridge, Mass.: Harvard University Press.

Vroman, Wayne. 2009. "Unemployment Insurance: Current Situation and Potential Reforms." Urban Institute, Washington, D.C., February 3. http://www.urban.org/Uploaded PDF/411835_unemployment_insurance.pdf (accessed February 15, 2018).

Waldfogel, Jane. 2013. "The Safety Net for Families with Children." In *Legacies of the War on Poverty,* edited by Martha J. Bailey and Sheldon Danziger. New York: Russell Sage Foundation.

Walker, Alexis. 2014. "Labor's Enduring Divide: The Distinct Path of Public Sector Unions in the United States." *Studies in American Political Development* (October): 175–200.

Weaver, R. Kent. 2015. "Temporary Assistance for Needy Families." In *The Oxford Handbook of U.S. Social Policy,* edited by Daniel Beland, Christopher Howard, and Kimberly J. Morgan. Oxford: Oxford University Press.

Weaver, Vesla M. 2007. "Frontlash: Race and the Development of Punitive Crime Policy." *Studies in American Political Development* 21: 230–65.

Wenger, Jeffrey B. 2014. "Improving Low-Income Workers' Access to Unemployment Insurance." In *What Works for Workers? Public Policies and Innovative Strategies for Low-Wage Workers,* edited by Stephanie Luce et al. New York: Russell Sage Foundation.

Wenger, Jeffrey B., and Vicky M. Wilkins. 2008. "At the Discretion of Rogue Agents: How Automation Improves Women's Outcomes in Unemployment Insurance." *Journal of Public Administration Research and Theory* 19: 313–33.

White, Jeremy, Robert Gebeloff, Ford Fessenden, Archie Tse, and Alan McLean. 2012. "The Geography of Government Benefits." *New York Times,* February 11. http://www.nytimes.com/interactive/2012/02/12/us/entitlement-map.html?_r=0 (accessed February 15, 2018).

White House. 2013. "Fact Sheet: The Tax Agreement: A Victory of Middle-Class Families and the Economy." Office of the Press Secretary, White House, Washington, January 1. http://www.whitehouse.gov/the-press-office/2013/01/01/fact-sheet-tax-agreement-victory-middle-class-families-and-economy (accessed February 15, 2018).

———. 2016. "Remarks of President Barack Obama: State of the Union Address, as Delivered." Office of the Press Secretary, White House, Washington, January 13. https://www.whitehouse.gov/the-press-office/2016/01/12/remarks-president-barack-obama—-prepared-delivery-state-union-address (accessed February 15, 2018).

Williams, Joan C. 2017. *White Working Class: Overcoming Class Cluelessness in America.* Cambridge, Mass.: Harvard Business Review Press.

Williams, Robertson C. 2016. "A Closer Look at Those Who Pay No Income or Payroll Taxes." Tax Policy Center, Washington, D.C., July 11. http://www.taxpolicycenter.org /taxvox/closer-look-those-who-pay-no-income-or-payroll-taxes (accessed February 15, 2018).

Wilson, William Julius. 1987. *The Truly Disadvantaged: The Inner City, the Underclass, and Public Policy.* Chicago: University of Chicago Press.

———. 1996. *When Work Disappears: The World of the New Urban Poor.* Chicago: University of Chicago Press.

Wolfinger, Raymond E., and Steven J. Rosenstone. 1980. *Who Votes?* New Haven, Conn.: Yale University Press.

Woodbury, Stephen A. 2015. "Unemployment Insurance Benefits." In *The Oxford Handbook of U.S. Social Policy,* edited by Daniel Beland, Christopher Howard, and Kimberly J. Morgan. New York: Oxford University Press.

Zedlewski, Sheila R., and Kelly Rader. 2005. "Have Food Stamp Program Changes Increased Participation?" *Social Service Review* 79(3, September): 537–61.

Ziliak, James P. 2006. "Understanding Poverty Rates and Gaps: Concepts, Trends, and Challenges." Boston: NOW.

———. 2008. "Filling the Poverty Gap, Then and Now." In *Frontiers of Family Economics,* vol. 1, edited by Peter Rupert. Bingley, U.K.: Emerald Publishing Group.

INDEX